FLORIDA STATE
UNIVERSITY LIBRARIES

OCT 10 1995

TALLAHASSEE, FLORIDA

Women, Politics, and the United Nations

**Recent Titles in
Contributions in Women's Studies**

Edith Wharton's Prisoners of Consciousness: A Study of Theme and Technique in the Tales
Evelyn E. Fracasso

Mothers and Work in Popular American Magazines
Kathryn Keller

Ideals in Feminine Beauty: Philosophical, Social, and Cultural Dimensions
Karen A. Callaghan, editor

The Stone and the Scorpion: The Female Subject of Desire in the Novels of Charlotte Bronte, George Eliot, and Thomas Hardy
Judith Mitchell

The Several Worlds of Pearl S. Buck: Essays Presented at a Centennial Symposium, Randolph-Macon Woman's College, March 26-28, 1992
Elizabeth J. Lipscomb, Frances E. Webb, and Peter Conn, editors

Hear Me Patiently: The Reform Speeches of Amelia Jenks Bloomer
Anne C. Coon, editor

Nineteenth-Century American Women Theatre Managers
Jane Kathleen Curry

Textual Escap(e)ades: Mobility, Maternity, and Textuality in Contemporary Fiction by Women
Lindsey Tucker

The Repair of the World: The Novels of Marge Piercy
Kerstin W. Shands

Clara Barton: In the Service of Humanity
David H. Burton

International Women's Writing: New Landscapes of Identity
Anne E. Brown and Marjanne Gooze, editors

"Some Appointed Work To Do": Women and Vocation in the Fiction of Elizabeth Gaskell
Robin B. Colby

Women, Politics, and the United Nations

Edited by Anne Winslow

Contributions in Women's Studies, Number 151

Greenwood Press
Westport, Connecticut · London

Library of Congress Cataloging-in-Publication Data

Women, politics, and the United Nations / edited by Anne Winslow.
     p.   cm.—(Contributions in women's studies, ISSN 0147–104X ; 151)
  Includes bibliographical references and index.
  ISBN 0–313–29522–0 (alk. paper)
  1. Women in politics—History. 2. Feminism—History. 3. United Nations. I. Winslow, Anne. II. Series.
HQ1236.W6395   1995
305.42—dc20   94–47415

British Library Cataloguing in Publication Data is available.

Copyright © 1995 by George Washington University

All rights reserved. No portion of this book may be reproduced, by any process or technique, without the express written consent of the publisher.

Library of Congress Catalog Card Number: 94–47415
ISBN: 0–313–29522–0
ISSN: 0147–104X

First published in 1995

Greenwood Press, 88 Post Road West, Westport, CT 06881
An imprint of Greenwood Publishing Group, Inc.

Printed in the United States of America

The paper used in this book complies with the Permanent Paper Standard issued by the National Information Standards Organization (Z39.48–1984).

10 9 8 7 6 5 4 3 2 1

Contents

Preface	vii
Acknowledgments	ix
1. Forerunners in Women's Quest for Partnership Margaret E. Galey	1
2. Women Find a Place Margaret E. Galey	11
3. World Conference of International Women's Year Virginia R. Allan, Margaret E. Galey, and Mildred E. Persinger	29
4. Losing the Battle/Winning the War: International Politics, Women's Issues, and the 1980 Mid-Decade Conference Jane S. Jaquette	45
5. Women and Power: The Nairobi Conference, 1985 Charlotte G. Patton	61
6. The Convention on the Elimination of All Forms of Discrimination Against Women (The Women's Convention) Arvonne S. Fraser	77

7.	The Politics of Women and Development Margaret Snyder	95
8.	Equality for Women in the United Nations Secretariat Kristen Timothy	117
9.	Women's International Nongovernmental Organizations at the United Nations Carolyn M. Stephenson	135
10.	Specialized Agencies and the World Bank Anne Winslow	155
11.	Conclusion	177
	Appendix I: Women's Right to Vote by Country and Date	185
	Appendix II: Priority Themes for the Period 1992–1996	187
	Selected Bibliography	189
	Index	199
	About the Editor and Contributors	211

Preface

It was June 1993. The United Nations (UN) World Conference on Human Rights had just ended. Hundreds of women's groups had participated. In the words of a Canadian Institute for International Affairs pamphlet (David Gillies, *Behind the Headlines*, 1993), the women had proved that "solid organization and careful planning could translate into positive action." Not so long ago human rights activists gave only a passing nod to women's rights. That time, the conference was fairly bristling with them. Women's rights were to be a "priority for governments and the United Nations." Violence "against women in public and private" was condemned. "Sexual harassment, exploitation and traffic in women as well as health care (including the widest range of family planning services)" were "finally understood as human rights issues."

One year later, at the close of the International Conference on Population and Development in Cairo, the *New York Times* (14 September 1994), reviewing the International Conference on page 2, declared that "progress for women is central to a new strategy." The opportunity for women to assert their rights and influence the course of history, not only in UN conferences on women but in the wider political arena, has now become not only a slogan but a reality.

Despite setbacks, the craggy indifference of male counterparts, and the closely knit fabric of male superiority woven over the centuries, women are finally getting things done.

The present volume seeks to shed light on the origins of the present strength and cohesion of women's movements. What forces have come into play? Have women gained a foothold in the political arena, long a predominant male preserve? What motivated women's interest in the UN? Did its very existence strengthen their bonds with each other? Men have always joined together in associations, but women, isolated and housebound for the most part, have had to learn the hard way that there is no strength without unity. Still another question, What have been the objectives of women working with the UN? Where are the successes, where are the failures? Has women's presence acted as a leaven in changing the agenda and the activities of UN organizations and bodies?

This series of chapters reflects the varying perspectives of the practitioner and the scholar. The practitioner sees the extent to which it has been possible to implement verbal promises. The practitioner asks whether the voices of grassroots' women have been heard and how much has seeped down unweakened and undistorted from headquarters to the field. The scholar, concerned with a broader canvas, looks at the ebb and flow of trends and their implications for the future.

The focus has been on the major instruments for women's action within the UN system. These include the UN itself as an institution and a political entity; the Commission on the Status of Women—a key point of entry; the three women's conferences, 1975, 1980, and 1985; and the Convention on the Elimination of All Forms of Discrimination Against Women. We also look at the origins of the women and development concept in post–World War II independence movements, and the influence of the UN Development Fund for Women and the International Training and Research Centre for the Advancement of Women—institutions that were created to be catalysts for women's interests in the UN development cooperation system. Also discussed is the condition of women in the Secretariat. How have they fared, trying to team up on an equal footing with their male colleagues? What influence have they had, and has their situation improved over the years?

Finally, there is a brief review of developments in five of the major UN–associated specialized organizations, those with which women have been most concerned. They are the International Labor Organization, the Food and Agriculture Organization, the UN Educational, Scientific and Cultural Organization, the World Health Organization, and the World Bank.

Acknowledgments

This study owes its inception and much of its forward momentum to Margaret E. Galey, an independent scholar and consultant, and to Victoria Schuck, former Professor of Politics at Mt. Holyoke College and later President of Mt. Vernon College. Professor Schuck's untimely illness unfortunately prevented her continuing participation in the project.

The editor and contributors wish to thank the Ford Foundation Division of International Affairs for a grant that helped to make possible the completion of this manuscript. They also wish to thank the Elliot School of International Affairs of George Washington University for its institutional sponsorship and for hosting a two-day meeting of contributors.

In addition, various present and former UN officials, delegates, and representatives of international nongovernmental organizations, too numerous to list, have generously shared their reflections, insights, and experiences with individual chapter authors who wish collectively to thank them and acknowledge their contribution. Their help in documenting the historical record was essential in providing as accurate a picture as possible of the developments analyzed.

Thanks are also due to the Esther Hymer Library at the UN Church Center as well as to the staff of the Government Documents Section of the Library of Congress and of the Foreign Affairs and National Defense Division of the Congressional Research Service for assistance in obtaining a number of verbatim records of UN meetings. The staff of the former UN Department of Social Development and Humanitarian Affairs, Division for the Advancement of Women, and its New York Liaison Office, and the UN Statistical Office have also given assistance in providing documents.

Contributors and the editor are grateful for valuable comments by Greenwood Press and by an anonymous reviewer on earlier versions of the manuscript.

Women, Politics, and the United Nations

1
Forerunners in Women's Quest for Partnership

Margaret E. Galey

Women's quest for full citizenship and partnership with men in politics and society, begun during the eighteenth century Enlightenment and political revolutions, reached global proportions two centuries later during International Women's Year (IWY) in 1975, the three United Nations (UN) women's conferences and the UN Decade for Women, 1976–1985. These UN activities mobilized a critical mass of women from around the world to formulate strategies and goals to achieve participation as full partners with men in all spheres of decision making and to gain equal access to opportunities offered by their societies. By the 1990s, women's issues had become legitimate subjects on the agendas of governments and international organizations, and women participated in public activity as never before.

Despite these developments, especially since the 1970s, there has been little real understanding of why and how women's activities achieved such global proportions. The social sciences, particularly history and sociology, and more recently political science have significantly contributed to understanding women in domestic society and polity. But women have remained invisible in scholarly analyses of international affairs, law, and organization until quite recently.[1]

Decades before the UN's establishment, women had begun to engage in several kinds of international activity that in turn shaped their efforts at the UN Charter Conference and afterward. First, women created their own international organizations, a phenomenon that paralleled the growth of international nongovernmental organizations (INGOs) generally in the late nineteenth and early twentieth centuries. Second, they began to serve as official delegates and as staff members of newly created international organizations (IGOs). Third, women representatives of INGOs, delegates in IGOs, and Secretariat staff formed informal networks through which they promoted measures to further equality within IGOs. Each of these activities is briefly discussed here.

WOMEN'S INTERNATIONAL NONGOVERNMENTAL ORGANIZATIONS

The creation by women of an increasing number of women's organizations in the late nineteenth century was a significant step in exercising democratic citizenship in partnership with men. Before achieving the vote or holding public office except in local governments, individual women joined together to create local and national societies to influence governments to grant suffrage, adopt temperance and other social measures, improve working conditions and achieve wider educational opportunity. To strengthen their appeal, they began to form international associations. Swiss national, Marie Goegg, is credited with the first International Association of Women in 1868. In the next decade, an International Women's Rights Conference convened in Paris.[2] And Josephine Butler (United Kingdom) organized the British, Continental and General Federation for the Abolition of State Vice.[3]

In the United States, women's crusade against the sale and consumption of alcohol resulted in the Women's Christian Temperance Union (WCTU) in 1874, and within a decade, WTCU's president, Frances Willard, established the World Women's Christian Temperance Union (WWCTU), which still exists.[4]

About the same time, international associations of women's religious groups were founded, such as the World Young Women's Christian Association (YWCA).[5] In the United States and United Kingdom, the women's club movement offered opportunities for civic and community action. By 1890, it became the General Federation of Women's Clubs, uniting women's clubs worldwide.[6]

Meanwhile, in Western Europe, as political parties developed, women's sections formed. Clara Zetkin, head of the women's section of the German Social Democratic Party (SPD) organized the first International Conference of Socialist Women, in conjunction with the 1907 International Socialist Congress, and later proposed March 8 as International Women's Day.[7]

In Russia, Alexandre Kollantai, who had helped orchestrate the 1917 Bolshevik revolution, supported the first International Communist Conference of Working Women in 1920 to define communist policy goals for women.[8]

As college-educated women grew in numbers, they formed national alumnae associations. Graduates in the United States, United Kingdom, and Canada took the lead in organizing the International Federation of Catholic Alumnae in 1914 and the International Federation of University Women in 1919.[9] Women's admission to nursing and medical professions inspired the International Council of Nurses (1899), Altrusa International (1917), and the Medical Women's International Association (1919). Professional women organized Zonta in 1919.[10]

The suffrage movement spawned great activity in the United States and Europe in the nineteenth century. The success of WWCTU led American suffrage leaders Elizabeth Stanton and Susan Anthony, in cooperation with their counterparts from eight countries, to create, in 1888, a federation of national councils of women, called the International Council of Women (ICW), to cooperate in efforts to achieve women's suffrage.[11]

When ICW's members later split over the priority given suffrage, Stanton, Anthony, and Carrie Chapman Catt organized the International Woman Suffrage Alliance (IWSA) in 1902 for the "enfranchisement of women of all nations" (the IWSA became the International Alliance of Women, or IAW, in 1926).[12] Like ICW, IWSA fostered new national societies and convened periodic international congresses to develop common agendas to advance women's status. On the eve of World War I, the IWSA even petitioned (unsuccessfully) the British foreign office and foreign embassies in London to prevent the outbreak of the war.[13]

At an International Congress of Women in The Hague in April 1915, presided over by America's leading social worker, Jane Addams, women drafted a peace plan for heads of warring and neutral governments. The women again failed, but they did establish the Women's International League for Peace and Freedom (WILPF).[14] Then, the World Union of Women for International Concord (WUWIC) was formed.[15]

PUBLIC INTERNATIONAL INTERGOVERNMENTAL ORGANIZATIONS

In the Western Hemisphere, the Latin countries and the United States established the Pan American Union (PAU) to encourage collaboration in health, sanitation, science, and cultural affairs. The first general purpose IGO, the League of Nations (LN), and a specialized organization, the International Labor Organization (ILO) (to promote social justice for working men and women), resulted from the Paris Peace Conference and Treaty in 1919. The LN, the ILO and the PAU stimulated women's interests in a new range of activities.

Pan American Union (PAU)

Before World War I, Latin and North American women had participated in PAU scientific congresses. Later, in connection with regular PAU meetings, a Women's International Committee was formed and sponsored a series of conferences, including one on suffrage. The latter inspired women delegates to the 1928 Conference of American States to propose an Inter-American Commission on Women (IACW) that was officially endorsed at the 1933 conference. The

IACW was the first regional intergovernmental body created to advance women's rights. Its members, appointed by governments, prepared an international treaty on the Nationality of Married Women (1933) and the Declaration of Lima in Favor of Women's Rights (1938). The IACW encouraged member governments to establish women's bureaus, to revise discriminatory civil codes and to take their demands to the LN in Geneva.[16]

Paris Peace Conference, 1919

As the delegates began to shape the structure of the LN, groups of women assembled in Paris to put forward their views. The French Women's Suffrage Union (FWSU) together with IWSA and ICW representatives formed a joint delegation, the Inter-Allied Suffrage Conference (IASC), and obtained permission from the Big Four nations to participate in certain peace conference commissions.

The women's delegation lobbied the Commission on International Labor Legislation, chaired by Samuel Gompers (U.S.), as it designed the future ILO. Margaret Bondfield, Executive Council member of the British Trades Union Congress, together with American labor leaders recommended an eight-hour day, a forty-four-hour work week, an end to child labor, support for social insurance, pensions and maternity benefits, equal pay, and minimum wages for housework. Although their proposals were politely received, they were quickly shelved as being too radical. Nevertheless, the women did manage to insert a reference into Article 23(1) of the League Covenant to "fair and humane conditions of labor for men, women and children."[17]

The women's delegation also met briefly with the fourteen allied government leaders in April 1919 and urged them to nominate women to positions of influence in the LN, abolish traffic in women and children and state-supported prostitution, recognize universal suffrage, adopt measures on the nationality of married women, create international education and health bureaus, and control and reduce armaments.[18] They helped to ensure wording of League Covenant Article 7(3) which obliged governments to permit all positions in the LN, including the Secretariat, to be open equally to men and women and of Article 23(c) giving the LN "supervision over the execution of agreements with regard to the traffic in women and children."[19]

Women and the League of Nations

Although the LN's Covenant opened the door for women to serve both as delegates and as Secretariat staff, no government ever appointed a woman to the LN Council. However, at each session of the Assembly, there were about a dozen women among the 250 delegates, some of whom were leaders of their respective national women's organizations.[20]

As Assembly delegates, women were usually assigned, despite their protests,

Forerunners in Women's Quest for Partnership 5

to its Committee on Social and General Questions dealing with "women's questions." Several also served on the LN's Advisory Committee on Traffic in Women and Children, the Expert Committee on the Legal Status of Women, and on delegations to League conferences on the traffic in women. A few women were appointed to the Conference on the Codification of International Law and on Disarmament Commission and two on the Permanent Mandates Commission.[21]

In the LN's Secretariat, most women held positions as secretaries and clerks, with two notable exceptions. From 1919 to 1930, Dame Rachel Crowdy (United Kingdom), headed the Social Section that shaped the work of the Advisory Committee on Traffic in Women and Children and prepared a Convention on the Traffic of Women and Children. The Social Section also helped the committee prepare a Convention on the Suppression of and Circulation of Obscene Publications.[22] When Crowdy left, Gabriella Radziwell (United Kingdom) in the Information Section became the most important contact for women's organizations.[23]

Leaders of an increasing number of international women's organizations had become "the voice of women" in Geneva. They created the Liaison Committee of Women's International Organizations and began informal liaison with the respective delegations and secretariats, addressing various proposals to them. One of these advanced by the executive secretary of IAW called for a permanent International Women's Office modeled after the ILO with a conference, governing body, and NGO representatives.[24] It failed to be adopted, since the LN Secretary-General, Sir Eric Drummond (United Kingdom), persuaded the women that a specially appointed Secretariat official in the Information Section would better enable women's voice to be heard.[25]

The Liaison Committee in Geneva monitored sessions of the LN and ILO and planned joint strategies to advance their aims.[26] But, increasingly it concentrated on the LN while working women and trades union groups devoted their energies to the ILO.[27] Both groups built alliances with the respective Secretariat staff and delegates to influence them informally to discuss women's issues. They were also often sources of new ideas: the draft of the Children's Charter, a memorandum on forced labor, petitions for arms reductions and collective security, and the Charter of the Rights of Mothers.

The Danish delegate, a WILPF member, had proposed and the LN agreed in 1921 to a Commission of Enquiry into the situation of deported women and children in Turkey. A decade later, after women protested the 1930 Hague Conference on Nationality because it did not deal with women's nationality, the LN Council placed the subject of the nationality of married women on the Assembly's agenda and created a Women's Consultative Committee on Nationality to study the question.[28]

Finally, at the urging of several women's organizations, the Assembly established in 1937 a Committee of Experts on the Legal Status of Women and authorized it to conduct "a comprehensive and scientific inquiry into the legal status of women in various countries of the world."[29] Consisting of seven experts and representatives of three international legal institutes—the Unification of Private Law, Public Law, and the International Bureau for the Unification of Penal Law—the Expert Committee first convened in April 1938 to plan the comprehensive study.[30] It held only two further meetings in January and July 1939. Then came World War II.[31] But, the Expert Committee's work offered an important starting point for the UN Commission on the Status of Women.

Women and the International Labor Organization

Stimulated by the goals of the ILO and its references to women, Rose Schneiderman and Mary Anderson, American leaders of the National Women's Trade Union League (NWTUL), convened the first International Congress of Working Women in Washington, D.C., in 1919 in cooperation with European trade union women. Out of this meeting emerged the International Federation of Working Women (IFWW) as well as a united approach to women's questions at the ILO's first annual conference.[32] Thereafter, women worked through the IFWW to influence ILO delegations to adopt humane labor measures. Among them were protective measures, such as the Conventions on Maternity Protection (1919), Night Work for Women (1919), and Underground Work by Women (1935).[33] ILO also approved equality measures such as the 1923 Labor Inspection Recommendation, which gave women inspectors the same powers, duties, and authority as men. The 1928 Minimum Wage-Fixing Machinery Recommendation asked governments, employers, and workers to include women on wage-fixing bodies.[34] Provisions regarding equal remuneration were discussed but not adopted until after World War II with encouragement from women's organizations.

WOMEN, WORLD WAR II, THE UNITED NATIONS, AND HUMAN RIGHTS

At the end of World War II, association leaders, fortified by their previous experience, resumed their activities and supported a new world organization to replace the LN. In the United States, President Franklin D. Roosevelt and Secretary of State Cordell Hull played a vital role in shaping the UN, as did James T. Shotwell of the Carnegie Endowment for International Peace; Clark Eichelberger of the Commission to Study the Organization of Peace; and Manley O. Hudson and Louis Sohn, professors of international law at Harvard University and members of the American Bar Association.[35]

Roosevelt and his advisors believed that a major cause of World War II had been the gross violation of human rights, especially Nazi atrocities, and insisted that human rights be given an international legal status in the charter of the new world organization. Human rights provisions were reflected in the U.S. government's "Tentative Proposals for International Organization" discussed by the

Allies at Dumbarton Oaks in Washington, D.C., in August and September 1944. But the British ambassador, Lord Cadogan, and the Soviet minister, Molotov, opposed them; therefore, along with the veto and membership issues, the proposals were referred to the Yalta Conference, which failed to produce the desired agreement. So Secretary Stettinius, who had replaced Cordell Hull, then went to Mexico City to enlist Latin American support for the U.S. proposals, including those on human rights. This highly successful mission resulted in an endorsement of the U.S. proposals, and several resolutions called on governments to the upcoming San Francisco Conference to abolish discrimination against women, adopt a charter for women and children, and appoint women as conference delegates.[36]

When the conference convened to discuss the Dumbarton Oaks proposals, it was evident that several delegations had taken the Chapultepec resolutions seriously. Three Latin women served as delegates: Minerva Bernardino (Dominican Republic), Berta Lutz (Brazil), and Isabel P. de Vidal (Uruguay). In Venezuela's delegation, Lucila L. de Perez Diaz and Isabel Sanchez de Urdaneta were counselors. From other regions came Cora T. Casselman (Canada), Wu Yi-Fang (China), Virginia Gildersleeve (United States)—all delegates. Ellen Wilkinson and Florence Horsbrugh were assistant United Kingdom delegates. The United States also had four women in its delegation as technical experts: Dorothy Fosdick, Marjorie Whiteman, Esther Brunauer, and Alice McDiarmid.[37]

In addition to establishing the general structure of the UN, which was based on that of the LN, three new features of special interest to women were introduced. These were the Economic and Social Council (ECOSOC), with authority to create subsidiary bodies; Article 71 of the UN Charter, which enabled qualified nongovernmental organizations (NGOs) to obtain consultative status with ECOSOC; and the broad human rights provisions.

Latin delegations and the American consultants representing forty-two national, professional, religious, labor, business, and women's groups strongly supported the human rights provisions. Women delegates from Brazil, the Dominican Republic, and Mexico had insisted that the phrase "to ensure respect for human rights and fundamental freedoms without discrimination against race, sex, condition or creed" be incorporated into the UN Charter. A similar proposal was offered by India. In its final form, the text referred to the promotion and protection of human rights without distinction as to race, sex, nationality, or religion as a principle UN Charter aim. The phrase was incorporated into four UN Charter Articles.[38] On a related matter, the women temporarily lost Brazil's proposed establishment of a separate Commission on the Status of Women. This met with strong opposition from Virginia Gildersleeve, the only woman on the U.S. delegation and a founder of the IFUW. Such a commission, according to U.S. policy, was contrary to the aim of no discrimination because of sex and a matter that the Commission on Human Rights could adequately manage.[39] As a result, the UN Charter provided for a Commission on Human Rights, but not a separate women's commission.

Delegations approved the UN Charter on 25 June 1945. It entered into force on 24 October 1945 after the fiftieth government ratification. Governments then convened preparatory meetings to discuss its implementation and agreed to inaugurate the new world organization in opening sessions of the UN General Assembly and ECOSOC in London in early January 1946.

The UN Charter gave women slim, formal recognition, but the human rights provisions gave women constitutional-legal leverage to renew their quest to improve their status, achieve full citizenship in partnership with men, and enter the world's political stage.

NOTES

The author wishes to thank an anonymous reviewer for helpful suggestions on an earlier version of this chapter.

1. See Fred Halliday, "Hidden from International Relations: Women and the International Arena," in *Gender and International Relations*, ed. Rebecca Grant and Kathleen Newland (Bloomington: Indiana University Press, 1991), 158–69; in the same volume, see Carol Miller, "Women in International Relations? The Debate in Inter-War Britain," 65–83. See also Hilkka Pietila and Jeanne Vickers, *Making Women Matter: The Role of the United Nations* (Atlantic Highlands, N.J.: Zed Press, 1990); Arvonne Fraser, *The UN Decade for Women* (Boulder, Colo.: Westview Press, 1987); Margaret E. Galey, "Promoting Non-Discrimination Against Women: The Commission on the Status of Women," *International Studies Quarterly* 23, no. 2 (June 1979): 273–302; Carol Lubin and Anne Winslow, *Social Justice for Women: The International Labor Organization and Women* (Durham, N.C.: Duke University Press, 1990); Irene Tinker and Jane Jaquette, "The UN Decade for Women," *World Development* 2 (March 1987): 419–27; Kathleen Staudt, ed., *Women, International Development and Politics* (Philadelphia: Temple University Press, 1990); Victoria Schuck, "NGOs at Nairobi," *Political Science and Politics* (April 1986); Natalie Kaufman Hevener, *International Law and the Status of Women* (Boulder, Colo.: Westview Press, 1983); Rebecca Cook, "Reservations to the Convention on the Elimination of All Forms of Discrimination Against Women," *Virginia Journal of International Law* 30 (1990): 643–709; Hilary Charlesworth, Christine Chinkin, and Shelley Wright, "Feminist Approaches to International Law," *American Journal of International Law* 85, no. 4 (October 1991): 613–45; Donna J. Sullivan, "Women's Human Rights and the 1993 World Conference on Human Rights," *American Journal of International Law* 88, no. 1 (January 1994): 152–66; Cynthia Enloe, *Bananas, Beaches & Bases* (Berkeley: University of California Press, 1990); Peter R. Beckman and Francine D'Amico, eds., *Women, Gender, and World Politics* (Westport, Conn.: Bergin & Garvey, 1994).

2. Richard Evans, *The Feminists* (New York: Barnes and Noble, 1977), 246–47.

3. Kathleen Barry, *Female Sexual Slavery* (New York: New York University Press, 1979), 14–15, 32–33.

4. Jack S. Blocker, Jr., "Separate Paths: Suffragist and Women's Temperance Crusade," *Signs* 11, no. 1 (Spring 1985): 460–76. See also Dorothy Staunton, *Our Goodly Heritage* (London: Walthamstow Press, 1956), 6–7; Mary Earhart, *Frances Willard* (Chicago: University of Chicago Press, 1944), 340–43.

5. Anna V. Rice, *A History of the World's Young Women's Christian Association* (New York: Woman's Press, 1947); Nancy Boyd, *Emissaries: The Overseas Work of the American YWCA, 1895–1970* (New York: Woman's Press, 1986).

6. Elise Boulding, *The Underside of History* (Boulder, Colo.: Westview Press, 1976), 661–66, 671.

7. Charles Sowerwein, "The Socialist Movement from 1850–1940," in *Becoming Visible*, ed. Renate Bridenthal, Claudia Koontz, and Susan Stuard (Boston: Houghton Mifflin, 1987), 403–22.

8. Barbara Jancar, "Women in Communist Countries," in *Women and World Change*, ed. Naomi Black and Ann Cottrell (Beverly Hills, Calif.: Sage, 1981), 140–41.

9. Edith Batho, *A Lamp of Friendship* (Washington, D.C.: American Association of University Women, n.d.), 5–6.

10. Mary E. T. Buchanan, ed., *World Directory of Women's Organizations* (London: Vail & Co., 1953), 13, 18, 22, 28.

11. International Council of Women (ICW), *Women in a Changing World* (London: Routledge & Kegan Paul, 1966), 15; Elizabeth Griffith, *In Her Own Right: The Life of Elizabeth Cady Stanton* (New York: Oxford, 1984), 192–96.

12. Arnold Whittick, *Woman Into Citizen* (Beverley Hills, Calif.: ABC-CLIO Press, 1976), 32–33, 288.

13. Ibid., 39, 63.

14. Catherine Foster, *Women for All Seasons* (Athens: University of Georgia Press, 1989), 14.

15. Buchanan, *World Directory*, 25.

16. Charles G. Fenwick, *The Organization of American States: The Inter-American Regional System* (Washington, D.C.: Kaufman, 1963), 450–58; Francesca Miller, "Latin American Feminism and the Transnational Arena," in *Women, Culture and Politics in Latin America*, ed. Emilie Bergmann et al. (Berkeley: University of California Press, 1990), 10–26; Paula Pfeffer, "A Whisper in the Assembly of Nations," *Women's Studies International Forum* (1985): 459–71.

17. ICW, *Women in a Changing World*, 45; Whittick, *Woman Into Citizen*, 70–74. See also Lubin and Winslow, *Social Justice for Women*, 21–23.

18. David Hunter Miller, *Drafting of the Covenant* (New York: G. P. Putnam's Sons, 1928), 2:360; Whittick, *Woman Into Citizen*, 70–71; ICW, *Women in a Changing World*, 45.

19. Lord Robert Cecil, UK Representative to the Paris Peace Conference and League of Nations Commission, proposed the reference to women. In Cecil's view, if a notion were not specified in the document, it would be excluded. Ibid., 1:348. See also Whittick, *Woman Into Citizen*, 71–72.

20. Carol Miller, "Women in International Relations," 65, 70. See also her "Interaction of National and Transnational Women's Networks with the League of Nations Secretariat," presented at the British International Studies Association, London, December 1991, 5 (mimeo).

21. Carol Miller, "Interaction." See also Egon F. Ranshoffen-Wertheimer, *The International Secretariat: A Great Experiment in International Administration* (Washington, D.C.: Carnegie Endowment for International Peace, 1945), 125–28; ICW, *Women in a Changing World*, 48, 70; F. S. Northledge, *The League of Nations* (Leicester, England: Leicester University Press, 1986), 198.

22. F. C. Walters, *History of the League of Nations* (New York: Oxford University Press, 1952), 1:176–87; Northledge, *League of Nations*, 184–86.
23. Carol Miller, "Interaction," 10.
24. Ibid., 4; Whittick, *Woman Into Citizen*, 76.
25. Carol Miller, "Interaction," 5.
26. Buchanan, *World Directory*, 21–22.
27. Whittick, *Women Into Citizen*, 37.
28. Ibid., 7–10, 12–16.
29. LN Assembly, 16th Session, Official Records, *Status of Women: Communication from Fifteen Delegations Regarding the Placing of the Above Matter on the Assembly's Agenda*, Annex 3, Off. No. A.8.1937.V. (1937), 45–46. See also idem., *Report on the Work of the League, 1937–1938*, Pt. 1, Off. No. A.6.1938 (1938), 178.
30. LN, *Report on the Work of the League, 1937–1938*, 179–80.
31. LN, *Report on the Work of the League, 1938–1939*, Off. No. A.6.1939 (1939), 160–61.
32. Even though the United States failed to ratify the League Covenant and ILO constitution, the first ILO conference was held in Washington, D.C. Lubin and Winslow, *Social Justice for Women*, 25.
33. ILO, *Conventions and Recommendations, 1919–1966* (Geneva: International Labor Office, 1966), 12, 15, 275.
34. ILO, *Conventions*, 71, 132, 155. Another was the Forced Labor Convention (1933). See also Lubin and Winslow, *Social Justice for Women*, 38–39.
35. Dr. Louis B. Sohn (Emeritus Research Professor of Law, National Law Center, George Washington University), personal communication, 16 July 1992. See also James T. Shotwell, *Autobiography* (New York: Bobbs-Merrill, 1961), 303–14; Harold Josephson, *James T. Shotwell and the Rise of Internationalism in America* (Cranbury, N.J.: Associated University Presses, 1975), 285–86.
36. Ruth Russell, *The History of the UN Charter* (Washington, D.C.: Brookings Institution, 1958), 555, 568–69.
37. UN, *Delegations and Officials of UN Conference on International Organization* Doc.693G/3(2) (1945), 17, 20, 23, 61–62, 65, 76–77.
38. UN Charter, Articles 1(3), 55, 68, and 76. Robert Divine, *Second Chance* (New York: Atheneum, 1967), 291–92; *The Jewish Position at the UN Conference on International Organization*, Report to the Delegates of the American Jewish Conference (New York: Parish Press, 1945), 16–17; Louis B. Sohn and Thomas Buergenthal, *International Protection of Human Rights* (Indianapolis, Ind.: Bobbs-Merrill Co., 1973), 508–14; Dorothy Robins, *Experiment in Democracy* (New York: Parkside Press, 1971), 100–140.
39. Virginia Gildersleeve, *Many a Good Crusade* (New York: Macmillan, 1954), 352–53.

2
Women Find a Place

Margaret E. Galey

When leaders of fifty-one governments that had ratified the United Nations (UN) Charter met in London in January 1946, their main preoccupation was the UN role in preventing future wars and in solving the pressing economic problems of a wartorn world. Few, if any, imagined that human rights, much less women's rights, would ever achieve such priority.

As in the case of the League of Nations (LN), women's place in the new public arena was almost invisible, a reflection of their subordinate position in national societies, governments, and world politics.[1] Several notable women served on General Assembly (GA) delegations as early as 1946, but their numbers rarely exceeded 5 percent—and this remained true even when the total membership increased. Fewer still sat on the Economic and Social Council (ECOSOC) and the Trusteeship Council (TC), and they were virtually absent from the Security Council (SC) and the International Court of Justice (ICJ).[2] But their turn would come in their own commission, a place of their own in which to press their case.

GA AND ECOSOC FIRST SESSIONS

In 1946, women served on eleven of fifty-one national delegations to the first GA. Five were delegates: Eleanor Roosevelt (United States); Minerva Bernardino (Dominican Republic); Jeane McKenzie (New Zealand); Evdokia I. Uralova (USSR), and Ellen Wilkinson (United Kingdom). Six were alternates or advisors on delegations from Czechoslovakia, Denmark, France, Greece, the Netherlands, Norway, the United Kingdom and United States.[3]

The women delegates met privately as the GA proceeded, drafted and signed an "Open Letter to the Women of the World." Referring to women's work during World War II, these delegates called on governments to encourage women everywhere to take a more active role in national and international affairs and in building peace. Eleanor Roosevelt presented the letter to the GA president, Paul Henri Spaak (Belgium) on February 13.[4] On the same day, delegates approved the first agenda item on women, the participation of women in UN conferences. This had been introduced by France's alternate, Marie-Helene LeFaucheux.[5]

During the debate, Bernardino proposed a committee under the statutory Commission on Human Rights (CHR) to work for women's rights. Peter Fraser (New Zealand), chairman of ECOSOC's Organization Committee, then announced, amid loud applause, that such a body would be recommended, and he called for understanding on the part of governments in different circumstances so that women of the world could march forward toward a better society, toward a world of peace, social justice, and equality.[6] Although no resolution was adopted at the time, President Spaak said the question of women's participation would receive "very serious consideration."[7]

Meanwhile, leaders of the British Federation of Business and Professional Women (BFBPW) had organized a Roundtable of Women's Organizations. They wrote President Spaak about their meeting and included their resolution calling for a UN convention removing discrimination against women. They also discussed this with the chair of ECOSOC, Sir Ramaswami Mudalier (India).[8]

Despite ECOSOC's charter responsibilities to "achieve international cooperation in solving international problems of an economic, social, cultural or humanitarian character" and "to promote human rights and fundamental freedoms for all without distinction as to race, sex, language or religion," women, as previously mentioned, played only a limited role for many years. Even in two ECOSOC subsidiary bodies of manifest interest to women, they fared little better. These were the Social Commission (SC) and the Population Commission (PC). The fifteen-member SC was responsible for social policy, social welfare, social defense, social work administration, and the advisory social welfare service program. It supplied social welfare advisors to assist governments of developing countries to create ministries of social affairs, some with divisions for women and youth. By 1952, the SC added community development to its agenda, and by 1954 it added housing and population questions. It also sponsored the *World Social Report*.[9] But neither the SC nor the *Report* dealt with the situation regarding women. By 1966, the SC became the Social Development Commission.

Few women were ever appointed to the SC, and fewer still to the PC. Only one woman attended before 1964. The PC took little specific interest in women's issues even though problems of international migration and population growth were on its agenda and special studies revealed the negative effect of rapid population growth. Not until the UN Secretariat sent a family planning mission to India at the government's request in 1964 did the PC, ECOSOC, and the GA begin to approve programs of this nature.[10] After that, several women were appointed to the PC.

The UN Department of Social Affairs provided staff for the SC and PC. Alva Myrdal (Sweden) headed it briefly. Julia Henderson (United States) became Director of the Bureau of Social Affairs in 1951. When Secretary-General (SG) Dag Hammarskjold reorganized the Secretariat in 1953, Henderson became Deputy Director of a combined Department of Economic and Social Affairs.[11]

At the first session of the Commission on Human Rights on 18 February 1946, Eleanor Roosevelt was elected chair. The same day, ECOSOC bowed to the persuasiveness of UN women delegates and NGO leaders and approved the Subcommission on the Status of Women. Nine governments were asked to appoint experts to draw up a charter and report through CHR to ECOSOC's June session of that year. The nine were China, Chile, Denmark, Dominican Republic, France, India, Lebanon, Poland, and the USSR.[12] Women thus gained modest recognition within the male-dominated world body.

SUBCOMMISSION BECOMES A COMMISSION

Seven of nine subcommission members met at the end of April 1946 in New York at Hunter College to prepare their program. They elected Bodil Begtrup (Denmark) chair; Minerva Bernardino, vice-chair, and Angela Jurdek (Lebanon), Rapporteur. They first reviewed the unfinished comparative legal study by the LN's Expert Committee, which Dorothy Kenyon (United States) urged them to complete as a priority. Mrs. Hans Mehta (India) presented a draft Indian Women's Charter of Rights and Duties. Mrs. W. S. New (Taiwan) reported on women in China. Bernardino told of the achievements of the Inter-American Commission on Women (IACW). Marie Helene LeFaucheux (France) proposed monitoring the status of women in trust and non–self-governing territories. Eleanor Roosevelt (United States), an ex-officio member, cautioned members to work in harmony with CHR.

After discussions between 29 April and 13 May, they unanimously approved a set of principles, policy aims, a thirteen-point program and four immediate tasks. The latter were (1) the creation of a Secretariat office headed by a competent woman; (2) the conclusion of the worldwide survey of laws on women; (3) the promotion of equal educational opportunity; and (4) a women's conference.[13]

The subcommission then reported to the CHR, which approved everything in the report except its policy aims and the proposed women's conference.[14] Immediately, Begtrup, Bernardino, and LeFaucheux sought out Roosevelt to gain her support for a full commission that could make independent recommendations. Contrary to popular belief, she initially opposed the idea, but then relented and influenced the U.S. government to support a full commission.[15] On 21 June, ECOSOC endorsed a U.S. resolution of support and authorized the Commission on the Status of Women (CSW) to complete a comparative legal study on the status of women, review its terms of reference, and report to the Council in 1947.[16]

The next February 1947, CSW amended its purpose, namely, to prepare recommendations and report to ECOSOC on promoting women's rights in political, economic, civil, social and educational fields with the object of implementing the principle that men and women shall have equal rights and develop proposals to give effect to such recommendations and consider urgent women's rights problems requiring immediate attention. It also recommended a fifteen-member body. The ECOSOC concurred, but retained authority over the conduct of business, the selection of members, and NGO observers as well as proposals for action.[17]

CSW INFLUENCE

The CSW's influence has been unique among UN bodies because of its connection with the international women's movement. It has always been an international intergovernmental body subsidiary to ECOSOC whose official members have been named by governments. But, unlike other such bodies, its official members, affiliated NGOs, and Secretariat staff have been primarily women.

In its early years, CSW members were usually experts who headed national women's organizations or held distinguished posts as parliamentarians, judges, lawyers, or, more rarely, UN ambassadors. As women moved into government officialdom in the 1970s, members were appointed from government ministries, and CSW became more purely political and less of an expert body. A Secretariat staff, the Section on the Status of Women, within the Division of Human Rights gave untiring support to CSW.[18]

The CSW, with council consent, collaborated with UN bodies as well as NGOs to promote its aims. The CSW sent a member to CHR meetings when the Universal Declaration on Human Rights and the International Covenants were discussed. The CSW staff kept members informed of developments in the SC and TC. At CSW's request, representatives of the International Labor Organization (ILO) and the UN Educational, Scientific and Cultural Organization (UNESCO) participated as nonvoting observers from 1947, and representatives of the World Health Organization (WHO) and the Food and Agriculture Organization (FAO) participated from 1951 and 1970, respectively. Also in attendance were representatives from the UN Children's Fund (UNICEF), the UN Development Program (UNDP), and the UN Fund for Population Activities (UNFPA). Beginning in 1948, the IACW was the first and, for more than two decades, the only non–UN intergovernmental body to observe CSW sessions. In 1974, the newly formed Commission on Arab Women also sent an observer.[19]

Of special importance were various international nongovernmental organizations (NGOs), especially women's organizations that enthusiastically participated in CSW. Upon gaining official consultative status with ECOSOC, fourteen NGOs attended CSW in 1950, thirty in 1974, and thirty-six by 1992. They publicized CSW decisions among their large memberships in various countries and in turn helped influence governments to undertake measures to improve women's condition.

The CSW members and NGO observers monitored ECOSOC and GA debates on CSW recommendations, offering explanations and support in both official meetings and in the corridors. As a result, the Council endorsed most recommendations and transmitted them to the GA and its Third Committee dealing with social and humanitarian affairs.

Though delegates often termed the CSW and the Third Committee the "women's committees," it was through them that women pressed the repeated adoption of international recommendations to influence governments' behavior and to establish women's issues as a significant priority on the UN agenda. It was also in debates in CSW, ECOSOC, the Third Committee, and particularly the UN women's conferences that the low politics of women's issues became linked with the high politics of security and economic matters.

Three distinct periods of CSW's political activity are apparent. In the first, CSW concentrated on defining the women's agenda, especially basic legal rights, and then expanded its program to encompass women's role in development. The second began with CSW's call for an International Women's Year (IWY), and continued through the end of the UN Decade for Women, 1976–1985. These initiatives facilitated the merging of the women's agenda with the larger UN political agenda and broadened CSW's program. A third phase began after the end of the Decade for Women when, in 1987, CSW reorganized its approach to an increasingly complex agenda to improve its ability to influence governments and international institutions to advance women's status to the year 2000.

Politics of CSW, 1947–1974

In the critical, formative period, Western and pro-Western members from Latin America, Asia, and the Middle East dominated the CSW as well as the UN generally. East Europeans were a minority. Ghana, the first African member state, was elected in 1962. In 1966, when CSW membership reached thirty-two, more African and Asian states joined.

In its early years, the East-West cold war conflict made itself felt in CSW in the 1950s over seating Taiwan's representative and over granting a visa to an East European–based NGO. In the 1960s there were tensions owing to the Arab-Israeli conflict, and in the 1970s there were clashes over petitions on violations of women's rights. But these issues were rarely disruptive since members, observers, and Secretariat staff predominantly reflected a traditional Western view of women's place in society and polity.

Having decided to complete the comparative legal study of women's rights, members asked the Secretariat to develop a comprehensive questionnaire for governments and NGOs. The first part dealt with public law, the second with property rights, and the third with family or private law. Based on replies, the Secretariat prepared various reports on women's political, economic, and civil status.

Political Rights

The CSW decided that the most important right not enjoyed by all women was suffrage. In June 1946, CSW asked for a report based on replies to the questionnaire on political rights. In its first resolution on women's issues, the GA adopted a draft introduced by Ambassador Begtrup. It called on all governments to grant women political rights immediately and to respond to the questionnaire.[20]

The preliminary report indicated that women had political rights in only forty-seven of seventy-four UN member states. The CSW promptly asked for further reports, including those on trust and non–self-governing territories so that members could keep a scorecard of government response. By 1949, since progress was slow, Amelia Ledon (Mexico) proposed a Convention on Political Rights to exert international legal pressure on governments to grant those rights. Kenyon (United States) argued initially that such rights were a domestic matter. It was up to women's organizations to work energetically to achieve them as they had in the United States. She also believed that the Human Rights Covenant before the CHR would make a treaty unnecessary.[21] However, when the CHR postponed action on the Human Rights Covenant the next year, the United States joined Mexico and others to support a convention. The United Kingdom preferred a public education campaign. Soviet and Polish members deemed political rights a matter of domestic jurisdiction. Nevertheless, CSW approved the Mexican–U.S. proposal and asked the Secretariat to submit a draft text in 1951.[22] After reviewing it for two years, CSW recommended a draft text that ECOSOC transmitted to the GA. The convention, approved by the GA, obliged ratifying governments to grant women the right to vote and stand for election, to hold public office, and to exercise all public functions on equal terms with men.[23]

The CSW then pressed governments to ratify and implement the convention. In 1953, it invited UNESCO to assess the extent to which women's legal equality was reflected in practice. With the help of the International Political Science Association, UNESCO surveyed seventeen countries. This study found public opinion unfavorable to women's participation in political life because of "an anti-feminist tradition . . . stronger in Latin than in the Anglo-Saxon and Nordic countries."[24]

To combat this bias, CSW supported citizen education for women, approving study guides and pamphlets on women's political rights for use by women's NGOs. Pakistan, in 1954, on behalf of the All Pakistan Women's Association, was the first to announce approval of the request for a UN expert to train a team of women leaders about their rights and responsibilities.[25] Similar requests soon followed.

Support also came through the UN Program of Advisory Services in Human Rights. Established in 1955, this program resulted from initiatives by the United States and Pakistan to expand the existing program of advisory social welfare services to encompass human rights, specifically women's rights.[26] The new program, administered by the Human Rights Division, helped UN members prepare legislation, organize government activities, create local societies, or convene regional and global seminars on human rights topics. The CSW held the first of several regional seminars in 1957 in Bangkok with its Asian members, representatives of the Economic Commission for the Far East (ECAFE), the Specialized Agencies, and women's NGOs to exchange views and recommend ways to improve women's participation in public life.[27]

The CSW meanwhile extended women's rights to encompass the UN Secretariat. In 1950, a U.S.–initiated report on women in the Secretariat revealed significant disparities between men and women in professional posts and gave rise to subsequent reports and CSW resolutions urging equal participation in the Secretariat and on national delegations.[28] In 1951, ECOSOC transmitted a CSW initiative by Bernardino urging the TC to appoint women to visiting missions to Trust territories. She reiterated the proposal in person before the TC, stunning delegates who never dreamed that women should or would join such missions.[29] Not until 1964 did a woman travel on a visiting mission when Angie Brooks (Liberia) was appointed.[30]

Economic Rights

Eventually, CSW turned its attention to an issue that had long preoccupied Eastern European countries—economic rights. (The socialist countries strenuously objected to the priority given by Western countries to political rights.)

In collaboration with the ILO, CSW embarked on a consideration of a wide range of subjects. When ILO representative Mildred Fairchild Woodbury advised CSW of ILO's intention to prepare a convention on equal pay, she invited CSW's views. After discussion and reports from the observers of the International Confederation of Free Trade Unions (ICFTU) and the World Federation of Trade Unions (WFTU), CSW approved a resolution combining proposals from China, the United States, and USSR. It reaffirmed the equal pay principle and asked governments to inform ILO of steps taken to implement it. Such measures included a pay rate for the job rather than a rate based on sex and the abolition of legal or customary restrictions on women's pay.[31] In 1952, CSW commended ILO's adoption of an equal pay for equal work convention and urged members that had not done so to ratify it and immediately enact implementing legislation.³² At CSW's request, ILO also prepared reports on a number of subjects ranging from day nurseries to tax legislation. These provided the basis for CSW recommendations to governments to establish such economic rights.

Education and Training

The CSW members and observers from NGOs, particularly the International Federation of University Women (IFUW), the International Federation of Women Lawyers (IFWL), and the International Federation of Business and Professional Women (IFBPW), as well as Unesco, understood that education was essential to exercising political and economic rights. In 1947, members called for a worldwide survey on education of women and girls and asked the Secretariat to circulate a comprehensive questionnaire to governments. The Unesco provided CSW with reports on primary and secondary education, access to higher and professional education, teacher training, and vocational training. The CSW urged governments to affirm women's access to all levels of education. The CSW discussions provided Unesco with views that were helpful in drafting the Convention on Eliminating Discrimination in Education, adopted in 1960.³³

Social Defense

In the LN, prostitution, traffic in women, pornography, obscene literature, and narcotics constituted "social defense," an antiquated term signifying a cluster of social evils that required concerted action to suppress. The ECOSOC gave responsibility for social defense to its SC, not CSW. When CSW sent a resolution on commercialized prostitution and venereal disease to ECOSOC for action by its SC and also to WHO, ECOSOC urged CSW not to duplicate the SC's effort.³⁴ Thus, CSW played no direct role in preparing the 1949 UN Convention for the Suppression of the Traffic in Persons and did not take up the matter again for almost thirty years.³⁵

Nationality

On another issue, CSW did contribute. An increasing number of women have faced a loss of nationality because of international marriages. Some wives have become stateless; others have acquired multiple nationality, and still others have been stranded in foreign countries through the death of husbands, legal separation, or divorce. The nationality of children from such marriages has also been an issue.

The 1933 Inter-American Convention on the Nationality of Married Women applied only to the Latin American Republics. The 1948 Universal Declaration on Human Rights proclaimed everyone's right to nationality but was not legally binding on governments. In 1948, Kenyon (United States) proposed that CSW give nationality rights to married women so that no woman would need to give up her country of birth. Bernardino agreed, seeing "nationality" as a "sacred right." The CSW then asked for a report on nationality laws and practices based on government and NGO replies to its comprehensive questionnaire.[36] Submitted in 1951, at the height of the cold war, the report precipitated U.S. and Soviet clashes. The Soviets viewed nationality as a domestic matter, not appropriate for an international convention. The United States backed a convention and persuaded a CSW majority to have the International Law Commission (ILC) rather than CSW, prepare one. The ILC had a crowded agenda and postponed action. After continued delay, CSW decided in 1955 to draft its own convention, and the following year its draft went to the GA.[37] When the GA's Legal Committee postponed action, Bernardino intervened to overcome the Legal Committee's procrastination, and GA approval was obtained in 1957.[38]

This convention drafted by CSW protects the nationality of the wife. It provides that neither the celebration nor dissolution of marriage between a national and an alien, nor the change of nationality by the husband during marriage, automatically affects the wife's nationality. The CSW publicized it in the *Legal Status of Married Women* and in the *Nationality of Married Women*.[39]

Ancient and Traditional Practices

Reports on trust and non–self-governing UN Charter territories requested by CSW spurred efforts to find ways to eliminate dowry, bride-price, sati, and child marriage. Learning of female circumcision from WHO's regional director for Africa in 1952, Latin members and Iran supported by NGOs at once urged governments to abolish all customs that violate the dignity and security of persons proclaimed in the UN Charter and Universal Declaration of Human Rights.[40] This recommendation was reiterated almost yearly by CSW without effect. When CSW asked WHO to investigate "ancient customs and ritual operations" in 1959, WHO's executive board said that the matter was cultural, not medical, and was thus outside its jurisdiction.[41] Later CSW dropped the subject when the ever-present suspicion of women from developed countries led African women at a 1964 seminar on family law in Togo to request that they, not Western women, deal with the matter.[42] However, an NGO, the Minority Rights Group, raised the subject in 1981 at CHR's Working Group on Slavery, which then named former CSW member Halina Embarek Warzazzi (Morocco) as special rapporteur to recommend measures to eliminate such practices.[43]

Marriage and Family Law

Perhaps the most significant area in which CSW worked to advance women's civil rights concerned marriage and family law. The CSW early influenced CHR to include a provision on the status of married women in the Universal Declaration on Human Rights.[44] In 1951, the Netherlands and Lebanon called for a report on family law and personal relations. Later Haiti and France encouraged CSW to recommend that governments ensure married women's right to independent work and to dispose of their earnings. But it was a provision in the final act of a 1956 conference approving the Supplementary Convention on the Abolition of Slavery, the Slave Trade, Institutions and Practices that precipitated CSW's comparative study of marriage.[45] The report, in turn, led Cuba, France, and Poland to propose an international convention on the minimum age for marriage. When ECOSOC rejected this in favor of a recommendation, CSW invited ECOSOC to reconsider its decision and asked the Secretariat to draft a text by 1960. On the basis of this draft, CSW prepared both a convention and a recommendation that were approved by ECOSOC and the GA.[46]

The Supplementary Convention established historic international standards: Marriage required full and free consent of both parties. Governments were to set a minimum age for marriage and were to designate a competent authority to record marriages in an appropriate registry. The Supplementary Convention acknowledged women's rights in marriage and accorded wives a status in civil law.

Later, CSW members asked for reports on parental rights and duties and developed by 1967 a set of international principles on equality in exercising such rights. To promote their acceptance, CSW publicized the principles and sponsored regional seminars on family law in which participants including NGOs exchanged views.[47]

Wider Horizons

Meantime, new African and Asian members who had joined the UN in increasing numbers saw CSW as a useful instrument to deal with questions of discrimination and economic development. The GA invited CSW to prepare a study of a Long-Term Program for the Advancement of Women as well as an instrument prohibiting discrimination against women.[48] In 1967 CSW responded to the latter with the Declaration on the Elimination of All Forms of Discrimination Against Women, the first comprehensive measure on women's rights. By 1979 it led to the convention on the subject.[49] Preparing the Long-Term Program challenged CSW members to rethink their views on the status of women and to emphasize increasingly women and development. Members of the CSW enlisted help from governments, UN programs, regional commissions, and Specialized Agencies. On the basis of the information collected, members assessed existing UN activities and resources, women's participation in community development, national commissions on the status of women, proposals for financing women's projects and centers for training cadres of women leaders. Their assessment along with a regional seminar on women and development in Manila in 1966 helped shape the Long-Term Program.[50]

Meanwhile, CSW pioneering action on family planning had also contributed to the Long-Term Program. A 1965 request from Australia, Finland, Egypt, and the United States, for a CSW study on the effects of family planning on women's life, education, and career plans, led to the nomination of Special Rapporteur Helvi Sipila (Finland) to prepare an in-depth study. The UNFPA lent its support for national surveys, and several valuable case studies were carried out.[51] The definition of family planning as a new human right soon gained international recognition and legitimation. At the UN Conference on International Human Rights Year in Teheran in 1968, Margaret Bruce (United Kingdom), UN Chief of the Status of Women Section and Conference Committee Secretary, presented a draft of the Long-Term Program and the 1967 Declaration. Then CSW member Sipila and representatives of such NGOs as the International Federation of Planned Parenthood (IPPF) lobbied conferees to refer to family planning, the Long-Term Program and the Declaration in the conference's Final Act. Later, CSW members and NGOs at the World Population Conference planted references to family planning and women and development in the 1974 World Population Plan of Action.[52]

In 1972, CSW made two important decisions that triggered even greater global recognition of women's issues. The first decision called for an IWY with the themes of equality, development, and peace; the second decision called for a conference to commemorate IWY.[53] The Conference on IWY in Mexico City resulted in the adoption of the first global public policy, to improve the status of women, entitled the World Plan of Action, with three goals: equality, development, and peace. The World Plan also reflected the merging of the women's agenda with the larger UN political agenda, linking for instance women's equality with the elimination of apartheid, the role of women in development with a New International Economic Order (NIEO), and women's contribution to peace with arms control and disarmament. The GA endorsed the conference report, proclaimed a UN Decade for Women, and asked CSW to prepare and implement a program for the Decade.[54]

CSW and the UN Decade for Women, 1976–1985

To fulfill its mandate to translate the World Plan of Action into an operating program for the UN Decade, CSW began a series of meetings. It convened in 1976 at the UN European headquarters in Geneva in September and again in December for two weeks each time. The sessions resembled miniconferences. Besides its thirty-two official members, an extraordinary number of official observers attended from governments, UN agencies and programs, NGOs, regional economic commissions, the Palestine Liberation Movement as well as the Council of Europe and the European Economic Communities.[55]

In drafting the program, members redefined priorities in terms of the broad outlines of the World Plan of Action: (1) policies, principles, and mandates; (2) specific areas for action; (3) information and educational activities for the UN Decade; and (4) review and appraisal of progress by governments, regional organizations, and international institutions. The CSW submitted the draft program to ECOSOC, which transmitted it to the GA.[56] The latter called for an annual report to be discussed by CSW on measures taken by governments and international institutions to implement the program. This new report reflected slow progress by governments and UN agencies in achieving the Decade goals.

To accelerate the pace, CSW, during its regular biennial meetings from 1976 through 1986, urged stronger national machinery (offices, bureaus, ministries) to enforce women's rights, better program coordination among international institutions, adequate staff and funding for regional organizations, and the incorporation of women's concerns in UN–sponsored conferences.[57]

Meanwhile, CSW addressed several new issues, including those raised in the Conference on IWY. Based on a report from Unesco, CSW decided in 1976 to appoint a Special Rapporteur to study and report on ways to eliminate stereotypes of women and girls in the mass media.[58] The CSW discussed the draft declaration on the participation of women in the struggle for peace, inspired by the German Democratic Republic, Libya, and Madagascar, following a 1977 GA initiative. Western members saw it as a propaganda ploy and sought to keep it from the Mid-Decade Conference. The CSW, however, invited government views and in 1980 submitted a revised draft that came before the GA for approval in 1982.[59]

In 1978, CSW held the first of a series of discussions on the effects of apartheid on women and children. On the initiative of France and Niger, CSW approved, over U.S. objection and Western European abstentions, a resolution condemning apartheid, urging all governments to isolate South Africa, inviting representatives of liberation organizations to participate in CSW sessions, and recommending that the item be included on the agenda of the 1980 conference.[60]

By 1980, CSW had determined the need to monitor the problem of women imprisoned or detained. Subsequently, at the United Kingdom's behest, CSW identified physical violence against detained women as a "trend" and asked for a report by 1986.[61] Western members as well as the Philippines, Trinidad, and Tobago then called for a study of domestic violence against women and for a seminar of experts on the subject. Later, a draft declaration was endorsed.[62]

The CSW had hoped to serve as the preparatory body for the 1980 conference, but ECOSOC decided, partly for budgetary reasons, to entrust the job to a twenty-three-member Preparatory Committee (PrepCom). The CSW sought, however, to make its influence felt. It supported, at India's behest, such conference subthemes as health, education, and employment, and an East European proposal for a review and appraisal of the Decade for Women aims during the second half of the Decade. The CSW also urged that the advancement of rural women be included in the conference agenda.[63] The conference approved the program for the second half of the Decade despite great contention. The CSW then amended the operating program for the UN Decade for Women to include new priorities, especially health, education, and employment.

As CSW began implementing the program for the second half of the UN

Decade, members expanded their consideration of women and development and also focused on newer issues. At France's behest, CSW asked for a Special Rapporteur to prepare a study of traffic in women and children with recommendations for remedial action.[64] Members endorsed an initiative urging governments to appoint women to delegations to the 1982 World Assembly on Aging and subsequently called for special reports on the situation of elderly women.[65] Recognizing that women comprised the vast majority of refugees, CSW requested studies with a view to alleviating the plight of refugees in Asia, the Middle East, and Southern Africa.[66]

In anticipation of the conference to commemorate the end of the Decade in 1985, the CSW successfully asserted its role as the conference preparatory committee. It met in special session apart from its regular biennial meetings to negotiate the draft entitled *Forward-looking Strategies for the Advancement of Women to the Year 2000* (FLS) for the Nairobi Conference. The FLS was ultimately approved by consensus.

Post-Decade Period, 1986–1995

In addition to its continuing responsibilities for the UN Women's Conferences and for monitoring the Forward-looking Strategies, CSW, at the initiative of Canada, Mexico, and the United States, began in the late 1980s to review and reorganize its program.[67] This had become essential in light of its increasingly heavy load resulting from the expansion of the women's agenda and its merging with the UN's political agenda. As a result, following a U.S. proposal, CSW has met annually and will do so until the year 2000. Members also agreed to organize its agenda by a thematic as well as a functional approach. The thematic approach, proposed by Egypt on behalf of the Group of 77, required a single issue within each of the three FLS goals—equality, development, and peace—to be selected for discussion and decision in cycles of five years each.[68] The functional approach adopted at Canada's suggestion has enabled CSW to focus on program monitoring and planning as well as policy development and coordination. The CSW also obtained permission to increase its membership from thirty-two to forty-five.[69]

When CSW held its first meeting of its enlarged membership, with Africans, Asians, and Latins outnumbering Western and Eastern Europeans, CSW devoted attention to a review and appraisal of developments since 1985. It was a mixed bag, members concluded. Women's efforts to achieve equality, development, and peace had begun to have an effect at the grass roots, but this had not yet been translated into action at the official level. Despite CSW's monitoring and assessment of old themes—like the effect of apartheid, women in political decision making, the relation of women's rights and human rights and violence against women, as well as newer themes like the role of women in environmental protection and their need to be legally literate—implementation of the FLS goals was deemed far behind.[70]

The CSW's efforts to influence the GA to commit adequate staff and resources to carry out its program had only limited success, owing in part—but not entirely—to UN budget constraints. Unless the pace of implementing the FLS is accelerated in the latter half of the 1990s, the progress of whole societies will be slowed and human resources wasted.[71]

The CSW approved a world conference to be held in 1995 and accepted China's offer to host it in Beijing. As the preparatory committee, CSW has drafted a platform of action structured to diagnose critical areas of concern and identify strategic goals and activities to achieve them at national, regional, and international levels.[72]

CONCLUSIONS

The determined women who created CSW in 1946 and their successors—members, Secretariat staff, and NGO observers—worked tirelessly to influence governments and international institutions to improve women's condition. Their efforts, as they have been reviewed in these pages, highlight the importance of a separate woman's place within the UN framework. Without such a place, women's rights, responsibilities, and contributions as citizens would probably not have been defined, elaborated, or advanced to the extent that they have been. It is also more than likely that women's issues would never have achieved the priority accorded them by the UN today.

NOTES

The author wishes to thank Margaret K. Bruce, former Director, Branch for the Advancement of Women; Dr. Julia Henderson, former Director, Social Affairs Division, and Mrs. Minerva Bernardino, Representative of the Dominican Republic to the UNCSW and Deputy UN Ambassador, for graciously granting interviews in connection with this chapter.

1. On the latter point, see Jeane J. Kirkpatrick, *Political Woman* (New York: Basic Books, 1974).

2. This is based on an analysis of UN delegations found in annual *Yearbooks of the United Nations*.

3. Women's Bureau, U.S. Department of Labor (USDOL), "International Documents on the Status of Women: Appendix B," *Bulletin*, No. 217 (Washington, D.C.: USGPO, 1947), 19–21; UN, "Annex I: Delegations to the UNGA, 1946–47," *Yearbook of the United Nations* (New York: UN, 1947), 304–10.

4. UN, GA, *Journal*, 1st Session, No. 30, 527–35.

5. Ibid., *Declaration on the Participation of Women in the Work of the UN: Report of the General Committee to the General Assembly*, A/46, 11 February 1946.

6. ECOSOC, Committee on the Organization of ECOSOC, *Proposals Concerning Terms of Reference of Commissions to be established by ECOSOC: Commission on Human Rights*, E/ORG./1 (2 February 1946), 1.

7. Women's Bureau, USDOL, *Bulletin*, No. 217, 73–78.

8. Dorothy V. Hall, *Making Things Happen* (London: Headley Bros., 1963), 232–33.

9. Robert E. Asher et al., *The United Nations and the Promotion of the General Welfare* (Washington, D.C.: Brookings Institution, 1957), 459, 500–549; unpublished interview with Dr. Julia Henderson, 21 June 1991.

10. Asher et al., *United Nations*, 459–63; Henderson interview.

11. Henderson interview; UN, *Yearbook of the UN* (1949), 164.

12. UN, ECOSOC, Res. 5, 18 February 1946.

13. UN, ECOSOC, Subcommission on Status of Women, *Summary Record*, 1st Meeting, E/HR/ST/3 (1 May 1946), 1; ibid., *Summary Record*, 2nd Meeting, E/HR/ST/7 (3 May 1946), 1–5.

14. Ibid., *Report to the Commission on Human Rights*, EHR/18/Rev.1 (13 May 1946), 170–71.

15. Personal communication with James F. Green, FSO assigned to Mrs. Roosevelt, 6 June 1975; Personal Communication with Bodil Begtrup, Copenhagen, Denmark, 17 July 1980; unpublished interview with Minerva Bernardino, New York, 3 and 5 December 1990.

16. James F. Green, *The United Nations and Human Rights* (Washington, D.C.: The Brookings Institution, 1956), 104; *Yearbook on Human Rights* (New York: UN, 1946), 437.

17. UN, ECOSOC, Commission on the Status of Women (CSW), *Report*, E/281 (18 February 1947), 1; UN, ECOSOC, Res. 48 (IV), 29 March 1947; UN, Doc. G/425, 1947.

18. Margaret K. Bruce, "An Account of United Nations Action to Advance the Status of Women," *Annals of the American Academy of Political and Social Science* 375 (January 1968): 164; unpublished interview with Mrs. Bruce, Larchmont, New York, 8 October and 6 December 1990.

19. M. E. Galey, "Promoting Non-Discrimination Against Women: The Commission on the Status of Women," *International Studies Quarterly* 23, no. 2 (June 1979): 273–302.

20. UN, GA, Res. 1(I), 16 December 1946.

21. UN, CSW, *Summary Record*, No. 41 (4 May 1949), 5.

22. Ibid., No. 84 (10 May 1951), 11.

23. UN, GA, Res. 640(VII), 20 December 1952; UN, *Compendium of International Conventions Concerning the Status of Women* (New York: UN, 1988), 7–10. Table on dates when women achieved the vote appears in Appendix 1.

24. Maurice Duverger, *The Political Role of Women* (Paris: UNESCO, 1955), 9–10.

25. UN, CSW, *1955 Report*, 15.

26. UN, ECOSOC, Res. 385D, 27 August 1951; ibid., Res. 504J, I and II, 23 July 1953; UN, GA, Res. 729, 23 October 1953.

27. UN, CSW, *1957 Report*, 26.

28. Ibid., *1949 Report*, 6–7.

29. Ibid., *1951 Report*, 15; interview with Bernardino.

30. UN, "Appendix III: Structure of the United Nations," in *Yearbook of the United Nations* (New York: UN, 1964), 621. Miss Brooks became vice-president of the TC in 1966.

31. UN, CSW, *1949 Report*, 12–13.

32. Ibid., *1952 Report*, 9–10; UN, *Compendium*, 62–63.

33. Jeanne Chaton, "Promoting Women's Education," *Annals of the American Acad-*

emy of Political and Social Science (January 1968), 145–53. UN, *Compendium* (1988), 102–5.

34. UN, ECOSOC, *Traffic in Women and Children* (1949), 1–6; UN, CSW, *1947 Report*, 10; ibid., *1948 Report*, 23.
35. UN, *Compendium* (1988), 25–27; CSW, *1982 Report*, 4.
36. UN, CSW, *Summary Record*, No. 89 (16 May 1951), 8.
37. Ibid., *1956 Report*, 14–15.
38. Interview with Bernardino; UN, CSW, *1956 Report*, 14–15; ibid., *1957 Report*, 21–22; UN, GA, Res. 1040, 29 January 1957.
39. UN, CSW, *Legal Status of Married Women* (New York: UN, 1958); ibid., *Nationality of Married Women* (New York: UN, 1963).
40. Ibid., *1952 Report*, 5; UN, ECOSOC, Res. 445C, 28 May 1952; UN, GA, Res. 843, 17 December 1954.
41. UN, CSW, *1959 Report*, 8; ibid., *1960 Report*, 22.
42. Interview with Margaret K. Bruce; UN, CSW, *1961 Report*, 6–7, 31.
43. UN, ECOSOC, CHR, *Report of the Working Group on Traditional Practices Affecting the Health of Women and Children*, E/CN.4/1986, 42, 4 February 1986.
44. UN, CSW, *1948 Report*, 12–13.
45. Ibid., *1957 Report*, 22.
46. Ibid., *1958 Report*, 7–8, 21; ibid., *1961 Report*, 7–11, 31–32; UN, GA, Res. 1680, 18 December 1961; ibid., Res. 1763, 7 November 1962.
47. UN, *Parental Rights and Duties* (New York: UN, 1968).
48. UN, GA, Res. 1777 (XVII), 7 December 1962.
49. Ibid., Res. 34/180, 18 December 1979.
50. UN, CSW, *1963 Report*, 41–44, 68; ibid., *1965 Report*, 34–43, 97–99; ibid., *1966 Report*, 50–54, 58–64, 107–10; ibid., *1967 Report*, 90–98, 128–29; ibid., *1968 Report*, 31–38, 54–56; ibid., *1969 Report*, 24–32; ibid., *1970 Report*, 7–20; ibid., *1972 Report*, 44–51.
51. Ibid., *1965 Report*, 42–44; ibid., *1966 Report*, 54–56; ibid., *1967 Report*, 93–94; ibid., *1968 Report*, 39–45; ibid., *1970 Report*, 21–23.
52. Interviews with Margaret K. Bruce and Dr. Julia Henderson. Unpublished interview with Helvi Sipila, 3 November 1989; UN, *Final Act of the 1968 Conference on Human Rights*, A/Conf. 32/41 (New York: UN, 1968), 3–5, 10–11; ibid., *World Population Plan of Action*, A/Conf. 60/19 (New York: UN, 1974).
53. UN, GA, Res. 3010, 18 December 1972; ibid., Res. 3276, 10 December 1974.
54. Ibid., Res. 3490, 12 December 1975.
55. UN, CSW, *1976 Report*, 92–94.
56. Ibid., *1976 Report*, 63–68, 89–90.
57. Ibid., *1978 Report*, 1–6, 13–15; ibid., *1980 Report*, 2, 9–10; ibid., *1982 Report*, 11–12; ibid., *1984 Report*, 12–13.
58. Ibid., *1976 Report*, 22–23, 81–82; ibid., *1980 Report*, 51–55.
59. Ibid., *1978 Report*, 6, 34; ibid., *1980 Report*, 33–37, 76–78; UN, GA, Res. 38/105, 16 December 1983.
60. UN, CSW, *1978 Report*, 11–12, 40–44.
61. Ibid., *1980 Report*, 16–17; ibid., *1984 Report*, 11–12.
62. Ibid., *1984 Report*, 5–6, 25–26; ibid., *1988 Report*, 25–26; ibid., *1992 Report*, 14–15, 48. The GA adopted the Declaration in Res. 48/104, 20 December 1993.
63. UN, CSW, *1978 Report*, 7–12, 31–36; ibid., *1980 Report*, 3–4, 22–32.

64. UN, CSW, *1982 Report*, 4, 50.
65. Ibid., *1982 Report*, 6–7; ibid., *1984 Report*, 4–5.
66. Ibid., *1982 Report*, 2–3, 7–9; ibid., *1984 Report*, 9–11, 48–50.
67. UN, GA, Res. 40/108, 13 December 1985, asked CSW to strengthen its ability to implement the FLS. UN, CSW, *1986 Report*, 21, 50–51. Unpublished telephone interview Maureen Reagan, U.S. Representative to the CSW, 17 July 1992.
68. UN, CSW, *1987 Report*, 6–8, 10–13; ECOSOC, Res. 1987/21 and 1987/22, 26 May 1987. Priority themes for 1992–1996 appear in Appendix 2.
69. UN, CSW, *1987 Report*, 7–8, 10, 30–31, 45–48; ibid., *1988 Report*, 25, 35–38; UN, ECOSOC, Res. 1987/23, 26 May 1987; ibid., Res. 1988/125, 27 May 1988; ibid., Res. 1987/23, 26 May 1989.
70. UN, CSW, *1990 Report*, 21–32; UN, *Women in Politics and Decision-Making in the Late Twentieth Century* (Dordrecht, Netherlands: Martinuus Nitjhoff), 1992.
71. UN, CSW, *1990 Report*, 21–32; unpublished telephone interviews with Chafika Sellami-Meslem, former Director, UN Division for the Advancement of Women, 6 November 1991, and with John Mathiason, Deputy Director, UN Division, 2 and 3 July 1991.
72. UN, ECOSOC, Res. 1987/21, 26 May 1987; UN, CSW, *1990 Report*, 17–18; ibid., *1992 Report*, 4, 36–42; ibid., *1993 Report*, 27, 79–84.

3
World Conference of International Women's Year

Virginia R. Allan, Margaret E. Galey, and Mildred E. Persinger

The real significance of the Conference of International Women's Year (IWY), held in June 1975 in Mexico City, is not merely that it was the first historic world conference of governments on the subject of women, nor that it produced the first international public policy to improve women's status (the World Plan of Action), nor that it was the largest consciousness-raising event held on this subject and advanced women's claim to full citizenship, nor that it fixed the status of women's questions on the United Nations (UN) agenda forever.

All of these were undoubtedly important. But the real significance of the Conference on IWY was that the occasion marked the beginning of the bringing together of two distinct agendas: the women's agenda, defined and developed by the Commission on the Status of Women (CSW) over thirty years, and the larger political agenda of the UN, articulated within its major political bodies. The merging of the two agendas was not complete at the end of the Conference on IWY. That process continued through the UN Decade for Women and the 1985 Nairobi Conference and is still continuing.

Women's groups, as mentioned previously, had called for an international conference of governments shortly after World War I and again at the first session of the CSW in 1946. Their call was finally answered in 1975.

Persistent activity by women scholars, diplomats, bureaucrats and nongovernmental organizations (NGOs) had helped change perceptions of women's role in society by 1970 when the UN General Assembly (GA) approved the Long-Term Program for the Advancement of Women. The 1974 UN food and population conferences helped expand the traditional view of women as reproducers and child bearers by highlighting their role in population policy, as producers of world food supplies and educators of children.[1] The CSW initiatives for IWY and the Conference on IWY continued to focus governmental attention on women's social issues and their relation to major world problems.

Commission members welcomed Romania's 1972 proposal on behalf of the Women's International Democratic Federation (WIDF), to proclaim IWY's twin goals: to promote equality and to increase women's contribution to development.[2] A third aim, women's increasing contribution to friendly relations among states and to world peace, was added by Greece and the Eastern Europeans in the GA. Thus, IWY's three goals became equality, development, and peace. Despite little indication that delegates understood the far-reaching nature of the resolution, the GA approved the decision on IWY and authorized the Secretariat to prepare a program on IWY for CSW's 1974 session.[3]

IWY PROGRAM

Based on suggestions from a few governments and UN agencies, the Secretariat presented a four-part program: (1) significance of IWY, (2) objectives and goals, (3) activities at the national level, and (4) activities at the regional and international level to be taken by governments as well as Secretariats of the UN, the UN Specialized Agencies and programs. With input from delegates and NGOs, CSW approved the program and a voluntary fund to which members invited governments, NGOs, and interested individuals to contribute.[4]

WORLD CONFERENCE OF IWY

Pat Hutar, U.S. member on CSW, proposed a world conference as the focal point of IWY. Initial State Department resistance had weakened as it became apparent that the world congress for the IWY, slated for 20–24 October in East Berlin, would be the only large international women's conference on the IWY.[5]

The CSW members welcomed the U.S. proposal. Chile, Colombia, Costa Rica, the Dominican Republic, Kenya, Liberia, Nigeria, the Philippines, and Thailand cosponsored it. But some worried about its cost. Others questioned its purpose. And still others thought it unnecessary in view of the East Berlin Congress. Still others feared that a conference might divide men and women in the world. Hutar emphasized that it would offer an opportunity to assess CSW's work over the last twenty-five years. When Colombia volunteered to host it, CSW quickly approved the proposal and in doing so began to connect the women's agenda with the larger UN political agenda as illustrated in IWY's stated purpose: to examine the extent to which CSW's recommendations had been implemented; to consider further programs to encourage the full integration of women, with special attention to rural areas; to develop an action plan to increase women's contribution to the achievement of the goals of the Second Development Decade; and to recognize the importance of women's increasing contribution to friendly relations, cooperation, and world peace.[6] The Economic and Social Council (ECOSOC) added the related purpose: elimination of racism and racial discrimination.

The GA approved the IWY program as well as the Conference on IWY on 10 December 1974 and also named a consultative committee to advise the Secretariat on an international plan of action.[7] The same day, Princess Ashraf Pahlavi (Iran), presented UN Secretary-General (SG) Kurt Waldheim with a Declaration of Support for IWY, signed by over sixty heads of state.

Then, unexpectedly, the Colombian government, which planned to host the conference, fell from power. Mexico, said to be seeking world prominence for its president, seized the chance and offered its capital as the conference site. The UN agreed.

Against this background, IWY officially began on New Year's day, 1 January 1975. Helvi Sipila (Finland), UN Assistant Secretary-General (ASG) and secretary-general of the Conference on IWY, declared that IWY would usher in a new era in international history. She appealed to governments to set aside prejudices of race, sex, language, or religion in order to confront problems affecting everyone. Her personal extensive travel to government capitals around the world to build understanding and interest in IWY and the conference encouraged vast activity as well as unexpected participation in the Mexico City Conference.[8]

The UN agency and program heads acknowledged the IWY in special reports, seminars, or ceremonies. Within the UN Administrative Coordination Committee (ACC), an Ad Hoc Inter-Agency Committee was established to review and coordinate IWY activities among UN agencies. The UN commissioned an official IWY emblem: a graphic integration of a stylized dove, the biological symbol for woman and the mathematical sign for equality. The Branch for the Advancement of Women issued a series of IWY bulletins; and on 8 March 1975, International Women's Day sponsored an "encounter" of eminent personalities at UN headquarters to discuss the topic "Women and Men: The Next Twenty-Five Years."[9]

Almost one hundred countries observed IWY before and after the Conference on IWY. Heads of state and senior government officials issued proclamations, declarations, and decrees. Over eighty governments created national commissions or committees or IWY centers and promoted seminars, lectures, symposia, conferences, or other special events.[10]

Women's NGOs formed an IWY committee to publicize IWY and sponsor special seminars and ceremonies.[11] These events highlighted awareness and spurred substantive preparations by governments and international institutions for the Conference on IWY.

Neither time nor money permitted appointing a special preparatory committee for the Conference on IWY, and CSW itself was not due to meet until 1976.

With a seemingly impossible deadline, the Secretariat undertook the main preparatory work for the Conference on IWY. By the end of March 1975, it had drafted an international plan of action to be reviewed by a twenty-three–member consultative committee and compressed into six months a preconference work load that normally required two years.[12] Guided by ECOSOC and GA resolutions as well as by recommendations from regional seminars and UN agencies, the Secretariat's draft plan of action emphasized guidelines for national, regional, and international action; research; data collection and analysis; mass media; and attitudes toward women.[13]

The consultative committee met at UN headquarters from 3 to 14 March 1975 to review this draft plan of action. Responding to Iran's prominent role and pledge of $1 million to a UN voluntary fund, committee members elected Princess Ashraf (Iran) as chair. Its ten-day discussion foreshadowed political divisions in the conference. The Group of 77 (G-77) supported the New International Economic Order (NIEO) and the Charter of Economic Rights and Duties of States (CERD). Eastern Europeans emphasized decolonization, detente, and disarmament. The United States asserted that such references detracted from the goal of equality. The committee then revised the draft text for circulation to governments for comment before the Conference on IWY.[14]

Meanwhile, the Secretariat, with borrowed staff from other UN divisions and three consultants, worked at fever pitch to complete, translate, publish, and ship necessary conference documents and background papers to Mexico City in time for the opening day, 19 June.

Opening Session

That day, about 5,000 participants gathered for the opening ceremony at the Giamnasio Juan de la Barrera when UN Secretary-General Kurt Waldheim called the Conference on IWY to order. He remarked that equality of men and women was essential to a more equitable international economic and social system and that equal rights of women, too long regarded a luxury, were vital to a world struggling with worsening poverty and ignorance. He urged representatives to regard sex discrimination as intolerable as race discrimination. The president of Mexico, Luis Echeverria Alvarez, appealed to women, the natural allies in the struggle against oppression, to improve their conditions by linking national action with international action and, specifically, with a new international economic order. The Conference on IWY acclaimed Pedro Ojeda Paullada, Mexican attorney general, as conference president. He promptly endorsed NIEO and expressed the hope that the conference would make it a reality.

Finally, Helvi Sipila, conference secretary-general, addressed the historic meeting. She pointed out that women constituted 49.8 percent of the world's 3.98 billion people and 500 million of the world's 800 million illiterates. Social and economic ills were rooted, she said, in the denial of women's rights and opportunities, a situation profoundly dangerous to world order. Sipila urged the conference to forge a new approach to development and to work for partnership between women and men in implementing the World Plan of Action.[15]

Delegates then approved the conference agenda and in doing so implicitly endorsed the bringing together of the women's agenda with the larger UN political agenda. Substantive items were (1) the aims and goals of the IWY; present policies and programs; (2) involvement of women in strengthening international peace and in eliminating apartheid, race discrimination, colonialism, and alien domination; (3) current trends and changes in the status of women and men, as well as obstacles to be overcome to achieve equal rights, opportunities, and responsibilities; (4) the integration of women in the development process; and (5) the World Plan of Action.[16]

Conference Proceedings: Consciousness Raising and Issue Expansion

Beginning on 20 June, official delegates and representatives of UN bodies, Specialized Agencies, and NGOs discussed the status of women in a plenary and two committees. By the early hours of 3 July, they had approved the first comprehensive global policy on women, called the World Plan of Action, as well as a Declaration of Mexico and thirty-four resolutions.

One hundred and thirty-three national delegations, 3 non-UN observer delegates, representatives of 8 UN Specialized Agencies, 13 UN programs, 8 national liberation movements, 6 non-UN IGOs and 192 NGOs in consultative status made up the roster of the Conference on IWY. Over 6,000 participants came to an unofficial parallel conference, an IWY Tribune, at the opposite end of Mexico City.

In contrast to sixty-five previous UN conferences, women were an unprecedented majority: 73 percent of government representatives and 85 percent of delegation heads.[17] But only one of three women heads of government or state, Sri Lanka's prime minister, Sirimavo Bandanaraike, was able to attend. Argentina's president and India's prime minister cancelled at the last minute because of domestic emergencies.

Wives of the presidents or prime ministers of Egypt, Pakistan, Jamaica, Israel, and the Philippines, the wife of Cuba's defense minister (and sister of President Castro), as well as the twin sister of the Shah of Iran, headed their delegations and gave the Conference on IWY international visibility.

Valentina Tereshkova, president of the Soviet Women's Association and the world's first woman astronaut, led the Soviet delegation. But most delegation chairs hailed from national ministries, especially domestic ministries of social and/or family affairs, women's affairs, labor or justice. Fewer came from foreign ministries. Fifteen members of parliament, mainly from Asian states, headed their delegations. The U.S. delegation was cochaired by the U.S. member of CSW and the U.S. Agency for International Development administrator. The latter planned a three-day stay but was the victim of domestic politics. After a violent attack by organized tomato-throwing agitators at an IWY Tribune session Friday afternoon and severe recrimination from American chicanos and blacks at a Saturday morning briefing at the U.S. Embassy, he returned to Washington, D.C.

Whether first ladies or sisters, ministers or members of parliament, many delegation chairs also headed national nongovernmental organizations. In addition, some eight delegation heads presided over government-backed women's organizations.[18]

Delegations ranged in size from one to forty-three (United States). But size did not predict influence in the Conference on IWY where the UN's rule—one state, one vote—prevailed. Majorities of varying sized delegations formed when voting occurred, usually when the women's agenda mingled with certain political agendas.

In the plenary, most delegates, describing their country's policies and programs to achieve the goals of IWY, articulated connections between the women's agenda and the larger political agenda. Debate ran into the late evening and early morning hours and two full days beyond the seven planned.

Almost all speakers referred to the interrelation of conference goals—equality, development, and peace—and urged action to achieve them. Several said that women's emancipation was inseparable from that of the nation and its peoples or from social and economic questions. Others referred to the neglect of women's rights in the context of human rights. Still others considered revolutionary change necessary to promote the liberation of women and ensure their equal rights.

Delegation heads denounced sex discrimination, although the Eastern Europeans claimed it did not exist in their countries because their national constitutions prohibited it. The Sri Lankan prime minister characterized women as "this forgotten half of humanity." Iran's princess spoke of ingrained prejudices against women and the deep and general movement for the emancipation of women, not only educated elites, but peasants of forgotten lands. Nigeria stated that discrimination against women was the worst form of discrimination because of its universality and because discrimination permitted a son to discriminate against his mother, a father against his daughter, and a brother against his sister.[19]

The U.S. cochair found sex discrimination the most widely known kind of discrimination and found equal rights and responsibilities for women essential.[20] But when Australia's advisor to the prime minister defined sexism—the only delegate to do so—most were mystified. Despite her definition of sexism as the artificial ascription of role, behavior, and even personalities to people on the basis of sex alone, occurring in societies ruled by men who colonized women by mute consent, the conference rejected the word *sexism*.[21] Many delegates thought it meant preoccupation with sex.

To achieve equality, countries such as Norway and Canada, supported domestic legislation. The latter referred to the first royal commission study on the status of women as a source of prospective legislation.[22] However, India asserted that no legislation could ensure women a rightful position. Others supported improved education, coeducation, and training, especially agricultural training. Still others called for national committees on women and for eliminating media stereotypes. Sweden's prime minister, Olaf Palme, said women's emancipation required the liberation of men, who had too little time with their children.[23]

Virtually all supported one international strategy to end sex discrimination: completion of the aforementioned Convention on the Elimination of All Forms of Discrimination Against Women, being elaborated in CSW. Apart from this strategy, Eastern European and Third World delegates stressed women's need to implement NIEO and CERD and to participate in the struggle against colonialism, racism, apartheid, and foreign occupation. China added superpower hegemony to this list of oppressive institutions but was quickly rebuffed by the Soviet and U.S. delegates. The Soviets charged China with "driving a wedge in the anti-imperialist front" and trying "to weaken the will of the people for a just peace." China in reply charged the USSR with engaging in arms expansion with other superpowers, citing, "huge munitions deals to reap fabulous profits from war." The U.S. and Western delegates rejected NIEO and CERD. Australia and France asserted that such programs alone would not change women's status. Instead, they supported bilateral and multilateral development programs.[24]

On peace issues, where there was little official clarity about women's role, delegates offered their personal and political agendas. European and Third World delegates called for ending the arms race, reducing military budgets, and convening a world disarmament conference. The United States urged internationally supervised general and complete disarmament and the need for women to so influence their governments.[25] Greece announced that women, as mothers and wives, were responsible for men who killed and sold arms to others to kill and urged women to eliminate crimes and scars left by foreign invasion and rape.[26]

Egypt's chief delegate asserted that "women's vocation is peace, we are the natural enemies of war, let us try to be the bearers of those principles of justice and mutual respect." But the Holy See disagreed, saying, "Woman is not automatically a peacemaker." Gabon called for ending tribal wars. Vietnam demanded U.S. withdrawal from Korea and Guantanamo. Morocco chided Spain for exploiting its peoples, which the latter denied. The representative of the Palestine Liberation Organization (PLO) labelled the U.S. Information Agency actions in Chile as evil. Sri Lanka and Mauritius urged maintaining the Indian Ocean as a zone of peace. Panama railed against the United States for its "illegal 1903 treaty" and exploitation of the Canal Zone.[27]

Inevitably political issues of the Middle East and South Africa arose. When Israel's chief delegate addressed the plenary, Arab delegations walked out, protesting Israeli government policies. Israel's delegate calmly responded that the walkout had no place in a conference on women's issues in which Israeli and Arab women should cooperate on common problems.[28] But delegates from Iraq,

Jordan, Libya, Morocco, and Somalia, following government policy, condemned Israeli practices, as did the PLO representative, who also urged the conference to support Palestinian self-determination.[29] Israel replied that Arab governments, not Israel, wanted to keep Palestinian refugees in camps at the expense of the international community.

Virtually all supported an end to apartheid. The Sudan urged moral support for the struggle of peoples in Rhodesia, Namibia, South Africa, and the occupied territories.

Conference Committee I

This committee met as a Committee of the Whole, to consider the principal conference document, the World Plan of Action. Chaired by Jeanne Martin Cisse (Guinea), committee members elected women officers from Bangladesh, Czechoslovakia, Uruguay, and Australia. The plan as revised by the twenty-three–member consultative committee, dealt with measures to advance IWY goals, specifically, (1) minimum national targets to be achieved by 1980; (2) specific areas for national action, including political participation, education, and training, as well as employment, health and nutrition, the family, population, housing, and other social questions; (3) research and data collection; (4) media and communications; (5) international and regional action; and (6) review and appraisal.

Most delegations wanting to leave their mark on the historic document proposed, within two days, upwards of 800 amendments to the draft plan. To cope with them, Committee I formed an informal working group and two subgroups. Sub-Group A discussed the purpose of the plan. Sub-Group B considered Chapter I, National Action, including minimum targets to be achieved. The working group, owing to time constraints, later approved the remaining chapters (II through VI) of the World Plan, as submitted to the conference, and appended their views to it along with regional plans of action developed at earlier UN regional seminars.[30]

Sub-Group A discussed the plan's relatively noncontroversial purposes. Then, Mexico, G-77 chair, proposed adding its own political agenda by inserting references to the NIEO and various *isms*: colonialism, foreign domination, racial discrimination, apartheid, and neocolonialism. The U.S. and Western delegates opposed "the NIEO" but after intense negotiation agreed to insert "a NIEO," meaning one of several possible international economic orders, in the "Introduction." The West then consented to refer to various oppressive institutions as among the greatest obstacles to full emancipation of women and to the progress of developing countries and peoples.[31]

Bringing together the women's agenda and the political agenda on questions of language in the Plan of Action required heavy negotiation. For example, the words "powerful revolutionary force" in the phrase "women as a powerful revolutionary force" appeared in Paragraph 8 of the draft plan. The United States insisted that no government wanted to invite its own overthrow and proposed women's ability to revolutionize the social, rather than political, order. Delegates agreed.

Links between both agendas were also reflected in new Paragraph 13 on the "special suffering of women in regions of alien domination" and in new Paragraph 23 that defined true international cooperation as national independence and sovereignty, sovereignty over natural resources, noninterference in internal affairs of states and peoples, the promotion of a just international economic order, and the end to practices and institutions of colonialism, fascism, foreign occupation and apartheid.

Sub-Group B discussed Chapter I of the draft Plan of Action. Delegates expanded the scope of women's concerns by enlarging the set of minimum targets proposed by the consultative committee to be achieved by 1980 to include health and family equality, recognition of the economic value of women's work in the home, education to stress women's roles as individuals, the promotion and establishment of women's organizations, and the development of rural technology to reduce the workload of farming women. They also referred to the need for national machinery (government offices, bureaus) to promote equality for women, and they referred to the active role of NGOs and to CSW as the UN focal point for implementing the plan. They then approved a revised Chapter I and recommended the World Plan as a whole to the conference plenary.

But before concluding, Committee I approved six draft resolutions, most of which expanded the women's agenda, as well as the Declaration of Mexico, for plenary action. The drafts elaborated several recommendations of the World Plan. They called for adequate public health investment, prevention of assault and cruelty against women, improved medical research on women's diseases; adequate staffing and funding to implement the World Plan; a Training Center for the Advancement of Women in Africa in cooperation with ECA's (Economic Commission for Africa) Research and Training Centre for Women, and the appointment of women delegates to the GA's 1975 Special Session. One draft linked women's concerns with the adverse effects of apartheid on women. But several Western states abstained because of the resolution's reference to sanctions against South Africa.[32]

Declaration of Mexico

After Committee I approved various draft resolutions, the G-77 pushed its political agenda and introduced its Declaration of Mexico, which Mexico's representative had proposed at an earlier UN seminar in Caracas. To forestall the G-77, just after the conference opened, the Federal Republic of Germany, the United Kingdom, and the United States introduced their own draft Declaration. The Western Declaration, replete with democratic principles, supported the maximum participation of women and men as necessary to the full and complete development of any country; equal access to education, decision-making positions in all spheres of activity, equal pay for work of equal value, and joint parental responsibility. It even called for balanced international economic relations; self-determination; noninterference in the internal affairs of states; and efforts to eliminate race discrimination, imperialism, and colonialism.[33]

Several Arab diplomats pressed their political agenda. In the G-77 caucus, Secretariat officials and several delegates, notably Leticia Shahani (Philippines) who chaired the drafting committee, negotiated the elimination of some of the most controversial political provisions of the declaration, including most G-77 references to Zionism and racism, while retaining social provisions actually more progressive than the Plan of Action. The negotiations split the Arabs, but by a single vote the caucus decided to introduce the declaration. It accented women's self-assertion, if not self-determination, in cooperation with men. It supported equality in family responsibilities and the right to plan families, the importance of opportunities to develop intellectual and spiritual potentials, and women's right to work with equal pay and participate in political life. It also identified women's responsibilities to educate themselves and to teach respect for the physical integrity of the human body—a negotiated substitute for the proposed wording of women's "right to control their own bodies"—and called for ending human rights violations against women and girls. But four paragraphs in the G-77 draft still referred to Zionism and racism.[34] After much hard bargaining, Committee I approved the declaration: eighty nine (USSR and the Third World) to one (Israel) and fourteen (United States and the West) and with the amended World Plan of Action and six draft resolutions sent it along to the plenary.[35]

Conference Committee II

On 20 June, Committee II, chaired by Iran, elected its officers, almost all women, from Belgium, Ghana, Hungary, and Jamaica. In general debate on current trends and changes in the status and role of women and men and the integration of women in development, delegations introduced about 168 draft resolutions. Combined ultimately into twenty-seven, the resolutions were reintroduced and circulated for discussion.[36] Many expanded the women's agenda.

Several resolutions invoked existing principles or standards on women and communications, education, health, and UN prohibitions against discrimination and prostitution.[37] One resolution was approved that urged states to protect the family and permit freedom to determine the number and spacing of children: thirty-eight for (Latin American and Western states), one against (the Vatican), and thirty-two abstentions (Asian and African).[38]

Still others recommended government-supported credit mechanisms for women, bilateral and multilateral agency support for rural development programs for poor women, and social and rehabilitation services for physically, mentally, or economically handicapped women of all ages.[39] Some were designed to improve research and data collection, widely recognized as essential to policy development, and to enhance programs on women and development.[40]

Delegates recommended two new institutions. The International Research and Training Institute for the Advancement of Women (INSTRAW) was proposed by Iran. A pilot UN voluntary development fund for women to support innovative programs proposed by the United Kingdom and Philippines later became the UN Development Fund for Women (UNIFEM).[41]

Finally, in Committee II several drafts linked women with peace and security matters: the Panama Canal, aid to Vietnamese people, the situation of women in Chile, and women's contribution to the structure of international peace and security. The most controversial was the G-77's proposal on Palestinian and Arab women. It appealed to women to proclaim their solidarity with Palestinian self-determination. But a controversial reference in its preamble listing Zionism with racism, colonialism, neocolonialism, and apartheid led to a vote after strenuous debate: seventy-one for (Eastern Europeans and G-77), three against (United States, Israel, and the Bahamas), and forty abstentions (mainly Western states).[42] All drafts were submitted to the conference plenary.

Final Plenary

Twelve days after it opened, conference delegations approved the World Plan, the first comprehensive global policy on the status of women, without a vote, and endorsed the reports of both conference committees and their draft resolutions. The draft Declaration of Mexico, which attempted to amalgamate the conference's political and social agendas, was left until last. Ultimately, the conference approved the text as a whole: eighty-nine (G-77), three negative votes (Israel, United States, and Denmark) and eighteen (mainly Western) abstentions.[43] The reference to Zionism was said to taint the victory that women won in the approval of the World Plan of Action.

In closing, Helvi Sipila found the epoch-making meeting a turning point in history. Women, the silent half of the world's population, had become vocal. Conference president Ojeda applauded the Declaration of Mexico, reiterated the importance of the CERD and called on governments to implement the Plan of Action.[44]

IWY TRIBUNE

When the UN had accepted Mexico's offer to host the conference, it became quickly apparent that potentially thousands of observers would flock to the site. To enable them to ally themselves with the UN drive for women's partnership in economic, social, and political life, a planned program was obviously needed.

The IWY Tribune convened at the same time as the official conference, 19 June to 2 July, but at the Convention Hall of the National Medical Center. A third of the participants came from Latin America, another third from North America, and a third from Europe, Africa, and Asia. In attendance were leaders of NGOs and of new local and national women's organizations; interested individual legislators, judges, lawyers; women teachers and faculty; members of professional associations; and a large contingent of Americans, including feminists Betty Friedan, Bella Abzug, Gloria Steinem, Jane Fonda, and Angela Davis. Spiritual leader Mother Teresa participated actively. Unknown grassroots leaders, such as fiery Domitila Barrios de Chungara, a Bolivian tin miner's wife, spoke of her experience and became an overnight celebrity. There were also professional agitators and large numbers of the press and media, mostly men.

Rosalind Harris and Mildred Persinger, long-time NGO leaders based in New York, organized the IWY Tribune in cooperation with the government of Mexico. Harris' success in arranging the tribune at the 1974 World Population Conference caught the interest of Don Antonio, Mexico's foreign minister. He prevailed on Harris to plan a similar meeting in Mexico City. Then president of the Conference of NGOs (CONGO) in consultative status with ECOSOC and UN Representative of International Social Service, Harris invited Persinger, UN Representative of the World YWCA, to chair the organizing committee. They met with Mexican officials in late February 1975 in Mexico City where they were asked to outline in detail the program for the two-week IWY Tribune.[45]

With three months to prepare, the 12-member planning committee then hired Marcia Bravo, a veteran of the tribune staff of the 1974 World Population Conference, to coordinate the program. Sympathetic governments, foundations, NGOs, and planning committee members enabled the committee to defray expenses of two staff members and a part-time secretary, fund publication of a daily newspaper, *Xylonen*, distributed daily to both the UN conference and tribune, and support travel costs of Third World speakers and resource persons from all walks of life. Using its NGO networks, the organizing committee sent out literally thousands of letters inviting registration on a first-come basis.

Tribune participants found the committee's planned program of twenty-five sessions organized around IWY themes, morning briefings on official proceedings, and plenary sessions, so stimulating that they held almost two hundred impromptu meetings.[46] For almost ten days, one such meeting brought from different countries forty to fifty women who constituted "an open and representative committee" to prepare thirty pages of "suggested revisions" to the text of the official World Plan of Action.[47] After submitting the draft to an ad hoc plenary at Centro Medico, these women expected to present it to the IWY Conference, but their hopes were dashed when Sipila advised them that official rules precluded unaccredited individuals or groups from submitting a text. Sipila urged the women to go home and work to implement the World Plan of Action. Despite the women's disappointment, collaboration on this common goal resulted in an empowering sense of cooperation, a precedent for the future.

The IWY Tribune has been judged of equal significance to the official conference because it joined countless men and women in the worldwide effort to advance women's status and it raised worldwide consciousness of the meaning of equality, development, and peace, as well as the workings of international institutions and procedures.[48] Subsequently, the IWY Tribune became the International Women's Tribune Centre (IWTC), a permanent center for responding to requests for information and for developing communication methods and educational materials for women and men throughout the world. Directed by Anne Walker, it mobilized support for the plan of action and for participation in the 1980 and 1985 forums held in conjunction with the UN conferences and their programs.

BERLIN CONGRESS

Many of those who had attended the Conference on IWY and IWY Tribune in Mexico City went on to participate in the World Congress in East Berlin, 20–24 October 1975. Sponsored by the Women's International Democratic Federation, which had initiated the proposal for IWY, the World Congress was attended by 2,000 women from 141 countries. The participants met for three days in nine commissions to discuss and exchange views on a full range of social problems confronting women, to reiterate support for the World Plan of Action and the Declaration of Mexico, and to adopt a Statement and Appeal to Women of the World, which the UN published and circulated as official documents.[49]

POSTCONFERENCE ACTION BY UN BODIES

As required by UN procedure, the IWY conference report containing the World Plan of Action, thirty-four resolutions and the Declaration of Mexico, was submitted to ECOSOC and the GA. Both approved it. The GA did so, however, only after heated debate on the Declaration of Mexico and separate votes on its controversial paragraphs, before adopting it as a whole: 107 (G-77), 1 (Israel), 26 (Western group).[50]

Over strenuous Western opposition, the GA also approved Resolution 3379, which equated Zionism with racism and aimed at discrediting Israel and, by association, Western—especially United States–Israeli—policy. Professional diplomats despaired. Israel's Ambassador Herzog called the GA a "theater of the absurd" and the Declaration of Mexico and Resolution 3379 an international scandal of major proportions.[51] Henry Kissinger, U.S. secretary of state, instructed U.S. Department of State officials henceforth to denounce the phrase whenever it appeared, and he prohibited U.S. officials from talking with the PLO. U.S. support for the UN immediately declined, ironically, just as IWY, one of the most successful UN-sponsored years, drew to a close and just as Americans were pressing for their own national IWY conference.

CONCLUSIONS

Three global events—the IWY, the Conference on IWY and the IWY Tribune—ushered in a new era. Despite abbreviated preparations and inadequate conference financing, the World Plan of Action affirmed an expanded women's agenda, one that had begun to join, however awkwardly, the world's political agenda. As the first comprehensive international public policy for women, the World Plan set forth goals and guidelines for governments, intergovernmental institutions, and NGOs. But implementation by all of these would be crucial to promoting equality, development, and peace, thus enabling women to move closer to full citizenship.

NOTES

The authors are grateful to Margaret Bruce—former director of the Branch for the Advancement of Women and Men, UN Secretariat and deputy director-general of the Conference on IWY—for her informed, judicious comments on an earlier draft of this chapter. Thanks are also due to Helvi Sipila, former ASG for Social Development and Humanitarian Affairs and IWY Conference SG; Pat Hutar, U.S. Representative to CSW; and Rosalind Harris, president of CONGO, for their willingness to grant interviews on the various aspects of this chapter.

1. Unpublished interview with Helvi Sipila, SG of the Conference on IWY, New York, New York, 3 November 1990. See Hilkka Pietila and Jeanne Vickers, *Making Women Matter* (Atlantic Highlands, N.J.: Zed Press, 1990), 74–75.

2. Pietila and Vickers, *Making Women Matter*, 73–74; CSW, *1972 Report*, 87–88.

3. UN, GA, Res. 3010, 18 December 1972.

4. UN, CSW, "Res. I: International Women's Year" and "Res. II: Establishment of a fund for voluntary contributions," *1972 Report*, 1–2.

5. Patricia Hutar, former Republican National Committee Cochair, was named by President Richard Nixon and reappointed by President Gerald Ford as U.S. representative to CSW. Unpublished interview with Pat Hutar, 14 September 1990, Washington, D.C.

6. UN, CSW, *1974 Report*, 3, 26–27.

7. UN, GA, Res. 3276, 10 December 1974, was adopted 124–2 (Israel and Nicaragua) −2 (Malawi and Saudi Arabia). UN, GA, Res. 3277, 10 December 1974, adopted 125–0–2 (Malawi and Saudi Arabia).

8. UN, ECOSOC, Consultative Committee, *Draft Report*, Pt. I, E/CONF.66/CC/L.3 (12 March 1975), 1–2. Unpublished interview with Mrs. Sipila, 3 November 1989. Unpublished interview with Mrs. Bruce, 6 December 1990, Larchmont, New York.

9. Interview with Mrs. Bruce.

10. UN, GA, *International Women's Year: Measures and Activities Undertaken in Connexion with International Women's Year*, A/10263, 2 October 1975. See also Australian National Advisory Committee, *Report on IWY* (Canberra, Australia: Australian Government Publishing Service, 1976); Women's National Commission/International Women's Year Coordinating Committee, *International Women's Year 1975 in the UK*, vols. 1 and 2 (London: Women's National Commission, 1976); U.S. Center for IWY, *The Year That Became a Decade* (Washington, D.C.: U.S. Center, 1976).

11. Unpublished interview with Esther Hymer, UN Representative of International Federation of Business and Professional Women and Church Women United, Shrewsbury, New Jersey, 16–17 August 1990.

12. Johan Kaufmann, *Conference Diplomacy* (Leyden, Netherlands: A. W. Sitjhoff, 1968), 45–65. Basic documents prepared by the UN Secretariat were *Report on Current Trends and Changes in the Status and Roles of Women and Major Obstacles To Be*

Overcome in the Achievement of Equal Rights, Opportunities and Responsibilities, E/CONF.66/3 and Add. 1 and 2; *Report on The Integration of Women in the Development Process as Equal Partners with Men,* E/CONF.66/4; *The UN System and the Elimination of Discrimination Against Women,* E/CONF.66/BP/1. FAO, UNESCO, WHO, and ILO each prepared background reports, as did the UN World Food Program, UNICEF, and the UN Development Program. Expert consultants prepared the *Report on Certain Aspects of the Integration of Women in Development,* E/CONF.66/BP/5; *The Situation of Women in the Light of Contemporary Time Budget Research,* E/CONF.66/BP/6; *Report on the Implications of Scientific and Technological Developments for the Situation of Women and Their Integration in Development,* E/CONF.66/7.

13. UN, World Conference on IWY, *Regional Consultation for Asia and the Far East on Integration of Women in Development with Special Reference to Population Factors: Plan of Action,* E/CONF.66/BP/2, 28 February 1975; *Regional Seminar for Africa on the Integration of Women in Development with Special Reference to Population Factors: Plan of Action,* E/CONF.66/BP/3, 4 March 1975; *Regional Seminar for Latin America on the Integration of Women in Development with Special Reference to Population Factors, Declaration and Recommendations of the Seminar,* E/CONF.66/BP/17, 9 June 1975.

14. UN, Consultative Committee for the World Conference on IWY, *Draft International Plan of Action: Revised Proposals and Suggestions on Chapters I and II,* E/CONF.66/CC/L.4, 12 March 1975.

15. UN, *Meeting in Mexico* (New York: UN, 1975), 7–11. See also UN, *Report of the World Conference of IWY,* E/CONF.66/34 (1976), 123–26.

16. UN, *Report of the World Conference of IWY,* 128–29.

17. Based on an analysis of the list of participants at the World Conference of IWY.

18. Ibid. See also Jennifer Whitaker Seymour, "Women of the World: Report from Mexico City," *Foreign Affairs* 54, no. 1 (October 1975), 174.

19. UN, *Report of IWY Conference,* 132–34; UN, Office of Public Information (OPI), Press Release IWY/30 (24 June 1975), 2; ibid. IWY/32 (24 June 1975), 1–2.

20. Statement by Patricia Hutar, Chair, U.S. Delegation to the World Conference on IWY, 20 June 1975; *Department of State Bulletin* (18 August 1975), 2.

21. UN, *Meeting in Mexico,* 12–13.

22. UN, OPI, Press Release IWY/29 (24 June 1975), 4; ibid. IWY/38 (26 June 1975), 1–2.

23. Ibid. IWY/29 (24 June 1975), 1–2.

24. Ibid. IWY/33 (24 June 1975), 4–5.

25. Statement by Patricia Hutar, *Bulletin* (18 August 1975), 3.

26. UN, OPI, Press Release IWY/30 (24 June 1975), 3–4; ibid. IWY/37 (26 June 1975), 5; ibid. IWY/42 (27 June 1975), 4–5; ibid. IWY/48 (30 June 1975), 2.

27. Ibid. IWY/32 (24 June 1975), 3; ibid. IWY/45 (30 June 1975), 5; ibid. IWY/48 (30 June 1975), 1–3.

28. Ibid. IWY/35 (25 June 1975), 4–5, 6.

29. Ibid. IWY/45 (30 June 1945), 5–7, 9.

30. UN, *Report of IWY Conference,* 140–52.

31. United States, Department of State, *Report of US Delegation* (1975), 20–21.

32. UN, *Report of IWY Conference,* 146–50.

33. UN, World Conference on IWY, *Draft Declaration,* submitted by FRG, UK, and USA, E/CONF.66/C.1/L.22, 25 June 1975.

34. Ibid., submitted by sixty-four states, E/CONF.66/C.1/L.37 (28 June 1975), 1–6. See also UN, *Meeting in Mexico*, 25–28.
35. UN, *Report of IWY Conference*, 150.
36. Ibid., 153–74; United States, *Delegation Report*, 31.
37. UN, *Report of IWY Conference*, 163–66.
38. Ibid., 87–88, 164.
39. Ibid., 82, 86, 96–99.
40. Ibid., 86–87, 102–3.
41. Ibid., 84–85, 102.
42. Ibid., 110–13, 166–68.
43. Ibid., 150–52, 165–74; UN, *Meeting in Mexico*, 28–36.
44. UN, *Report of IWY Conference*, 180–81.
45. Unpublished interview with Rosalind Harris, New York, New York, 9 October 1990. Unpublished interview with Mildred Persinger, Rosalind Harris, Virginia Saurwein, and Virginia Hazzard, New York, New York, 10 August 1991. See also UN, *Meeting in Mexico*, 37–42.
46. Rosalind Harris and Mildred Persinger, "Report: International Women's Year Tribune, 1975," mimeographed.
47. "The World Plan of Action," *Women in Action* Pt. 2 (Berkeley, Calif.: Al-Ber Costa Chapter, UNA/USA, 1976), 1–70.
48. One was Betty Friedan, "Scary Doings in Mexico," in *It Changed My Life* (New York: Random House, 1976), 344–65.
49. Women's International Democratic Federation, *Women of the Whole World* 1 (1976), 4–5, 26–32, 34–36.
50. UN, GA, Res. 3520, 15 December 1975.
51. UN, GA, 30th session, Official Records Plenary Meeting No. 2441, vol. 3, pp. 1334–35, 1341.

4
Losing the Battle/Winning the War: International Politics, Women's Issues, and the 1980 Mid-Decade Conference

Jane S. Jaquette

The second conference of the UN Decade for Women convened in Copenhagen on 14 July 1980. In retrospect, it was the most conflictive of the three conferences held during the Women's Decade. At its close, in the early hours of 31 July, four countries—the United States, Canada, Australia, and Israel—voted against the Programme of Action; the rest of the Western delegations abstained. The Palestine Liberation Organization (PLO) declared the conference outcome a "victory," and the U.S. press labelled it a diplomatic defeat. Many left Copenhagen convinced that the international women's movement had been irrevocably damaged.[1]

This outcome was not inevitable: The draft Programme of Action that emerged from the Preparatory Committee in April did not include the three paragraphs attacking Israel that produced the final vote. These were a product of the conference negotiations in Copenhagen. The main issue addressed by the existing literature is why a conference ostensibly devoted to women's issues ended in a deadlock on Middle Eastern politics. Now, over a decade later, with the Eastern European bloc dissolved and the "South" in disarray, additional questions deserve our attention.

This chapter will address the politics of the vote, but it will also ask why ninety-four countries, most of which have done little to recognize women's contributions or alter centuries-old patterns of discrimination, voted for a document that commits them to do both. It will assess the long-term effects of the Mid-Decade Conference on defining an international agenda for women and on focusing the attention of the international community on those issues.

Despite the impression given by journalists and shared by many participants that the United States and its closest allies had suffered a stinging defeat, the Mid-Decade Conference has received little attention in the international relations literature. The few articles that appeared in the women's studies journals and in the newsletters and magazines of the women's movement were largely personal accounts. The most detailed assessments were prepared by the U.S. delegation and by the congressional staff members who helped staff the delegation.[2]

These accounts focus on the politics and personalities of the Mid-Decade Conference from very close range, defending the U.S. position and often justifying specific actions taken by the delegation in the heat of battle. They conclude that the conference might have gone more successfully for the United States if the U.S. delegation, appointed late in the spring and chosen to represent U.S. women's constituencies rather than to maximize diplomatic experience, had been better led and prepared. They argue that the conference secretariat was not a neutral arbiter in the conflicts between the United States, Israel, and the Western bloc, on the one hand, and the developing countries and the Eastern European bloc, on the other. Some accounts see an immature international women's movement unable to hold on to its own agenda; they point to the moments when the conference was "politicized," often by men who took over from women delegates to press for language on the New International Economic Order (NIEO) or to condemn Israel.[3]

This chapter draws on that material but attempts to go beyond the conference itself to understand its dynamics and consequences within the broader context of international politics, taking Southern perspectives into account.

THE INTERNATIONAL CONTEXT

In the UN context, the lopsided vote in Copenhagen was not an anomaly but a consistent part of an overall pattern of growing U.S. isolation in the General Assembly (GA). During the 1940s and 1950s, the United States and its Western European and Latin American allies controlled a voting majority in the GA, which in turn became an international resource for the West in its confrontation with the USSR. The GA vote to support an international "police action" in Korea is the case that defined the era.

In the 1960s, as the newly emerging Asian and African states of the "South" began to overtake and then decisively outnumber the votes of the "North," the UN agenda changed to reflect Southern interests, and the United States was increasingly on the defensive. By the 1970s, a new pattern was established in which the GA became the forum where the developing countries could call for a New International Economic Order. South Africa was effectively marginalized from the UN as the GA voted to condemn and sanction apartheid.[4]

By the mid-1980s, Israel had come under similar scrutiny with regard to its policies toward the Palestinians; during the Decade for Women, the GA stepped up the pressure on Israel to negotiate with the PLO and loosen its grip on the "occupied territories." Israel, with the full backing of the United States, resisted these efforts. The 1970s also marked the high point of military rule in Latin America, as the policies of right-wing military allies of the United States frequently came under attack in the GA. The United States and sympathetic Western bloc allies counterattacked, questioning the ideological neutrality of the UN by pointing out the GA's "double standard" of criticizing right-wing, but not left-wing, dictatorships.[5]

Through the 1960s and 1970s, the South elaborated and sharpened its own agenda. Two overlapping blocs, the Non-Aligned Movement (NAM) and the Group of 77 (G-77), came to dominate the GA. With the East/West stalemate in the Security Council, these two caucuses could effectively define UN policies. The key principle uniting the NAM was anticolonialism, which in practice meant pressure on South Africa and, as Arab influence increased, on Israel. The NAM's strength was in Asia and Africa; it gave largely rhetorical support to the movements of national liberation and criticized the Latin American military dictatorships, reliable anticommunist allies of the United States.

The Latin Americans took the lead in the more inclusive G-77, formed in 1964 to caucus for changes in the international regime of trade and aid. The G-77, which had over one hundred members by 1980, took as its main premise the view that the international economic system was unjust; it promoted the NIEO to increase the flow of capital from North to South, to gain access to Northern markets, and to stabilize and improve the prices of Southern agricultural and raw material exports.

The one nation–one vote rule in the GA both anticipated and exaggerated the shift in power toward the South. In the late 1970s, the North/South confrontation was heightened by a series of international events. The overwhelming success of the Organization of Petroleum Exporting Countries (OPEC), which tripled the price of oil, revealed the economic vulnerability of the West and greatly increased the influence of the Arab states. The U.S. failure in Vietnam, followed by victories for the revolutionary movements in Iran and Nicaragua in 1979, seemed to prove that the United States was a superpower in decline. The Carter administration's progressive attempt to engage in a North-South dialogue won it few points and actually seemed to enhance the widespread impression that the United States was in serious trouble.

As the decade grew to a close, the unity of the Western bloc declined and the United States increasingly stood alone. One indicator of deepening U.S. isolation was the growing number of U.S. negative votes in the GA: In 1960 the United States cast two negative votes; in 1970 the number was seventeen, but in 1980 the United States voted against the majority forty-five times. Between 1975 and 1980, the United States accounted for one-fourth of all the single negative votes cast.[6] In 1976, the United States dropped its uncompromising opposition to sanctions and to language supporting NIEO; but the one issue on which it did not compromise was support for Israel. Thus, it is not surprising that a conference marked by a high degree of North-South tension would be stalemated by Middle Eastern issues.

UN CONFERENCES

The political dynamics of the Women's Decade conferences differed in some important respects from the other global issue conferences sponsored by the GA. In most UN conferences, the nongovernmental organizations (NGOs) are largely in agreement about what the problem is and what needs to be done. Consensus is hammered out by "networks of knowledge-based experts," using scientific research to reinforce their positions. In addition to consciousness raising,[7] the conferences typically provide an arena for North-South bargaining, with the North agreeing (on paper) to compensate the South for at least part of the costs of change.

By contrast, the NGO base for the women's conferences was ideologically divided and weak in cross-national linkages: Even the term *feminism* was unacceptable to most Third World women.[8] The Women's Decade conferences did not call for the redistribution of resources between North and South, but for the reallocation of existing resource flows between men and women. Under pressure from its domestic women's movement, the United States had a stake in having the conference produce a strong document on gender equality, but it had little economic or moral leverage to bring this about.

Ultimately, consensus emerged through "women's linkage" politics: Women's claims to resources were linked to larger development issues that had broad support in the GA. But there was no prior "epistemic community" of agreement, and the conference could easily have foundered had the South chosen to defend cultural nationalism or to define the Northern agenda as "feminist imperialism."[9]

Delegates brought to the conference a "bloc perspective" on women's issues. Western delegates had traditionally emphasized equal rights for women, especially legal rights. Events in the 1970s added the "women-in-development" agenda, which sought to guarantee women's access to development programs and resources and provided a bridge to the interests of Third World women. For their part, many women from the developing countries felt strongly that the most important factors determining women's status were economic and that apartheid and other "vestiges of colonialism" prevented women from exercising their most basic rights.

Fresh from a decade of fighting for women's equality in male-dominated democracies, most Western delegates were suspicious of the South's "structural" agenda, which they saw as diversionary and thus as "politicization" of the conferences. Similarly, as Mallica Vajrathon wrote afterward, even the feminists from the South rejected the view that the Western delegates should decide what was "political" and what was a "women's issue." "It is simplistic," she argued, to think "that all women in the world would see the struggle to improve their lives only in male versus female terms."[10] The West's bid to limit the discussion to women's issues, narrowly defined, was seen as self-serving because it left Western economic and neocolonial domination unchallenged.

The Eastern bloc, which could have taken a more purely Marxist position on women's issues, confined itself to defending the point that women had already achieved equality under socialism and to calling for women to promote peace and disarmament in the Programme of Action. Politically, it aligned itself with the G-77 and NAM, leaving the often divided and ambivalent Western bloc to defend its interests from a weak minority position.

CONFERENCE AUTHORIZATION AND PREPARATIONS

In December 1975, following a recommendation in the Plan of Action agreed upon in Mexico City earlier in the year, the GA voted 1975–1985 the "Decade for Women" and approved a Mid-Decade conference to be held in 1980 to "review and evaluate progress." Shortly thereafter, the UN Economic and Social Council (ECOSOC) asked the Commission on the Status of Women (CSW) to begin planning the 1980 conference.

However, in May 1977, as part of a larger reorganization plan, ECOSOC named a preparatory committee of twenty-three states. Six states (including the United States) were from the North; three (including the USSR) were from the East; and the rest were from the South: four each from Asia and Africa, three (including Cuba) from Latin America and the Caribbean, and two from the Middle East. Iran was included, since it was anticipated that the conference would be held in Teheran.

In February 1978 Secretary-General Kurt Waldheim appointed Lucille Mair, a Jamaican historian and diplomat, as secretary-general to the conference, in charge of the conference secretariat.[11] Mair had a strong background in women's issues, but was also very committed to Third World positions; she had served in several UN posts including vice-chair of the social committee of ECOSOC and the Third Committee of the GA. Her role in the conference would be controversial.[12]

The first preparatory committee (PrepCom) meeting was held in New York in June 1978; it was chaired by Lena Gueye of Senegal. The second was held in the fall of 1979, staffed by Mair and the new secretariat, and chaired by Maimouna Kane, also from Senegal. In December 1979, the GA added two new items to the conference agenda. The first stipulated a review of the "effects of Israeli occupation on Palestinian women in the occupied territories" and the second called for a review of the conditions of refugee women—a new topic and one that had strong Western support. The GA also called on the conference to consider measures to integrate women in development.

When the third PrepCom met in April 1980, with Kane again in the chair, it reviewed the reports submitted by the five UN regional commissions. The report on Palestinian women, submitted by the Economic Commission for West Asia (ECWA), was met with strong objections by the Western delegates to the PrepCom on the grounds that it was biased against Israel. Despite these objections, but in keeping with the usual practice with regard to regional commission reports, it was accepted as an official conference document.[13]

In preparation for the Conference, the secretariat under Mair prepared nineteen documents reviewing the progress on the Plan of Action; eleven of those were based on national questionnaires to which ninety-six governments eventually responded.[14] Mair also commissioned reports, including one by Ingrid Palmer that reviewed the treatment of women in other global issue conferences held under UN auspices; this study showed that women and women's concerns were often ignored, even in obvious cases like the first Population Conference, held in Budapest in 1974.[15]

THE CONFERENCE

The main purpose of a UN issue conference is to produce international agreement on a final document that outlines origins of the issue at hand and sets out the means by which the UN, and the international community more broadly, should address the problem.

It was anticipated that the Programme of Action would produce debates that would divide the delegates along both feminist and bloc lines. The causes of women's low status, discussed primarily in the first forty-six paragraphs of the Programme of Action, was understood by Western delegations largely as discrimination but was understood by the South (with support of the Eastern European countries) as a product of international economic exploitation and colonialism. The introductory section of the draft Programme of Action emerged from the PrepComs with many paragraphs bracketed for further discussion.

The emphasis on Palestinian women and apartheid showed the impact of the GA in setting the agenda and made confrontations between North and South over sanctions and the Middle East almost inevitable. The NIEO language appeared throughout the draft Programme; it was resisted by the West, but perhaps most persistently by Japan.

One hundred and forty-five member states sent delegations to the Mid-Decade Conference. In addition, twenty-three UN offices were represented, nearly half of which had not sent anyone to the World Conference of International Women's Year (IWY) in Mexico City. The UN High Commissioner for Refugees (UNHCR), the World Health Organization, and the International Labor Organization substantially increased their participation. The UN University, the International Research and Training Institute for the Advancement of Women (INSTRAW), the UN Conference on Trade and Development (UNCTAD), and the regional commissions (each of which had held its own meeting to develop a regional agenda) were also present, as were the UN Council for Namibia and the Special Committee on Apartheid. Observer delegations included the PLO (twenty-three members), SWAPO (South West Africa People's Organization, seven members), ANC (African National Congress, one member) and the Pan Africanist Congress of Azania (three members). Of the non–UN intergovernmental organizations, the European Economic Community (EEC) sent the largest delegation (nineteen members); the League of Arab States sent four. Many NGOs with UN consultative status sent observers.

The United States had the largest national delegation (fifty), followed by Italy and Kenya. Those countries with over twenty delegates included the Nordic countries, France, West Germany, the Netherlands, and Belgium from Europe; Mexico and Venezuela from Latin America; Australia, China, and Indonesia from Asia; and Iraq and the USSR. Most delegations had fewer than nine members. In contrast to the Conference on IWY in Mexico City, fewer than 10 percent of the delegations were headed by men. As usual, most female delegates came from government departments traditionally associated with women's issues (such as health and social welfare), although there was a visible trend toward women from women's parties and women's bureaus.[16]

A preconference session, chaired by Kane, set the tasks of the three conference committees. The domestic dimensions of the program were assigned to the First Committee, while the Second Committee took the international dimensions and the item on refugees. A newly formed Committee of the Whole was set up to negotiate the ideologically sensitive introductory section.

The speeches given by Secretary-General Waldheim, Queen Margrethe of Denmark, and Lisa Ostergaard, head of the Danish delegation and chair of the Mid-Decade Conference, provide evidence of not only the degree to which the UN leadership was responding to the strength of the alliance between South and East but also the deep ambivalence of the Western bloc. Waldheim emphasized the South's structural position, arguing that global problems are "interlocked" (thus, women's issues cannot be dealt with in isolation), and he deplored the arms race, having just received a disarmament petition signed by 1,500 Nordic women.

Queen Margrethe praised the Declaration of Mexico, the document denounced by the United States and others because of its equation of Zionism and racism. Her plea that the effort to achieve equal rights for women should "take due account of the personal capacity of the individual" could be seen as a subtle attack on affirmative action. Her closing remarks warned the participants at the Mid-Decade Conference not to act in a "political vacuum" and called for efforts to strengthen "international development and peace." Ostergaard alone gave equal weight to the views of Western feminists and Southern structuralists. Sensing the conflicts ahead for the delegates, Ostergaard pledged to "spare no effort" to produce a consensus on the Programme of Action.[17]

As part of the preconference ceremonies, sixty nations signed the Convention on the Elimination of All Forms of Discrimination Against Women (CEDAW).[18]

THE FIRST AND SECOND COMMITTEES

The thesis that the dynamics of the Mid-Decade Conference itself made a crucial difference in the outcome receives some support from the analysis of the First and Second Committees. The First Committee, chaired by Maimouna Kane, reached agreement on the language of Part 2 of the Program of Action and on ten of eleven resolutions it submitted to the plenary.

By contrast, the Second Committee, chaired by Sheila Kaul of India (which chaired the G-77), was much more contentious. Of the thirty-four draft resolutions considered in the Second Committee, thirteen required a vote, and three of those were roll call votes. Members of the U.S. delegation attributed the consensus achieved in the First Committee to Mrs. Kane's leadership;[19] it is also clear from the debates that India played a major role in challenging the West, and the United States in particular.

The First Committee was not without its dramatic moments, however. Of the eleven resolutions sent to the plenary, all but one, on disabled women, produced reservations on the part of some delegations. The family planning resolution prompted reservations from six Latin American delegations, Romania, and the Holy See; and the USSR and Czechoslovakia had reservations about a resolution on battered women, on the grounds that this was not a problem in socialist countries.

Nine countries, including the United Kingdom, Belgium, West Germany, and the United States, expressed reservations about a resolution calling for support for CEDAW on the grounds that it contained what became known as an "isms" paragraph, a list of condemned "isms"—colonialism, neocolonialism, imperialism, and so forth: by which the South pinned responsibility for underdevelopment and oppression on the North. The Western bloc objected to this paragraph on principle, even though it did not contain any reference to "Zionism."[20]

The First Committee heard bitter reports on the condition of Palestinian women. Israel countered by declaring the ECWA report "malicious, tendentious and inaccurate," and argued that Zionism was not racism but the "national liberation movement of the Jewish people." Syria attacked the Camp David accords as an attempt to "liquidate" the Palestinian cause and declared that Israel's "expansionist" policies in South Lebanon proved that "Zionism was not a liberation movement but racist in both its structure and practices."[21] The Western delegations repeatedly called for these issues to be dealt with in more appropriate UN forums.

Given the political salience of the racism/Zionism equation, the State Department at first resisted the idea, raised by ninety African-American women who were attending the NGO Forum, that the U.S. delegation take a resolution on racism to the floor. On 19 July the African-American women held a press conference to present a draft resolution that condemned racism and defined it in terms much broader than apartheid, for which it had been a synonym in UN debates. Women of color on the U.S. delegation immediately supported the initiative and, overcoming State Department hesitation, the delegation introduced the racism resolution in the First Committee.[22]

Minority women on the U.S. delegation lobbied hard for support among their Third World allies, and it appeared that the U.S. resolution might win majority support. But when Mrs. Kane was replaced in the chair by Madame Groza of Romania, who "ruled in favor of the Eastern bloc" and prolonged the debate, many of the delegations left the hall.

In the end, the United States withdrew its resolution in response to hostile amendments introduced by Syria, Cuba, East Germany, and Egypt. According to Western accounts, the Third World delegates were "taken by surprise" at the U.S. withdrawal, and Angola hastily reintroduced the U.S. resolution with the four hostile amendments intact. The United States then moved to amend the Angolan resolution to strike the hostile amendments but lost by a vote of 46 to 42, with 12 abstentions—the narrowest loss (or the closest that the United States came to a win on a contested issue) of the conference. The Angolan resolution passed by a vote of 66–5–39, with West Germany, Israel, the United Kingdom, and the United States in the "no" column. (Lesotho also voted no, but later declared that it meant to vote yes.) In the final plenary, the vote was 78–3–39, with Lesotho voting in favor and Israel abstaining.[23]

On 25 and 26 July, the Second Committee took up the issue of women refugees, an issue that was raised for the first time at a UN meeting. The United Nations High Commissioner for Refugees (UNHCR) report underlined the magnitude of the problem: Approximately 80 percent of the world's refugees are women and children, and women are especially vulnerable to sexual abuse and exploitation. The report made the delegates aware of the difficulties faced by women who take the responsibility for maintaining cultural traditions for their children, while trying to obtain food, housing, and medical care under adverse and often dangerous conditions.

Here the United States again took the initiative, introducing a resolution that was adopted as orally amended. Then, apparently not wanting a U.S.-backed resolution to go unchallenged, Pakistan introduced another resolution that condemned "foreign aggression, racism, oppression, *apartheid*, colonialism, neocolonialism, the use of inhumane weapons and methods of war" and "indiscriminate hostilities," as the causes of the refugee problem. The United States was the sole negative vote; but thirty countries, including the Western bloc, but also Grenada, India, and Suriname, abstained. Here, as in the racism issue, UN politics, and particularly the goal shared by the South and the East of isolating the United States, were significant factors. The resolutions went through, carrying the substantive message that the United States wanted, but not under U.S. sponsorship and not without additional—and from the U.S. standpoint, objectionable—baggage.[24]

The issue of Palestinian women also led to a heated debate in the Second Committee. Israel attacked the position taken by the ECWA report that the PLO should be the conduit for assistance. India then moved to amend Paragraph 244 of the draft Programme of Action to specify that assistance should be given to Palestinian women "in consultation and cooperation with the PLO, the representative of the Palestinian people." After an extended debate, which required a cloture vote, the amended paragraph passed by a vote of 85-3-21, with Canada, the United States, and Israel opposed.[25]

There were three roll call votes in the Second Committee: the vote on the Pakistani resolution on women refugees, as noted above; a vote on a resolution on the situation of women in Chile; and a vote on assistance to Sahrawi women.

The resolution on Chile, which condemned the authoritarian regime, was introduced by eleven of the Non-Aligned states, including Algeria, Cuba, Mozambique, and Nicaragua. It was passed by a vote of 70-7-38, with the Latin American military dictatorships (Argentina, Brazil, Chile, Guatemala, Honduras, Peru, and Uruguay) voting against and the United States and many Western countries abstaining. (The practical issue for the West may have been loyalty to anticommunist allies in the cold war, but the ideological issue was the "double standard.")

The resolution on Sahrawi women (women in territory in the Western Sahara, under contested Moroccan rule) was sponsored by the radical states in the Southern bloc, but it did not yield a unified vote. Fifty-five countries voted in favor, but eight African countries, including Tunisia, and the United States voted against. Some delegations, including Brazil and Argentina, who had voted against the resolution on Chile on the grounds of noninterventionism, voted for UN intervention in the Western Sahara. Others, like Peru and Paraguay, maintained a consistent anti-interventionist stance.

Of the ten resolutions that went to a vote, three resolutions condemned the repressive policies of particular governments: Lebanon, El Salvador, and Bolivia, where a military coup was mounted against a woman president while the Mid-Decade Conference was taking place. Of those, the United States voted to censure only Bolivia.

Four resolutions went to a vote because of resistance in the West to language promoted by the other blocs. Two of these resolutions involved sanctions against South Africa (Resolutions 16 and 45); another called for women's participation in "preparing societies for a life of peace (Resolution 7); and a fourth (Resolution 11) called for women's participation in strengthening "peace and security" and in "the struggle against colonialism, racism, racial discrimination, foreign aggression and occupation, and all forms of foreign domination." Resolution 47 called for implementation of the goals of the Decade "within the framework of the NIEO," and Resolution 26 reaffirmed the right of all countries to receive aid from any source—a complaint by the South against the tendency of the superpowers to demand loyalty in return for aid.

Only one resolution went to a vote on differences that divide men and women. Resolution 17, noting that migration is a cause of the growth in the number of female-headed households, urges governments to enter into agreements to "ensure that alimony will be paid to the abandoned wife." The vote was 52–0–53, indicating the unwillingness of a number of governments to take responsibility for ensuring male support of the family. This vote did not follow bloc lines.

What was most striking about the work of the two committees was the overwhelming consensus on a detailed women's agenda. Much of the draft Programme of Action was approved without debate, including a paragraph urging that customary laws that discriminate against women be identified and changed. This consensus was not unlimited, and the Australian attempt to have sexism listed among the "isms" condemned in Paragraph 12 of the Programme of Action illustrates the resistance to feminist language. Many delegations objected that the term *sexism* did not exist in their language. In the end, the Australians won an awkward victory of sorts.[26] Paragraph 12 condemns "*de facto* discrimination on the grounds of sex," with a footnote that reads, "Which in some countries is called sexism." Australia and New Zealand were persistent in pressing for independent recognition of male power as a cause of women's low status and of the ways in which women were exploited because of their reproductive roles, but the Programme of Action contains very few references that are feminist in this antipatriarchal sense.[27]

THE COMMITTEE OF THE WHOLE

The Committee of the Whole returned to the Mid-Decade Conference unable to resolve disputes over Paragraphs 2 and 5. On 30 July, the conference met in plenary session to hammer out the language on these two remaining paragraphs. Mr. Tukan of Jordan, vice-chair of the committee, suggested language for Paragraph 2 that included references to the Declaration of Mexico and to the Conference of Non-Aligned and Developing Countries, which had been held in Baghdad in May 1979.

Both references were unacceptable to the United States. Paragraph 2 was adopted by a roll call vote of 89–7–23, with Australia, Canada, Paraguay, Peru, and the United Kingdom joining the United States and Israel among the seven "no" votes; the rest of the Western bloc and Japan abstained, along with Chile, Uruguay, the Dominican Republic, the Vatican, Guatemala, Thailand, and Upper Volta (now Burkina Faso).

Turning to Paragraph 5, the conference debated a text suggested by India. The critical sentence recognized the Western interest in promoting women's *rights*, but added "Zionism" to the list of isms. This, of course, was unacceptable to the United States and Israel. Senegal moved that the vote be declared procedural and not substantive; the motion carried by vote of 59–37–13. The paragraph was adopted by a roll call vote of 69–24–25, with the Western bloc voting against, along with Guatemala, Paraguay, and Peru. Abstentions were Chile, Colombia, Costa Rica, Ecuador, Mexico, Suriname, and Uruguay from Latin America; Barbados, the Dominican Republic, Jamaica and Trinidad and Tobago from the Caribbean; Gabon, Ghana, Ivory Coast, Lesotho, Swaziland,

United Republic of Cameroon, and Zaire from Africa; Bhutan, Fiji, Papua New Guinea, and Thailand from Asia; as well as Greece and Spain.

With the adoption of Paragraphs 2 and 5, the United States called for the final vote. The Programme of Action passed by a vote of 94 to 4 (Australia, Canada, United States, and Israel), with 22 abstentions (the Western bloc, minus Japan, Greece, Portugal, and Spain, which had often voted with it, in addition to Chile, Guatemala, Paraguay, Peru, Thailand, and the Vatican). The final plenary adjourned at 2:35 A.M.[28]

THE LONG-TERM IMPACT OF THE MID-DECADE CONFERENCE

Many have argued that, because the Mid-Decade Conference was so contentious and politicized, Copenhagen's importance lies not in the official meeting but in two events that took place in conjunction with the conference: (1) the signing of CEDAW and (2) the NGO Forum.

This position has much to be said for it. The importance of the convention, signed at the conference by 60 governments (and ratified by 134 as of May 1994), is without question the most significant international document on the equality of women produced thus far. Like the Plan of Action and draft Programme of Action, from which many of its themes were drawn, the convention calls for women's legal equality as citizens and for women's rights in domestic relations and as workers; it also claims women's rights to health care, employment, and education. The convention represents a new international set of norms for women, using the most powerful mechanism for compliance, short of the use of force, that is available to the international community. Once a state has ratified a convention, it is expected to change its domestic laws to conform to its principles, and domestic and international groups have been able to use the ratification of the CEDAW to reinforce changes in laws and behavior at the national level.

Many would argue that the Forum was a more significant international meeting than the official conference. It drew more than 8,000 participants, over 3,000 from outside Europe. The United States and Canada accounted for 937 participants; Asia and the Pacific, for 836; and Latin America and the Caribbean, 398. There were 245 African participants, and 147 from the Middle East.[29]

The Forum continued the process, begun in Mexico City, of consolidating the base of the international women's movement, as seen in the growing number of women's groups at all levels, the widespread diffusion and exchange of information, and the creation of grassroots networks of women's organizations. Because the Forum participants were not constrained by diplomacy, many felt that the Forum dealt more directly with the issues and made more progress on a women's agenda than the official conference.[30]

However, the politics of the conference were played out on a very public stage at the Forum as well. There were shouting matches over the issue of Israeli treatment of Palestinian women, and the hostility toward Israel expressed in these debates was seen by many in the United States (and to a lesser degree in Europe) as a return to the overt anti-Semitism of the 1930s.[31] The results were long term: After the Forum was over, many women's groups in the United States lobbied to cut funding to UN programs for women, specifically the Voluntary Fund for Women (now UNIFEM), a small-scale development assistance program, and INSTRAW, the research and training center located in the Dominican Republic. This funding was only partially renewed in the late 1980s.[32]

But a case can be made that the Mid-Decade Conference has been dismissed too readily and that its long-term impact is more positive than the conventional wisdom allows. The Programme of Action is an important bridge between Mexico City and Nairobi, giving strong international legitimacy to the international norm of legal equality for women and elaborating a more effective and detailed women-in-development agenda. The Programme of Action breaks new ground on a number of issues, including a recognition of violence against women, an emphasis on the importance of women-headed households, encouragement of women's empowerment through grassroots organizations, and attention to racism and refugees.

Lucille Mair's strategy, however repugnant to those Western delegates who wanted her to be a feminist first and "Third Worlder" second, was appropriate to the GA context within which she was working. Her strategy was to argue that attention to women was crucial to achieving the goals that the GA had identified as its priority issues: opposition to apartheid and support for NIEO and PLO. Mair's report to the GA in October 1980, set out a women's agenda couched in goals and principles that the men in the GA could not disavow. One linkage established by Mair in that speech deserves more attention: She argues that the issue of violence against women should be taken up by the UN as part of its commitment to the "struggle for peace." Women's recapturing of the peace issue, which had been dominated by the Eastern European bloc, would be one of the important successes of the Nairobi Conference in 1985.[33]

Mair achieved her immediate purpose—the explicit recognition of women in the International Development Strategy that the GA passed in the fall to set the stage for the Third Development Decade. Longer-term results included thirteen resolutions from ECOSOC in 1982 and active preparations for the End of the Decade Conference to be held in Nairobi.[34]

Finally, the "politicization" of the conference served the international women's movement in two important ways. The debates over structuralist and feminist perspectives changed views on both sides and helped contribute to the consensus that was later forged in Nairobi—the "coming of age" of the international women's movement. The vote in Copenhagen, though difficult for the United States and Israel, helped legitimize women as an issue not just for the West but for the world. It is hard to argue that a document that the United States, Canada, and Australia voted against, and on which the Western bloc abstained, is simply a "Western" document. The outcome in Copenhagen was a "Third World victory," but women won a victory that we may well look back on as the high point of international consensus on the universality of women's rights.

NOTES

1. For a review of U.S. and international press reports, see U.S. Embassy, "Danish Press at a Glance" (July 1980), mimeographed; *Berlingske Tidende*, 26 July 1980.

2. But see Arvonne Fraser, *The UN Decade for Women* (Boulder, Colo.: Westview Press, 1987); Hilkka Pietila and Jeanne Vickers, *Making Women Matter: The Role of the United Nations* (London: Zed Press, 1990); Georgina Ashworth, "The United Nations 'Women's Conference' and International Linkages in the Women's Movement," in *Pressure Groups in the Global System*, ed. Peter Willetts (New York: St. Martin's Press, 1982).

3. *Report of the United States Delegation to the World Conference of the United Nations Decade for Women* (hereafter *US Delegation Report*) (1980), 137. My understanding of the delegation's position is also based on interviews with Vivian Derryck, Arvonne Fraser, Margaret Galey, and Barbara Good; I also consulted the *Staff Report* (see n.17, below).

4. See Thomas M. Franck, *Nation Against Nation* (New York: Oxford University Press, 1985), chaps. 10–13; Daniel Patrick Moynihan, *A Dangerous Place* (Boston: Little, Brown, 1975); Charles William Maynes, "The UN in Today's World," in *The US, the UN and the Management of Global Change*, ed. Toby Trister Gati (New York: New York University Press, 1983).

5. Franck, *Nation Against Nation*, chap. 12; Jack Donnelly, "Human Rights at the United Nations, 1955–1988: The Question of Bias," *International Studies Quarterly* 32 (1988), 275–303. Robert A. Mortimer, *The Third World Coalition in International Politics* (Boulder, Colo.: Westview Press, 1984).

6. Miguel Marin-Bosch, "How Nations Vote in the General Assembly of the United Nations," *International Organization* 41, no. 4 (1987): 195–204. See also Donald J. Puchala, "American Interests in the United Nations," in *The Politics of International Organizations*, ed. Paul F. Diehl (Chicago: Dorsey Press, 1989), 226–41.

7. Peter M. Haas, "Epistemic Communities and International Policy Coordination," *International Organization* 46, no. 1 (Winter 1992): 1–35. On UN "consciousness raising" conferences and the role of parallel NGO meetings, see A. LeRoy Bennett, *International Organizations: Principles and Issues* (Englewood Cliffs, N.J.: Prentice-Hall, 1988), chap. 7.

8. See Irene Tinker, "A Feminist View of Copenhagen," *Signs* 6, no. 3 (Spring 1981), 531–37.

9. Mallica Vajrathon, "The Success of the Copenhagen World Conference: A Feminist Perspective," New York, Tribune Centre, 1980, mimeographed.

10. Ibid., p. 94.

11. The chronological account of the preparatory committees and the Mid-Decade Conference, the voting statistics and committee membership and leadership that appear in this chapter are from the *Report of the World Conference of the United Nations Decade for Women: Equality Development and Peace*, A/CONF.94/35, 1980 (hereafter *UN Report*).

12. Interviews with Galey and Derryck (see n.3); *US Delegation Report*. But see Fraser, *UN Decade for Women*; see also Lucille Mair, *International Women's Decade: A Balance Sheet* (New Delhi: Center for Women's Development Studies, 1985).

13. Vivian Derryck, personal interview, July 1980 and April 1992; Arvonne Fraser, personal interview, April 1992.

14. Ashworth, "United Nations," 131.

15. Ingrid Palmer, *Recommendations Relating to Women and Development Emerging from Conferences Held Under the Auspices of the United Nations or the Specialized Agencies* A/CONF.94/19, 1979, analyzed in Pietila and Vickers, *Making Women Matter*, chap. 4.

16. UN delegation data supplied by Margaret Galey.

17. *UN Report*, 121–23. For the U.S. view, see Congressional Staff Advisors to the U.S. Delegation, *UN World Conference of the UN Decade for Women* (Washington, D.C.: US GPO, 1980) (hereafter *Staff Report*); *US Delegation Report*; Ashworth, "United Nations," 125.

18. The figure used by the U.S. Committee for CEDAW is fifty-two; *Forum 80* used fifty-three in its 21 July issue.

19. See *Staff Report* and personal communication from Margaret Galey, January 1993.

20. *US Delegation Report*, 125. *Forum 80*, 29 July 1980, 1.

21. *UN Report*, 152, 164–69; *US Delegation Report*, 71–86.

22. *US Delegation Report*, 118–19; *Staff Report*, 18–19.

23. *UN Report*, 153–55.

24. *US Delegation Report*, 94–95.

25. *UN Report*, 164–69.

26. John Rowley, "Counting Down . . . ," *Forum 80*, 29 July 1980, 1.

27. The *US Delegation Report* lists twenty-three ways in which the Programme's feminist language was strengthened (78–80); Australia and New Zealand often took the lead.

28. *UN Report*, 194–95.

29. The NGO Planning Committee, *Report of NGO Activities at the World Conference of the UN Decade for Women* (New York: n.d.); Ashworth, "United Nations," 136–41.

30. Irene Tinker and Jane Jaquette, "The UN Decade for Women: Its Impact and Legacy," *World Development* 2 (March 1987): 419–27.

31. Helen S. Lewis, "Reflections on a Chilling Experience: 1980 Conference Seen as Throwback to the 1930s," *Pioneer Woman* (November 1980), 15–24; Judy Drausz, "The Anguish of Copenhagen," *Pioneer Woman* (November 1980), 18–26; Letty Cottin Pogrebin, "Anti-Semitism in the Women's Movement," *Ms. Magazine*, June 1982, 45–49.

32. Vera Gathright, Washington representative for the International Fund for Agricultural Development (IFAD), personal communication, November 1992.

33. Statement of the Secretary-General of the World Conference of the UN Decade for Women, 1980, Mrs. Lucille M. Mair, to the Third Committee of the 35th Session of the General Assembly, 15 October 1980.

34. International Women's Tribune Centre, "Resolutions and Decisions Referring Specifically to Women," *International Women's Tribune Centre*, 2 vols. (New York: 1982).

5
Women and Power: The Nairobi Conference, 1985

Charlotte G. Patton

It was July 1985! Planeload after planeload of women arrived in Nairobi, Kenya, to attend the last conference of the United Nations Decade for Women, 1976–1985, and the parallel nongovernmental organization (NGO) Forum '85. The numbers—under 1,900 official delegates, over 1,400 women, over 400 men, and more than 14,000 NGO representatives (women and some men)—strained hotel facilities and totally surprised the Kenyan government conference hosts and the NGO forum organizers. The purpose of the Nairobi Conference was for governments and international organizations to review and appraise the achievements of the Decade and to adopt the major Conference document, Nairobi Forward-looking Strategies for the Advancement of Women (FLS). The parallel NGO meeting, Forum '85, had no planned outcome, although its leaders issued a summary report in 1986. But the thousands of participants in its panels and workshops testified to the fact that the global women's movement had gained new strength and visibility during the Decade for Women; underlying that movement was women's increased political and public participation. As the last official event of the Decade for Women, the Nairobi Conference created the FLS, a design for the women's movement in the future.

The Nairobi Conference needed to "succeed." Delegations, Secretariat staff, and the press continued to express fears of failure. East-West antagonisms and North-South differences threatened to isolate women's issues and deny women's perceptions about their relationship to global issues. Renewed cold war rhetoric had attended the increased competition between the United States and the Soviet Union. Women's concerns were generally out of favor in the 1980s with conservative governments in the United States, the United Kingdom, and the Federal Republic of Germany. The rich states of the industrial North and the economically poor Southern states were deadlocked over solutions to growth and Third World debt; financial crises preoccupied multilateral institutions and their member governments. To the very end, assembled delegates were never certain that they would approve the FLS by consensus. That they did testified to some delegates' new knowledge of how to use power to accomplish what they wanted.

At Copenhagen in 1980, African delegates had gained acceptance for a resolution on behalf of a third women's conference to conclude the Decade for Women. That year in the UN General Assembly (GA), Venezuela, on behalf of the Group of 77 (G-77), proposed "a World Conference to Review and Appraise the Achievements of the United Nations Decade for Women." The United States, Canada, and Israel eventually opposed the GA resolution approving the Copenhagen Conference Report because two paragraphs referred to UN Women's Conference documents linking Zionism with racism (categorized as imperialism, colonialism, apartheid, etc., as obstacles to women's equality and participation).[1] That resolution was nevertheless approved with Eastern and G-77 support.

In 1981, the GA confirmed Secretariat proposals to consult with the Commission on the Status of Women (CSW) in order "to give priority, to the question of the preparations for the World Conference . . . to be held in 1985." Then, in 1982, the GA[2] confirmed the CSW request that it be the preparatory committee (PrepCom), authorized it to meet in extra sessions, and requested the UN Secretary-General (SG) to appoint the secretary-general of the conference.

CONFERENCE PREPARATIONS

At the Vienna UN headquarters, CSW scheduled extra meetings for 1983, 1984 (in conjunction with a regular session), and 1985. In December 1984, the Branch for the Advancement of Women, located in the Vienna UN Center for Social Development and Humanitarian Affairs, produced an elaborate draft FLS, based on an inquiry to governments, in favor of historical and thematic continuity with the Decade for Women, an array of other UN sources, and then PrepCom discussions among delegations along with representatives of consultative NGOs.

Letitia Shahani had been one of two vice-chairs of the Philippine delegation in Mexico City, and then head of the Philippine delegation in Copenhagen, from which position she had campaigned to be executive director of the Vienna UN Center and an assistant secretary-general; the SG appointed her secretary-general of the conference before the second PrepCom—a position that the Asian caucus thought was rightfully theirs. Chafika Sellami-Meslem, head of the Algerian delegation in Mexico City and a member of the GA Third Committee between 1969 and 1975, had gained the approval of the Department of International Economic and Social Affairs (DIESA) directed by Jean-Paul Ripert, who appointed the French-speaking Sellami-Meslem as head of the branch. From that position she became the deputy secretary-general of the conference.

Before the third PrepCom, 4 to 13 March 1985, delegations had already agreed on the conference dates, 15 to 26 July 1985, with two preceding days of preconference consultations; accepted general UN procedure that the representative of the host country would be president of the conference; organized the conference into a plenary and two committees; and agreed to invite all states as well as NGOs in consultative status with the Economic and Social Council (ECOSOC).

Then, delegations set out to revise and amend the 279-paragraph FLS, divided into such subjects as obstacles, strategies, and measures for implementation in chapters on development; international and regional cooperation; equality; the introduction; areas of special concern, and then peace (listed here in descending numerical order by numbers of paragraphs). The delegates faced a draft which retained continuity with the Mexico World Plan of Action and the Copenhagen Programme of Action but emphasized practical actions by governments, by international and regional organizations and NGOs to affirm the goals of the Decade and to identify "concrete measures to overcome the obstacles to their achievement."

Nongovernmental organizations—acknowledged as critical, if informal, players in UN women's issues, in consultative status with ECOSOC under Article 71 of the UN Charter (generally, international organizations)—and their UN representatives had lobbied for the incorporation of many items in the draft FLS. Thus, it reflected NGO interests; the item on elderly women (under "Special Concerns"), for example, gave recognition and support to the NGO community.

Delegations bargained in political blocs—the Western European and Others (WEO), the Eastern Socialist States (ESS), and G-77—sponsoring amendments in conference room papers. They came to so little agreement that the PrepCom could only recommend that the draft FLS be sent as it was to the Conference. Maureen Reagan, daughter of the president and then alternate U.S. delegate at the PrepCom, thought that result was a prescription for disaster. The ESS conference room paper included "Zionism, racism"; the G-77 had not. Maureen Reagan, who thought that "Zionism, racism" might end up in the FLS, returned to Washington, determined to make full U.S. participation in the conference a reality and to forestall any such inclusion.

Working through missions in New York—the Canadian, and U.S., among others—delegates won GA Resolution 39/459 on 12 April, requesting that the PrepCom meet in resumed session from 29 April to 7 May. Maureen O'Neil (Canada) continued to lead the WEO; Leila Emara (Egypt) chaired the G-77; and Mrs. T. N. Nikolaeva (USSR) chaired the ESS. Rosario Manalo (Philippines), an accomplished diplomat who had chaired the second and third

PrepComs, set up "Friends of the Chair," a negotiating procedure she used later in Nairobi to promote agreement on the text. Deliberating on the draft FLS paragraph by paragraph, the blocs focused the paragraphs yet more specifically on women and negotiated on more gender/feminist concerns, for example, linking peace to the prevention of violence against women in all its manifestations: in international war, poverty, neighborhoods, families, or between men and women. The relationship between women's rights and peace became more elaborate and more inclusive. Bloc negotiations resulted in expanded chapters, although by numbers of paragraphs the development chapter dominated the draft. Drawing also on the reports of the regional intergovernmental meetings[3] of Africa, Asia, Latin America, and the Caribbean, the G-77 promoted references to the Declaration of Mexico and the inseparability and interdependency of the objectives of equality, development, and peace from the Latin meeting in Havana. Delegates devised linkages on apartheid, Palestinians, and women to a broadly defined peace.

The resumed PrepCom brought the FLS to a near completion. Delegations felt they had a sufficiently agreed upon document to take to Nairobi, even though 20 percent of the document, or seventy-six whole/partial paragraphs, was in dispute: Zionism/racism, women and children under apartheid, Palestinian women and children, the new international economic order, and the character of the global economic crisis—whether a crisis, recession, or neither.

The U.S. delegation, whose alternate delegate Maureen Reagan, was to chair in Nairobi, fought for a change in two proposed decision-making rules: Rule 32, which provided for decision making at the conference by "general agreement," and Rule 34, which provided for decision making by two-thirds majority on substantive matters of those present and voting. The U.S. delegation held out for consensus on the FLS because Congress under the Kassebaum Amendment had directed the U.S. government to avoid a "politicized" conference. Later, at the resumed ECOSOC session on 20 June, action on the U.S.–sponsored resolution to adopt the FLS by consensus was postponed, 26–2–12. Some support for consensus decision making gradually emerged as delegations from Canada, United Kingdom, France, Japan, Federal Republic of Germany, Turkey, and Sweden explained their abstentions, and the Zimbabwian and Moroccan delegations explained their vote for postponement.

The contentious prestige issue was the size of the General Committee, the number of vice-presidents of the conference to be allotted to each regional group. If the General Committee of the conference had followed the format of the GA General Committee, its size would have been twenty-nine members; the Latin Americans wanted more than four vice-presidents, their allotment under the GA formula. The Swedish delegation, aided by the Pakistani, announced the compromise expansion of the General Committee to thirty-four, by the addition of a vice-president from each region, except Africa (where the representative of the host state, Kenya, was president of the conference). Insiders say that the generosity of the Africans made the compromise possible.

Nevertheless, with the conference less than a month away, no one really knew if delegates could, or would, agree to consensus decision making in order to avoid political confrontation.

FORUM '85: NGO MEETING IN NAIROBI, 10–19 JULY 1985

The NGO forum opened at the University of Nairobi on 10 July, preceding the intergovernmental conference. Over 14,000 women from more than 150 countries attended the tumultuous and festive forum.[4] The Conference of Nongovernmental Organizations (CONGO) had about two years earlier created the organizational structure: the NGO planning committee in New York, subcommittees there, in Geneva and Vienna, as well as the on-site Kenyan committee for the Forum, under Eddah Gachukia. Dame Nita Barrow, recently retired as World President of the World Young Women's Christian Association, later governor-general of Barbados, served as convenor; Virginia Hazzard, just retired from the UN International Children's Emergency Fund, as coordinator. Although there was no official relationship between the conference and the forum, CSW had encouraged the parallel NGO meeting.

The networking and strategies initiated in Mexico and further developed in Copenhagen matured at Forum '85, an embodiment of the global women's movement much as the Peace Tent symbolized the breakdown of barriers among women. Forum '85 wound down as the official conference began.

THE CONFERENCE OPENS: 15 JULY 1985

Secretary-General Perez de Cuellar, opening the conference at the International Kenyatta Conference Center, noted the growing recognition of the interrelationships between women's advancement, development, and peace, and acknowledged the challenge that lay ahead to achieve the full partnership among men and women, without which the Decade "goals would remain elusive."[5] Next, Kenya's President Daniel arap Moi recognized the "duty of governments to take action," but he also noted that "the onus remained on women to unite and take full advantage of the opportunities so created." Then, the conference delegates elected by acclamation the Head of the Kenyan and host delegation, Margaret Kenyatta, president of the conference.

Conference Participation

One hundred fifty-seven governments sent delegations to Nairobi. Of the 1,899 members of governmental delegations—delegates, alternates, and advisors—1,546 were women.[6] Sixteen delegations were headed by men; less than 10 had no women. Of the 668 delegates, 114 were men; of the 648 alternates, 106 were men; and of the 583 advisors, 133 were men. Thus, 83 percent of the delegates, 83.6 percent of the alternates, and 78 percent of the advisors were women. Women were at a UN conference in greater numbers than ever before.

In attendance were representatives, or observers, from five UN Secretariat offices, from four UN regional commissions, from eighteen UN bodies and programs, from eight specialized agencies and related organizations, from four liberation organizations, and one each from the UN Council (Namibia) and Special Committee (Apartheid), as well as seventeen other intergovernmental organizations.[7]

The major players were delegations whose role in decision making was to come to agreement on the FLS. Members of the Secretariat worked with delegations in many capacities, finally demanding decisions in order for the conference to succeed. Consultative NGOs, lobbying at Forum '85 and into the portals of the intergovernmental Conference itself, numbered 154; their representatives, about 605 persons.[8]

The Conference Proceeds

At the second plenary session, the President of the conference, Kenyatta announced a carefully worded statement on conference decision making: "Without prejudice to the rules of procedure of the Conference which have been adopted, in particular rule 34, and without setting a precedent, a general understanding has emerged as a result of consultations whereby all documents of the Conference, in particular the Forward-looking Strategies document under item 8 of the Conference agenda, should be adopted by consensus."[9]

How this "general understanding" would take effect or whether delegations might revert to voting created tension throughout the conference. The compromise reached during preconference consultations that lasted into the morning hours of the opening day of the conference had been given enormous assistance by the SG. Agreement between the U.S. and Soviet delegates was a next significant factor. But the compromise resulted from the work of many delegates. The Canadians sought out conciliatory language from another UN conference in order to show how to proceed; the G-77, led in this instance by Mervat Tallawy (Egypt), with internal disagreements on this matter, accepted the compromise of "without prejudice" and "no precedent" on this issue, the language of compromise worked on by the UN legal counsel.

Margaret Kenyatta moved the adoption of the agenda and the election of other presiding officers. Still in pursuit of the prestige that they felt was lacking, the Latin American regional group demanded (and gained) the chair of Committee One for Cecilia Lopez, Colombia's Minister of Agriculture. PrepCom chair Manalo had been scheduled as chair of Committee One; at the last minute, Manalo was acclaimed chair of Committee Two, dealing with the "Introduction," "Areas of Special Concerns," and "International and Regional Cooperation." Colombia's Lopez, who had never before attended an international conference, was acclaimed chair of Committee One, which focused on the national as well as the international aspects of equality, development, and peace, and on selections from the "Areas of Special Concerns." Politically and procedurally, Committee One carried a heavier burden than Committee Two, the "technical" committee. It began with 231 paragraphs to Committee Two's 132; it faced 47 bracketed paragraphs to Committee Two's 29. Opposing coalitions fought out the "high politics" issues in Committee One.

The conference process occurred at many levels. At the same time that the two committees met, delegates were making statements on national review and appraisal in the ongoing plenary. NGO statements were fitted in when time was available, often at the end of the evening.

Behind small groups in the committees were other groups, including the official regional groupings and the bloc groups; and deep in ongoing negotiations were the contact groups, each a very small number of selected delegates to whom the most contentious issues were referred. The contact groups enabled women to demonstrate their negotiating skills as equals with men, who were more active in these groups than in the other committees.

Committee One Negotiations

Cecilia Lopez presided, assisted by Laetitia van den Assum (Netherlands), Olimpia Solomonescu (Romania), and Kulsun Saifullah (Pakistan) as deputies, and Diaroumeye Gany (Niger) as rapporteur. Committee One's delegates negotiated and approved the revised FLS chapters on equality, development, and peace as well as the selections from "Special Concerns." Of Committee One's total paragraphs, 120 went from the resumed PrepCom to Committee One to the plenary unchanged, including three bracketed. Eighty-nine went to plenary with some recommended changes. Blocs remained in confrontation over the most controversial paragraphs and could reach no agreement on nine paragraphs, which went to plenary for its decision. Three of the four paragraphs bracketed by the PrepCom that went to Committee One were voted on in the plenary; the other controversial paragraph also voted on had been introduced to Committee One.

Eventually, the delegates arrived at consensus on new conceptualizations of women's issues: Equality centered on the elimination of de jure as well as de facto discrimination against women, on the achievement of equality between women and men dependent on constitutional and legal changes, and on the many forms of social and political participation. Obstacles to women's advancement were deeply embedded in international, national and local politics; measures to be taken were focused in the subparagraphs of the development section, including, but not limited to, employment, health, and education. Peace could be strengthened by the efforts of women, whose participation at all levels of society on an equal basis with men advanced with gains in development.

Coalitions of delegates from the three blocs struggled, as they had at Copenhagen, over the "high politics" conflicts located in paragraphs that (1) criticized the developed countries for lacking the political will to restructure international economic relations on a democratic basis; (2) called apartheid a hindrance to peace in the African region and wanted sanctions applied to South Africa; (3) wanted Israeli settlements stopped in the West Bank and Gaza Strip and supported Palestinian self-determination and an independent state; and (4) stated that coercive measures, including blockades and other economic measures, were in violation of the UN Charter and prevented the integration of women into development. Western delegates wanted no language to bind them in later fora; they argued that the Women's Conference was not the forum of decision in which to discuss these issues. These conflicts ended up in the contact groups.

NGO representatives lobbied in both committees, establishing coalitions with Third World delegates. As an example, Housewives in Dialogue gained Committee One acceptance for their wording of Paragraph 120 on the recognition of "unremunerated contributions of women to all aspects and sectors of development"—namely, the inclusion of such unremunerated contributions in the "gross national product" and then "concrete steps . . . to quantify the unremunerated contribution of women to agriculture, food production, reproduction and household activities."

Negotiations in Committee One were endlessly delayed; delegations often refused to deliberate without translation into their official UN languages. The shape of the room, like a gladiators ring, epitomized sharp negotiations between blocs right to the very close of Committee One. By contrast, Committee Two proceeded without the volatile dynamics of Committee One.

Committee Two Negotiations

Rosario Manalo presided; Billie Miller (Barbados) chaired the working group responsible for the specific negotiations of contested language in FLS. The other deputies were Konjit Sine Giogis (Ethiopia), chair of the working group on resolutions; Eva Szilagyi (Hungary); and the rapporteur, Helen Ware (Australia). Delegates in this committee came from donor aid agencies and from the many more—from 1980 to 1985—domestic ministries established on behalf of women or that women headed.

Committee Two was charged with approving the "Introduction" of the FLS: historical background, with its emphasis on the Decade for Women and conference actions and on UN human rights charters as well as the critical global economic situation; substantive background of the FLS, especially the interrelationship of the Decade for Women themes; current trends and perspectives to the year 2000, with its controversial Paragraph 35's references to the Declaration of Mexico (Zionism/racism); and the FLS basic approach, "a practical and effective guide for global action." Its mandate also included "Areas of Special Concern" and "International and Regional Cooperation."

Ambassador Manalo took charge of her committee and directed the negotiating dynamics toward approval of the paragraphs.[10] With diplomatic aplomb, she gained acceptance of the principle of an open-ended working group, that is, the right of all delegations to participate on an equal basis in negotiations. The chairs of G-77, WEO, and ESS, as well as the chairs of the regional groups, were to be included in the working group. The Committee Two chair from G-77, Egypt's Emara, suggested that all other participants in the working group be witnesses, that is, not full members. Chair Manalo ruled for—and the committee accepted—the principle of an open-ended working group. The committee considered each paragraph in order. To resolve disagreements, Chair Manalo requested the negotiating delegates, those who opposed each other, to meet informally, then to return to the committee with agreed-upon wording. Difficult conflicts were promptly dispatched to the working group, to forestall voting.

Committee Two approved all of its assigned paragraphs except Paragraph 35 (final document), which mentioned the Declaration of Mexico, ("Zionism/racism") as one of the valid bases for "concrete measures to be pursued up to the year 2000."

NGO representatives also lobbied delegates in Committee Two, where, for example, the International Business and Professional Women gained additional wording to final Paragraph 288 on "Abused Women," which urged governments to "suppress degrading images of women" and "to encourage the development of educational and re-educational measures for offenders," those who had committed violent crimes against women.

At the last session of Committee Two, one delegate congratulated Chair Manalo as a successful chair by comparing her to a schoolmarm. The room had the characteristics of a classroom: a headseat, chairs and tables across the room with a center and two side aisles, the rows one behind each other. Manalo was a very skilled negotiator who brought her committee to a well-crafted finish.

By the second night before the end of the conference, Secretariat staff—mostly women—in their bureau meeting were expressing concern about the possible failure of the conference. They said so—openly! The plenary was left with little time for resolving conflicts.

Plenary Deliberations: Committee Reports

The two committees submitted their reports to the plenary for final decision making. The plenary opened early Thursday evening, 25 July, then abruptly adjourned. Reconvening after midnight, delegations agreed to review the FLS, in numerical order, paragraph by paragraph. Led by Margaret Kenyatta, the plenary accepted the contested Paragraph 35, delegation reservations to be noted in a footnote, and moved on!

Sixty paragraphs later, the delegates took their first vote: 94 bis (final 94), "coercive measures" applied by some developed states against underdeveloped ones, including blockades, embargoes, in violation of the UN Charter. The Latin American and Caribbean group had gained its acceptance from the G-77. Eastern delegates had also accepted it, but Western delegates had rejected it in Committee

One. A senior Latin delegate identified sanctions against Nicaragua as the apparent inspiration of the paragraph.[11] The roll call vote was 109–0–28.

Next, the plenary confronted bracketed Paragraph 95 (final), naming apartheid, "racism, Zionism," along with "imperialism, colonialism, . . . domination and hegemony" and "the growing gap between the levels of economic development of developed and developing countries" as obstacles to the advancement of women. The United States delegation had made it known that it was prepared to walk out of the conference if the phrase "racism, Zionism" was retained; the U.S. government had lobbied other governments for support on this issue. Margaret Kenyatta called a recess to resolve the phrase with substitute language, deleting "Zionism" and inserting "all other forms of racism and racial discrimination."

The political complexity of decision making on this issue was reflected in the "quid pro quos" that governments exchanged! Insiders say that the president of Kenya was involved in this decision to offer the alternative language, that Secretariat officials were critical to its acceptance, and that any voting could have become a knotty procedural/political affair. When the plenary resumed hours later, Margaret Kenyatta announced the substitute and then dropped her gavel, signifying the end of discussion and consensus approval of the paragraph just before the Iranian delegation sought a vote on the substitute language. The second vote, this one requested by the United States, followed hard upon the Zionism/racism deliberations and consensus acceptance of two more paragraphs: Paragraph 98, inequality among women in developing countries explained by the "lack of political will of certain developed countries" to restructure international economic relations on a democratic basis, including certain GA/New International Economic Order (NIEO) resolutions. Western delegates objected to reference to the GA/NIEO resolutions that had been hotly contested in the GA; the vote was 103–1 (United States)–27.

But the U.S. delegate Alan Keyes was booed when he requested a vote on apartheid. The vote on FLS final Paragraph 259, "Women and children under apartheid," was 122–1 (United States)–12. Later, along with other delegations, including United Kingdom, Sweden, Federal Republic of Germany, Belgium, and the Netherlands, all of whom abstained, the United States objected to breaking all relations with South Africa, but in particular to the call for Security Council sanctions and the support of liberation movements, as the paragraph demanded.

The U.S. delegation then followed with a request for a vote on Paragraph 260, "Palestinian Women and Children," 98–3 (Australia, Israel, United States)–28. The blocs had come to no agreement in Committee One because WEO delegates wanted no language preemptory of their foreign policies included in the paragraph. The plenary resumed discussion and finally approved the entire FLS by consensus. After delegations made statements on their votes or expanded upon their selected reservations and thanked the host government for the Conference, Margaret Kenyatta closed the conference at 4:30 A.M. on Saturday morning, 27 July—with the clock stopped on Friday, 26 July 1985.

THE CONFERENCE CONCLUDED, THE DECADE COMPLETED

The plenary deliberately avoided a draft declaration but agreed to append it and the resolutions from both committees to the Report! The conference, a creature of the GA, reported to it, which adopted the conference report without a vote by Resolution 40/108 on 13 December 1985 but took no action on any of the appended resolutions nor on the draft declaration.

Many delegations took the conference and the FLS home in the form of reports to their congresses, parliaments and governments: United States, Yugoslavia, New Zealand, Mexico, among others. As international public policy for UN agencies, the FLS was also national public policy, to be "acted upon" by each government. Nongovernmental organizations also took their experiences home, drawing on them to move the FLS into the future.

The success of the Conference is two-fold: The Conference itself was a success, as well as the long-term effect of the conference and the Decade on women and their conditions.

CONCLUSION: WOMEN, POLITICAL POWER, AND SUCCESS OF THE CONFERENCE

That the Nairobi Conference completed the FLS by consensus decision making meant that all delegations could claim the conference a success because blocs and delegations gained something that each wanted. Even though no one delegation/bloc gained everything that it wanted, women brought the conference and the Decade for Women to an acceptable, but not perfect, conclusion. Women were chairs of committees, they negotiated in the contact groups. The outcome of the conference suggested that women would work together in favor of women, in spite of, and along with, continuing foreign policy/bloc disagreements, reflected as reservations to FLS. Women had learned to manage power, and as one delegate said later, "they had grown up to be leaders." That is evidence of an impact of the women's movement on the UN, a major objective of the Decade for Women itself.

Can it be said that any one delegation determined the outcome of the conference? To put it differently, to whom should the success of the conference be attributed? Many participants had reasons to have the conference succeed, if not actively to make it a success. The desire of the Africans that a final conference be held on their continent, the large numbers of African, especially Kenyan, women at Forum '85 and also the large numbers of official delegates (the Kenyan delegation numbered 180) at the conference gave African political leaders stronger incentives for success than reasons to tolerate failure.

Neither the Soviet nor the U.S. delegations wanted to be blamed for any failures of the Conference. Maureen Reagan set out to develop working relations with her Soviet counterparts; she was also a person with access to the highest levels of the U.S. government. She helped to develop the U.S. position and to prepare the U.S. delegation so that the delegation could participate successfully in the conference.

The U.S. delegation had stood firm, often isolated, in its demand for consensus decision making. Although criticized for its demands on this, the U.S. delegation put forward a decision-making mechanism that other delegations used when constraints in foreign policy or domestic legislation or politics demanded, as already noted in Paragraph 35. The Holy See expressed reservations about family planning and related health issues (Paragraphs 29 and 156–59); Japan and Sweden voted for Paragraph 259 on women and children under apartheid but had reservations about the International Convention on the Suppression and Punishment of the Crime of *Apartheid*; Morocco and the United Arab Emirates expressed doubts about Paragraph 74, the right of married women to own property.

Conciliation in the negotiations was led by women, who were politically astute enough not to be aggravated by hostile and deliberately provocative language. Some delegates concluded that the USSR was not playing a "Copenhagen role" and that compromise might be possible. Even the PLO may have dropped its demands for "Zionism/racism," a strategy determined by then to be counterproductive.

If Committee One was the public sense of "high politics," then the language of FLS, where G-77 pushed its perspective, reflected their negotiating attitudes. Western delegations fought to prevent the acceptance of any new formulae on systemic issues, such as sanctions against South Africa or the global economic crisis, which could later be incorporated as acceptable policy compromises into other UN documents—in effect, a "no language, no precedents" policy. By contrast, Committee Two's paragraphs emerged as more conciliatory, more feminist language; its participants were less burdened with "high politics" language. In the end, FLS passed by consensus because the Western and G-77 blocs, led by women, had their say on issues of importance to each bloc.

The open demands by the Secretariat that the conference accomplish its purposes also contributed to the success of the conference. As one UN staff member later remarked, "If we hadn't brought the Conference to a successful conclusion, we'd have set the women's movement back fifty years."

If the conference was an immediate success in that delegates approved FLS by consensus, what were the strategies about which it was so important to be successful? The FLS was a political document, politically adopted; it was also agreed-upon international public policy, to take the women's movement into the future.[12] In what sense can it be for women, from women, on behalf of women, to women? Can it be called a feminist document, or did it and the conference processes remove women "from an identity group to which they owed allegiance" within the context of transnational relations back within the "focus on ... the state and its power as a unit of analysis"?[13]

We argue that, because of, not in spite of, the politics of negotiations, FLS advanced feminist positions and shifted conceptualizations. As already discussed, women depended upon peace at all levels, but peace would be strengthened when women could participate on an equal basis with men at all levels of society. Women's contribution to development had not yet been fully recognized and would not be until approaches to development underwent basic changes. Thus, FLS integrated issues on the basis of gender language: the *participation* of women in development and the recognition that current development strategies actually damaged women and their status; that structural adjustment policies were being carried out at the expense of the poor—and, thus, of women; the assertion of the right of women to control their own bodies and a mitigation of some feminist objections to population policy in favor of linkages between population policy and women; the recognition that violence at all levels was at the expense of women; the linkage of women's rights to a relationship between peace and the exercise of those rights; and an acknowledgment of divisions among women based on race, color, ethnicity, and national origin. Delegates ignored, eliminated, or expressed reservations on some issues: sexual preference/ same sex relationships, equal pay for work of equal value, the right of married women to own property.

There was a growing sense that women were significant political players and that they would be counted in significant ways, but that particulars could and would be worked out at the national and local levels. The FLS specifically called on men and women, those materially better off and in positions of influence, "in a spirit of solidarity," to work "to change the current inferior and exploited condition of the majority of women" (Paragraph 42).

Two immediate aspects of FLS stood out. First, women demanded that they no longer be excluded from the public world because of and by means of gender-based rules. By implication, the gender-based relationships in the so-called private world would have to change, and the call to governments to act on behalf of women presented a powerful statement to the international community for future action on behalf of women.

Second, in the context of expanded governmental domestic action on behalf of women, international organizations were in the future—with the regional and international mandate that was FLS—to improve, develop, strengthen, and monitor a whole range of actions on behalf of women, including the expansion of coordination by the Branch for the Advancement of Women under CSW and the inclusion of more professional women in professional posts. The CSW was to undertake "regular consultations" with UN agencies and organizations to exchange information and to coordinate future planning of women's issues. The strengthened role of CSW, later to hold annual meetings because the U.S. and USSR delegates agreed to support them, was an important outcome of the FLS, Nairobi Conference, and Decade. The UN itself was under challenge to expand its policy on and commitment to women.

What then about the long-term success of the Nairobi Conference and the Decade for Women? Any hypothesis about the establishment of a regime on women seems premature. One proposition some scholars have supported is that the Decade for Women led to "standards of behavior for governments and individuals" or to the "gaining of agenda status and arousing awareness among women."[14] Some governments may have intended consensus as support for implementation. One delegate suggested that her delegation's support for consensus was on behalf of a "commitment that the FLS would be implemented by the international community."

Some question the premises of success of the Nairobi Conference or the Decade for Women when women in many areas were worse off at the end of the 1980s than at the beginning. We suggest that the new standards of women's equality, recognition of social and cultural stereotypes about women as sources of discrimination, the acknowledgment of women's roles in peace and development, women's global movements for social reform, and adjustments in North-South issues in the global women's movement need to be understood as the very dynamic long-term consequences of the Nairobi Women's Conference, 1985.

APPENDIX: INTERVIEWS

My appreciation and thanks are due especially to Maureen O'Neil, Mildred Persinger, and Chafika Sellami-Meslem, for their detailed and thoughtful comments on the manuscript; to Mallica Vajrathon, for her remarks on the manuscript; and to Kay Fraleigh, for her generous sharing of documents and papers from the Church Center International Collection on Women. No direct citations of interviews have been made in the chapter, and we remain responsible for all interpretations of such interviews.

Members, Delegations in Nairobi

Canada: Christopher Greenshield, telephone, Ottawa, 4/30/91
Julie Loranger, microcassette, Madrid, 3/11/90
Lindsay Niemann, CEDAW, UN hdqts., New York City (the same for others at CEDAW), 1/90
Maureen O'Neil, telephone, Ottawa, 4/13/92

Egypt: Mervat Tallaway, CEDAW, 1/90

Italy: Ivanka Corti, CEDAW, 1/90

Mexico: Aida Martinez Gonzalez, CEDAW, 1/90
Olga Pellicer, New York City, 4/6/90

United Kingdom: Richard Fursland, New York City, 5/14/91
Anne Warburton, Diss., United Kingdom, 3/28/89

United States: Esther Coopersmith, Washington, D.C., 5/27/90
Alan Keyes, telephone, Washington, D.C., 5/2/91
Margaret Jones, New York City, 12/1/90
Maureen Reagan, telephone interview by Margaret Galey, California-

Pennsylvania, 7/17/92
Nancy Reynolds, Washington, D.C., 5/21/90

Yugoslavia: Zagorka Ilic, CEDAW, 1/90

Secretariat Officials, Nairobi

Alexander Berg-Oliver, New York City, 5/31/90

Aysa Kudat, telephone, Washington, D.C., 11/30/90

Chafika Sellami-Meslem, CEDAW, 1/90 and 1/92

NGO Representatives in Nairobi and New York City

Nita Barrow, New York City, n.d.

Virginia Hazzard, New York City, n.d.

Mildred Persinger, New York City, World YWCA, April and July 1992

Representative of International Federation of Business and Professional Women, Nairobi, 7/85

Representative of Housewives in Dialogue, Nairobi, 7/85

Others

Mallica Vajrathon, United Nations Fund for Population Activities (UNFPA), New York City, 6/25/92

NOTES

1. UN, GA, Plenary, Official Records, GA Res. 35/135.

2. UN, ECOSOC, Plenary, Official Records, 4 April 1982, ECOSOC Res. 1982/26; GA Res. 37/60 (1982).

3. UN, World Conference to Review and Appraise the Achievements of the United Nations Decade for Women: Equality, Development and Peace, Nairobi, Kenya, 15–26 July 1985, *Recommendations of Regional Intergovernmental Preparatory Meetings. Report of the Secretary-General*, A/CONF.116/9, 5 February 1985.

4. *For the Record ... Forum '85. The Non-Governmental World Meeting for Women, Nairobi, Kenya*, prepared by Caroline Pezzullo for the NGO Planning Committee, September 1986. For an account of the NGO Forum '85, see Victoria Schuck, "Forum '85 and the UN Decade for Women Conference," *Political Science and Politics* 18, no. 4 (Fall 1985): 907–11.

5. UN, World Conference (Nairobi), *Report*, A/CONF.116/28 (15 September 1985), 99–101.

6. Victoria Schuck undertook an extensive analysis of the makeup of the delegations to the Nairobi Conference, the data for which is based on A/CONF.116/INF/1, 22 July 1985.

7. A/CONF.116/28, 97–98.

8. The data on consultative status NGOs is drawn only from A/CONF.116/MISC.1, Add. 3, 17 July 1985.

9. A/CONF.116/28, 102–3.

10. Notes of Charlotte Patton, who observed Committee Two.

11. Article by Nadia Hijab, *Forum '85* (8 July 1985), 1.

12. For an analysis of FLS, see Hilkka Pietila and Jeanne Vickers, *Making Women Matter: The Role of the United Nations* (London: Zed Books, 1990).

13. Kathleen Newland, "From Transnational Relations to International Relations: Women in Development and the International Decade of Women," *Millenium: Women and International Relations* (special issue), 17, no. 3 (Winter 1988): 507, 513. For a positive appraisal on Forum '85 in its contribution to global feminism—that is, a diversity of feminisms—see Nilufer Cagatay, Caren Grown, and Aida Santiago, "The Nairobi Women's Conference: Toward a Global Feminism?" *Feminist Studies* 12, no. 2 (Summer 1986): 401–12; see also Jessie Bernard, *The Female World from a Global Perspective* (Bloomington: Indiana University Press, 1987).

14. Paul Taylor and A.J.R. Groom, eds., *Global Issues in the United Nations Framework* (New York: St. Martin's Press, 1989). See also chapters by Paul Taylor, "The Origins and Institutional Setting of the UN Special Conferences," 8 and R. H. Harrison, "Women's Rights, 1875–1985," 242 in this volume.

6
The Convention on the Elimination of All Forms of Discrimination Against Women (The Women's Convention)

Arvonne S. Fraser

When fifty-seven nations stepped forward to sign the Convention on the Elimination of All Forms of Discrimination Against Women during the opening ceremonies of the 1980 United Nations World Conference on Women in Copenhagen, a new era for women began. Encouraged by a 1975 Mexico City Conference resolution, women within the United Nations (UN) and in the international nongovernmental women's organizations (NGOs) that supported and encouraged them had pressed hard to finish work on this convention in time for the 1980 conference. Just over a year later, by 3 September 1981, twenty nations had ratified it and the convention became an international treaty. Never before had discrimination on the grounds of sex been defined internationally and equality between women and men sanctioned in all areas of life and work.

The convention and its predecessor, the Declaration on the Elimination of Discrimination Against Women, resulted from initiatives and long negotiations within the political organs of the UN, but with a unique difference. Women drafted these instruments. The Commission on the Status of Women (CSW) afforded women members, NGOs and female UN staff what feminists term a free space. There they forged an understanding of their common problems and ways to alleviate them. But CSW's recommendations require approval of the Economic and Social Council (ECOSOC) and the General Assembly (GA). Women delegates to CSW, and the GA succeeded in persuading these UN bodies to consent to both instruments. In doing so, they demonstrated their ability as consummate politicians and as feminists, though the record of discussion and debate never contained the word *feminist*.

By 1993, 120 nations had ratified the convention, putting women's human rights firmly on the international agenda. Full implementation of the treaty will take generations, for this is a revolutionary document covering both public and private acts. It requires that nations change laws and policies, that tradition and culture be modified, and that citizens and public officials alike change behavior. The Committee on the Elimination of Discrimination Against Women (CEDAW) officially monitors implementation of the convention by annually reviewing reports from ratifying countries. After over a decade of reviewing these reports, it has made general recommendations and comments that establish new international standards.

How and why women drafted the declaration and the convention, gained necessary approval of their numerous articles, and then advanced the principles of the convention within the political milieu of the UN is an essential chapter in the story of women and politics in the UN.

ORIGINS

The roots of the declaration and the convention lay not only in the common understanding of women's situation gained in the CSW but also in the equal rights provisions of the UN Charter and the Universal Declaration of Human Rights. Conventions on specific women's rights prepared earlier by CSW, the International Labor Organization (ILO) and the UN Educational, Scientific and Cultural Organization (UNESCO) were the foundation on which CSW members built. The international covenants on civil and political rights, on economic and social rights, and on eliminating race discrimination offered ideas, as did the UN concern with economic and social development. Political and intellectual support for CSW came from women's national and international organizations to which many members belonged.

THE DECLARATION

In November 1963, twenty-two developing and Eastern European countries introduced a resolution at the 18th GA session calling for drafting a declaration on eliminating discrimination against women.[1] None of the sponsoring countries were major Western powers, refuting the notion that feminism or women's rights is an industrialized country idea. Resolution sponsors argued that women's participation in the development of nations was essential and that discrimination impeded development. In 1963, ECOSOC also had before it a new *Report on the World Social Situation*, analyzing trends during the preceding decade. Population, health, nutrition, housing, education, and social services—all issues with which women were traditionally associated—were prominent in that report. The

Third Committee also had on its agenda that year a report on refugees; a CSW recommendation on consent, registration, and minimum age of marriage; declarations on religious intolerance and racial discrimination; and the international covenants on human rights. The *Report on the World Social Situation* noted that an important change in developing countries was the employment of women in new occupations and that recent UN work demonstrated the interrelationship of economic and social issues. The CSW members understood this interrelationship. They also knew that social and economic issues were political.

In the Third Committee debate on the declaration resolution, credit was given to CSW for its earlier work on women's employment and education and for drafting conventions on the political rights of women, on marriage law, and the nationality of women.[2] However, a strong difference of opinion surfaced over whether the commission should tackle practical, programmatic questions of women's integration in the development process or deal with law and policy reform to eliminate discrimination. The Western Europeans, reflecting their relative wealth, homogeneity, and reliance on social programs and administrative procedures, put more faith in tangible programs. The newly independent nations argued that a declaration was needed to ensure women's equality and enhance prospects for development. Their view prevailed. The final votes to begin work on a declaration were unanimous in both the Third Committee and in the General Assembly (GA).

The declaration resolution invited governments, UN specialized agencies, and NGOs to send comments and proposals to the Secretary-General (SG). This invitation combined political education and consensus building. By the 1965 CSW meeting in Teheran, the UN Secretariat had a memorandum ready with replies from thirty-three governments, fifteen NGOs and four UN specialized agencies.[3] The report identified issues that surfaced throughout drafting and adoption of the declaration, the convention, and beyond. There was almost unanimous agreement that women's education was a priority, and there was a strong sense that tradition and culture, especially as exemplified in marriage and family law, were major constraints on women's equality. Some respondents extolled women's roles as mothers and family members; the political argument was over whether women had primary or multiple roles.

Among the eight industrialized countries responding to the SG's request for comments, the Western Europeans all suggested that the new declaration either should be limited to melding together the existing women's conventions or should emphasize the importance of education, training, and social services so that women could engage in activities outside the home.[4] The United States was more enthusiastic, even hinting at the possibility of a stronger document later. Only three of the sixteen developing country sponsors of the original resolution on the declaration—Afghanistan, Argentina, and Morocco—responded.[5] Afghanistan said that overcoming discrimination required "combating of traditions, customs and usages which thwart the advancement of women ... (and) intense educational efforts ... designed to enlighten public opinion."[6] Anticipating the idea of affirmative action, Afghanistan also said that "amends must be made to women by granting them certain privileges." Other respondents emphasized the need for home and child care services to encourage women's outside activities—employment, education, or training—and the need for public education campaigns advocating equality. China noted that civil laws often denied married women rights to hold or inherit property or to be guardians of their children. Nepal made the interesting suggestion that no marriage be allowed if the age difference between spouses was more than twenty years. The United Arab Republic argued for equality in nationality and domicile, aid to widows and divorcees, and the need for educational campaigns to overcome discriminatory customs and tradition.

The seven Eastern European respondents all strongly supported the proposed declaration, submitting detailed suggestions and adding criminal law and the problems of unmarried mothers to the list of issues. Respondents of NGOs were almost unanimous in stating that a declaration would be particularly useful in illustrating worldwide discrimination against women. Only the Young Women's Christian Association (YWCA) demurred, saying adoption of a declaration might give the impression that CSW's work would be finished, a fear often expressed throughout deliberations on the declaration and convention. The NGOs also shared concerns about family and criminal law, discrimination against single women and female heads of households, prostitution, employment, and education.

Neither governments nor NGOs nor the World Health Organization mentioned women's health. This issue surfaced only during the final Convention drafting. The Food and Agriculture Organization (FAO) did point out that discrimination against rural women included lack of recognition of their work, especially in food production, and that they needed satisfactory housing and education, ideas found in the final convention. The UN Educational, Scientific and Cultural Organization (Unesco) indicated that although an existing convention on education allowed for equivalent education in separate male and female educational systems, coeducation would be better, an idea that was not followed up.

With this world survey of ideas before them in the SG's report, CSW meeting in Teheran appointed a twelve-member drafting committee composed of volunteers and members from the countries that had sponsored the original resolution.[7] The committee was urged to prepare a text based not only on the Secretariat's report but on all the proposals and suggestions that had been made within CSW since the declaration resolution had been adopted. Poland had a draft text and Ghana and the commission chair, Maria Lavalle Urbina of Mexico, had submitted working papers. Interest was high and CSW members were eager to begin work on the declaration.

Among those present in Teheran who continued with the commission as it drafted the declaration and then the convention were Helvi Sipila (Finland), later a UN Assistant Secretary-General; Aziza Hussein (Egypt) later head of International Planned Parenthood Federation; Jeanne Chaton (France); Helena Z.

Benitez (Philippines); Zofia Dembinska (Poland); Hannah Bokor (Hungary); Rachel Nason (United States); Annie R. Jiaggie (Ghana), who later became a judge; and Princess Ashraf Pahlavi (Iran), the Shah's sister. Present also were representatives of governments that were not members of the commission, UN specialized agencies, and twenty-two NGOs, all of which had submitted responses. The director of the Division of Human Rights also attended, as did Margaret K. Bruce, Chief of the Section on the Status of Women, representing the SG. It was a full house.

Poland's draft was selected as the committee's working document. Its preamble referred to previous UN actions promoting equal rights for women but noted that women's legal status did not correspond to their practical situation. Some countries still denied political rights to women; remnants of colonialism and feudalism were obstacles to women's full emancipation; and although women's role in national development was increasing, discrimination impeded development and peace. This linkage between equality, development, and peace—made in 1926 by the International Alliance of Women—later became the major theme of the UN Decade for Women.[8] The substantive text of Poland's draft began with a definition and condemnation of discrimination, followed by eleven articles covering every area mentioned in the government and NGO responses. The final article called on women's organizations to undertake educational campaigns to inform men and women of the declaration's principles. All the ideas in this first draft—except the reference to women's organizations—were destined to be included in the final convention but not without years of discussion, debate, and political maneuvering.

The 1965 drafting committee prepared a full text for the commission, but after a brief discussion it asked the SG through ECOSOC, to circulate the text and background materials for additional comments. This would test political sentiment, educate governments, and allow time for conciliation within CSW between those who wanted to concentrate on women's rights and those more interested in a programmatic agenda. Meanwhile, momentum for women's rights was building in the larger UN system. At the 1965 Third Committee meeting, twenty-nine female delegates spoke, reiterating ideas found in the draft declaration.[9] This committee had become another free space for women, even though men also served on it. Ider (Mongolia), who subsequently became CEDAW's first chair, reported on a UN Seminar on Participation of Women in Public Life held in her country and regretted that the commission had decided to postpone debate on the declaration. Mrs. Boulton de Bottome (Venezuela) articulated the free space theory, when she said the "Third Committee itself had become a most useful meeting place for women from different countries, some of which had only recently recognized the role of women in modern society."[10] Male committee members joined the debate. Mr. Hoveyda (Iran) pointed out that Islam was not opposed to the emancipation of women, noting that within Moslem countries a women's movement was gathering momentum. Mr. Baroody (Saudi Arabia) did not agree, raising a familiar cry: "The sacred unit of the family must be preserved at all costs; in particular it must not be sacrificed to so-called democratic principles purporting to put women on an equal footing with men."[11]

The debate continued. During its 1966 session, the commission appointed a style committee to make sure that provisions were clearly translatable into all UN languages and could be understood by both governments and ordinary citizens. The only substantive issue debated was the protection of women. A majority of the members agreed that protection of women often resulted in discrimination against them, an issue that would find its way into the convention. After lengthy discussion but a unanimous vote, the draft declaration went to ECOSOC. There, so many amendments were introduced that the draft was sent back for further consideration.

The declaration considered women to be individual citizens and called for abolishing customs and laws that perpetuated discrimination. This was anathema to those who put family first. Most commission members and the interested NGOs strongly supported freeing women from traditional constraints. NGOs, in responding to the ECOSOC amendments, argued that a declaration should set international goals and that the suggestion, for example, of limiting women from dangerous and arduous work was silly because women in both developing and industrialized countries consistently did such work. Women's legal capacity was also a deep concern. Should women be free to make contracts, obtain credit in their own name, inherit and manage property and be guardians of their children? Commission members knew that most legal systems designated the husband head of household and family representative. Every married CSW and NGO member was directly affected by such laws. Although the Universal Declaration of Human Rights recognized individual persons under law and freedom of movement, Article 12 left the issue of family ambiguous. The draft declaration's intent was to change the concept of family from *his* to *their*.

The commission went back to work. At its 1967 session, Urbina (Mexico) was selected chair of a new drafting committee and Chaton (France) as rapporteur. Both were thoroughly familiar with the declaration and the commission's views. The Committee decided only to consider changes proposed in ECOSOC and the GA. Then Urbina made an important political move. She invited all CSW members whose governments had submitted amendments to join the drafting committee. One of the major controversies was over the word "abolish" in Article 2 relating to discriminatory customs, laws, regulations, and traditions. Everyone understood change was essential. An amendment to substitute the phrase "modify or change" carried on a 7 to 6 vote, with 3 abstentions. The committee also rejected a proposal to limit guarantees of former employment after maternity leave.

When the committee's new text came before the commission, the chair put forth another unique suggestion: There would be no general debate. Rather, in light of the GA's resolution to review the text, they would look first at the new drafting committee's text which had taken the suggested amendments into account, compare it with the earlier draft, and if the new amendments were rejected, then they would vote on the original CSW text. Explanations of votes could be given and sponsors of amendments that had been withdrawn could explain their reasons. No new amendments would be considered.

The question of whether to abolish or modify discriminatory customs and traditions was the first major vote. Abolish won—overturning the drafting committee—by a vote of 15 to 14, with 2 abstentions. On this and other votes, the traditional UN political blocs did not hold. Feminism was international and the free space theory worked. Women could collaborate across geopolitical boundaries even when their governments differed. These women were canny politicians; they understood the advantage of off-the-record discussions and negotiations. They knew how to carry out their governmental responsibilities and still uphold their personal convictions.

In the controversy over women's legal capacity under civil law, Iran's representative proposed separate votes on each subparagraph. This gave members the right to express their nation's disapproval of some clauses without destroying the essence of the particular article. Representatives who might favor particular wording, but whose governments did not, could report to their governments that they either voted no or abstained on the controversial paragraphs. Before the final vote, representatives were allowed to explain their votes and ask that reservations be recorded. The commission then, on 2 March 1967, unanimously adopted the draft declaration with the final article stating that the principle of equality demanded implementation, an indication that some members were clearly thinking ahead. They knew that declarations were harbingers of conventions and looked toward a legally enforceable women's human rights instrument.

The CSW draft declaration contained eleven articles and a preamble, just as the original Polish draft had. The preamble asserted that discrimination against women was "incompatible with the dignity of women as human beings, and with the welfare of the family and of society" and prevented women's participation in political, social, economic, and cultural life, thus impeding development. Article 1 declared that discrimination is "fundamentally unjust and constitutes an offence against human dignity." (The definition of discrimination had been dropped, but would reappear in the convention.) Article 2 called for measures to abolish discriminatory laws, customs, and practices and for legal protection of equal rights. Article 3 dealt with changing public opinion and eradicating prejudice, while Article 4 folded in the principles of the 1952 Convention on the Political Rights of Women. Article 5 incorporated the women's nationality convention, adopted in 1957, and Article 6 insured equal legal capacity.

Article 7 on penal codes illustrated the intensity factor in politics. A critical mass of members insisted on this article and were vigilant during every drafting session. They understood sexual abuse in detention facilities as well as the common practice of prosecuting prostitutes but not their customers. These, they believed, were flagrant examples of double standard morality. Article 8, dealing with prostitution and trafficking in women, reflected the same outlook. Prostitution was not condemned; exploitation through prostitution was. Although there was a proposal to delete Article 8, it remained on a vote of 22 to 6, with three abstentions.[12]

Article 9 reflected the overwhelming consensus on the importance of women's education and included a phrase on ensuring the health and well-being of families, a precursor of convention language on joint parental responsibility in the rearing and support of children and on family planning. Article 10 called for free choice of profession, equal pay for work of equal value, and the right to paid maternity leave and social services so that women could be employed outside the home. The final article referred to the UN Charter's equal rights provision and to the Universal Declaration of Human Rights and urged implementation of the declaration.

On 7 November 1967, the GA adopted the Declaration on the Elimination of Discrimination Against Women, ending four years of political maneuvering between the more intimate commission and the more formal, male-dominated GA.[13] Women in the Third Committee were the intermediaries who moved the declaration from the commission to the GA. Unanimity was achieved only because this was a declaration, a statement of principles. A convention would be an international legal instrument, with mechanisms for monitoring and implementation, and consensus on it would not be as easily achieved.

From a Declaration to a Convention

Within a year, the Polish CSW member proposed elaboration of the declaration into a convention, noting that this was customary in the field of human rights. It was 1972, however, before the commission had an SG's report on provisions in existing conventions relating to the status of women and to provisions in the declaration.[14] By this time the commission was preoccupied with preparations for International Women's Year (IWY); therefore, a special working group was suggested to consider government replies to the idea of a convention and to begin work on one or more new instruments.[15] Attention was also drawn to a progress report of the special rapporteur on the status of women and family planning, and member states were requested to collaborate with her.[16] This effectively put everyone on notice that the issue would be part of any new instrument.

The ECOSOC appointed members of the special working group by geographic region. Experienced commission members were elected as working group officers. When the group met in January 1974, a representative of the SG discussed government replies, possible substantive and implementation provisions, and a draft text from the Philippines that its country's delegate hastened to say was preliminary and should not be construed as binding on the government.[17] The group quickly decided to draft a single, comprehensive document and soon had a compromise Philippines-USSR draft before it. They adopted the

Philippines' strategy of presenting a text without commitment; the draft would not bind governments represented on the working group. The group decided that where consensus could not be reached, alternative texts would be presented and CSW members could then choose between the alternatives. The speed and efficiency of this process was extraordinary, suggesting that a well-connected, politically effective group of women were again collaborating in their own free space, using their political knowledge and access effectively. Working group members were identified by name and country only in the annex to the document; elsewhere, actions or opinions are attributed to "one representative" or "some representatives."

The first draft of the new convention mirrored the declaration, although articles were reordered and the words "all forms of" discrimination were added to the title. One provision under Article 5 stated that advocacy of superiority or inferiority of one sex should be prohibited by law, raising the freedom of speech issue. A version of the nationality article included a controversial new provision granting women equal rights in conveying nationality to children, a troublesome issue for governments that held that only males could head families. Presented with this working group draft, the commission used the familiar tactic of deferring consideration, understanding that moving from a declaration to a convention was serious and governments needed time to consider the ramifications of this move.

Drafting of the convention was only one element of CSW work. Preparations for the 1975 world conference on women had priority. In addition, by the time the Mexico City IWY Conference was held, the UN had become more politicized around development issues and Soviet–U.S. relations. Demands for a new international economic order were made in every international forum with the Mexico City Conference no exception. Yet the Declaration of Mexico, written by the Group of 77 developing countries and led by Lucille Mair (Jamaica), took notice of the declaration and quoted from it.[18]

At the 1976 CSW meetings, the draft convention was only one of four major items on the agenda, and the politicization carried over into CSW deliberations. A new preambular paragraph linking international peace and security to the safeguarding of women's human rights was introduced by the German Democratic Republic. Senegal added a provision on the effect of apartheid on women. Both were accepted, making the convention's preamble a product of its time. However, these political questions did not impede the momentum for a convention. CSW's objective was to have a convention ready for the 1980 world women's conference.

Although CSW members expressed increasingly politicized views, personal views of members again played a part. Few votes were taken. Instead reservations or comments were made about provisions that were not in accordance with national law. For example, although the United States balked at a provision on equal pay for work of equal value, it did not demand a vote. On the question of special protections for women workers, the USSR favored protection; the

United States did not. Almost every nation that was represented joined the debate over a provision for special protection of employed pregnant women in types of work that were harmful to them. Compromise was reached with a statement that such legislation should be reviewed periodically in light of scientific and technological knowledge.

Another new element, foreshadowed during the declaration discussion, was introduced when an FAO observer, noting that a majority of the world's women lived in rural areas, drew attention to the numerous rural womens resolutions adopted at the Mexico City Conference and in the GA and suggested that they should not be overlooked in the convention.[19] Although the article that was subsequently adopted repeated subjects already covered in the convention, the momentum for the article was overwhelming, and it was adopted by consensus. Another major change was the inclusion of family planning as a right to be freely exercised. India proposed a new subparagraph on the right "to decide freely and responsibly on the number and spacing of their children and to have access to the information, education and means" to enable women to exercise this right.[20] And although the question of discrimination against single mothers and female-headed households proved to be a delicate one—with some countries insisting that female-headed households did not exist because no female could legally head a household—numerous CSW members insisted that it was a worldwide de facto phenomenon demanding attention. As a result, the phrase "married and unmarried" modifying the word "women" in numerous articles was retained, as had been suggested earlier by Eastern European bloc countries. In another astute political move, the divisive and contentious articles on women's legal capacity and marriage and family law were moved to last place. This meant that readers, and potential ratifying nations, would see the less controversial provisions first, building up to the logical conclusion that law, including marriage and family law, institutionalized inequality.

With agreement on the substantive articles, the commission moved to the question of implementation and monitoring. Were the commission members willing to give the task of monitoring progress under this new convention to a new international body? Could they monitor the new convention and the work on the Decade for Women that still had years to go? The disagreements were sharp. Should the international monitoring body be composed of government representatives or independent experts? Some argued, reflecting their own experience in the drafting committees and on working groups where they may have disagreed with their governments, that independent experts were preferable. Others simply did not want to give up commission control. The final decision was to have an ad hoc group of ten to fifteen persons, elected by the commission, as the monitoring body with members serving in their private capacity.

The next question involved the number of ratifying nations that would be required to make the convention an international treaty. The United States suggested one-third of all member nations; the USSR wanted a much lower number. Consensus was reached at twenty nations. With these decisions, the draft convention was adopted without a vote and the commission proceeded to drafting the Programme of Action for the 1980 world conference, confident that the draft convention would be considered by the GA promptly.

It took three more years. Treaties are legally binding documents. Precision in language and understanding of specific provisions and general concepts is required. A Third Committee working group scrutinized the CSW draft text article by article and word for word, clarifying every disputed or misunderstood provision.[21] The concept of social security was discussed at length, with final agreement that it meant a nation's whole system of social services. A new article was added ensuring equal access to health care services, including family planning. The contentious issues—protection of women workers, nationality, women's legal capacity, the married/unmarried clauses and the politicized preamble—were all debated again. Extensive revisions were made to the article concerning rural women with new clauses on women's participation in development planning and with the right to organize self-help groups and cooperatives added.

Again, the most difficult articles were left until last. The broad concept of equality before the law drew no opposition, but virtually all legal systems were threatened by specific provisions of Articles 15 and 16 that gave women equal legal capacity and equality under marriage and family law. These precipitated more than a full week's debate. Nations, in anticipation of possible ratification, were minutely scrutinizing the draft text. Individual members had to face the fact that legal discrimination becomes very personal, affecting the home and the person who owns and manages marital property and who has the right to establish domicile, make contracts, and be guardians of children. The CSW had been extremely direct and explicit, especially in a provision that said that contracts directed at restricting the legal capacity of women shall be deemed null and void. This, the Ecuador delegate asserted, would "create a disquieting legal vacuum."[22] Debates ensued over interpretations of private and public law and over civil law, which in some countries included commercial as well as personal or private matters. Finally, a near consensus was reached on the preamble and substantive text of the convention.

This again left the final provisions on reporting and implementation and a few provisions on which the working committee could not agree. It was late 1979, and four different proposals covering the structure of the monitoring body were before the working group. Sweden's comprehensive proposal was finally adopted, calling for a twenty-three member committee elected by ratifying countries (States Parties) from among their nationals at a meeting called for that purpose. Members would serve in their private capacity and would have four-year terms. The full membership would represent the principal legal systems of the world.

On 6 December, when the Third Committee took up the convention, the momentum for adoption was almost lost when the Mexican delegate proposed a stalling technique that governments should be given a year to consider and comment on the draft convention. The working group chair responded that by this time delegations knew their government's positions on all the controversial issues and appealed strongly for closure in time for the 1980 world conference. The Netherlands delegate, Ms. Van den Assum, saved the day. A young but experienced CSW and GA delegate who thoroughly understood UN procedures, she argued that since the Mexican amendment was not substantive, it should not be considered first. After consultations with the UN Legal Office, her position was affirmed and the committee moved ahead to adopt the Swedish monitoring body proposal and resolve most of the remaining issues. Earlier, the working group had added an article on reservations; moved the article on discrimination in penal codes into Article 2, and inserted a provision in Article 9 granting women equal rights with men as to nationality of children. In voting on the politicized preambular paragraphs, the United States stood alone in voting no, although many other Western nations abstained. The final Third Committee vote on the resolution sending the new convention to the GA was 112 to 1 (Mexico), with 13 abstentions.[23]

On 19 December 1979, the GA took up the draft convention. Only three issues required votes. The tenth and eleventh paragraphs in the preamble dealing with the controversial political issues—apartheid, colonialism, and nuclear disarmament—were adopted by a vote of 108 to 0, with 26 abstentions, including the United States and other industrialized countries. Paragraph 2 of Article 9, granting women equal rights to convey nationality to their children, was carried by a vote of 92 to 13, with 28 abstentions. Those voting against the article were Muslim countries and Brazil; those abstaining were all developing countries ranging from Afghanistan to Upper Volta. Paragraph 1(c) of Article 16, covering equal rights and responsibilities during marriage and at its dissolution, was passed by a vote of 104 to 0, with 32 abstentions. Again, those abstaining were all developing countries, primarily Muslim and Catholic. However, the final vote on adopting the convention as a whole was 130 to 0, with 11 abstentions.[24] Among those abstaining were three countries that had supported the original declaration resolution—Mali, Mexico, and Morocco—all countries with strong religious and family law traditions.

With this vote, a new human rights document was adopted, and the work of CSW and Third Committee women delegates was affirmed. Women now had an international legal instrument aimed at destroying thousands of years of tradition and custom under which they were considered subordinate to men. The convention gave women full citizenship under law, made marriage an equal partnership, called for affirmative action to eliminate discrimination, and asked that all appropriate measures be taken to modify or abolish discriminatory laws, customs, and practices. Legal and de facto discrimination were both attacked. Article 18 called for the submission of reports by ratifying countries on legislative, judicial, administrative, or other measures adopted to implement the convention. Subsequent articles allowed the monitoring committee to make recommendations and suggestions to the GA based on their reviews of country reports. Country reports were to be submitted within one year of ratification and every four years thereafter. CSW was to receive the committee's reports through the SG.

A Treaty in Place—Would It Be Used?

Attention then turned to the national level—to ratification by enough governments to give the document the force of law and to international monitoring. The required number of ratifications took less than two years. The world women's conferences in Mexico City and Copenhagen had generated a strong, new political constituency to which governments responded. By 3 September 1981, twenty nations had ratified the new women's convention and it entered into force.[25] In April 1982 representatives of the ratifying countries, called States Parties, met to elect members of CEDAW as provided under Article 17 of the convention. In October, the new committee met at the UN International Centre in Vienna. In opening the meeting, the director of the Branch for the Advancement of Women, which serves as the CEDAW secretariat, said a "new chapter in the long struggle for equality and the integration of women into the process of development had begun."[26]

Members of the CEDAW understood that the convention, despite the increasing number of ratifications, needed more publicity. More women needed to be aware of its existence, power, and scope, or national implementation would not proceed. It was also clear that what was supposed to be a committee of independent experts was a committee of government officials. They divided along political lines with the Soviet bloc dominating by electing Ms Ider (Mongolia) as chair. Organizational matters consumed CEDAW's early annual sessions since few governments had yet reported. By 1983, fifty-one states had ratified or acceded to the convention—seven each from Africa and Asia, ten from Eastern Europe, nineteen from Latin America, and eight from Western Europe, and others—and thirteen government reports had been received. Mrs. Sellami-Meslem, director of the UN unit that housed the CEDAW secretariat, attributed the increasing numbers of ratifications to the work of national and international women's organizations.

The CEDAW then proceeded to draw up general guidelines on the form and content of future government reports and agreed that six languages—Arabic, Chinese, English, French, Russian, and Spanish—would be the official languages of the committee, covering the major legal and political systems of the world.[27] The guidelines suggested that government reports be in two parts. The first should deal with how the nation was proceeding to eliminate discrimination under the convention, including legal measures adopted to facilitate implementation; whether institutions had been created to deal with equality issues, the means for promoting women's development and ensuring their human rights; and whether convention provisions could be invoked before or enforced by courts or administrative authorities. The second part was to give specific information on each provision of the convention. The committee wanted to know the de facto as well as the de jure situation of women, to be presented with statistics, and with what obstacles nations faced in moving toward equality.

By the 1985 world conference on women, CEDAW's work had gained little notice. Though women's groups had worked for ratification, they were not following the convention reporting and review process. Attention, instead, was focused on the world conference. Yet the idea that discrimination impeded development and that inequalities between men and women prevented women from achieving full citizenship was becoming widely accepted. The drafting and adoption of the convention and the push for ratifications had also contributed to a shift of focus within the UN and among NGO activists and scholars from almost exclusive concentration on women in development programs to increasing attention to equality issues and the influence of law and custom on women's status.

At the 1985 Nairobi NGO forum, four major groups held workshops that focused on the convention, legal literacy and services, and the power of NGOs to influence public policy. Over five hundred women and men from more than fifty countries attended a week-long workshop series cosponsored by the Commonwealth Secretariat's Women in Development office and two U.S. university-based development projects encouraged by CEDAW members. Out of these workshops, the International Women's Rights Action Watch (IWRAW) global network was formed with the objective of publicizing the convention and encouraging national implementation of its principles. At the other end of Nairobi, in the Kenyatta Center where the official UN conference was held, numerous paragraphs referring to the convention and the need for legislation, legal reform, and policy change to improve the status of women were introduced into the Forward-looking Strategies document adopted at the conference.

By 1991, only ten years after the convention became an international treaty, CEDAW had changed, becoming another free space for women. Although a number of CEDAW members were government officials, they guarded their right to serve in their personal capacity. An unwritten rule was established whereby no national could comment on CEDAW reports on her country. Although some governments were delinquent in their reporting obligations, the increasing number of ratifications meant that CEDAW could not keep up with its workload. Thanks to the work of interested NGOs, however, women's rights were beginning to be recognized as human rights, and cultural relativism was no longer an acceptable excuse for discrimination.

By this time, CEDAW was reviewing second and third reports from some countries and making general recommendations to the GA as provided under Article 21. At its 1990 session, CEDAW adopted general recommendations 14 and 15 concerning female circumcision and women with AIDS. These two topics were not specifically covered in the convention but they could be embraced by the fortuitous addition of the three small words in the convention's title, "all forms of" discrimination. At its 1989 session, CEDAW had responded to NGO concerns about violence against women with a short general recommendation that it expanded in 1992 with an explicit recommendation and series of comments showing exactly how violence was covered by the convention. An earlier recommendation calling for a UN study of the status of women under Islamic law created a furor in the GA and was rejected. Clearly, if this study were to be done, NGOs would have to do it. Women Living Under Muslim Laws, a new international NGO network headquartered in France, undertook the study.

Human rights treaties may be adopted, but changing laws, policies, and, above all, cultures, is another matter. While governments may change laws, enforcing them, especially when they cover private acts such as relationships within families, is often resisted by public officials to whom international treaties mean little. Change takes time, as does the creation of political will to make change. Delegates to CSW knew this when they suggested that national women's organizations conduct public education campaigns about the declaration. Today, women in the UN and in NGOs at the national and international level are working at creating the necessary political will. The UN Division for the Advancement of Women has sponsored regional training seminars on the convention and women's groups have succeeded in having some provisions of the convention melded into the new constitutions of Brazil, Colombia, and Zambia.[28] Legal literacy and services projects have been mounted in many countries to teach women their rights and to take cases into local and national courts; and more scholars—including development country scholars—are writing about law, custom and stereotyping, and specific women's legal issues. New women-and-the-law research groups are being organized and human rights groups in developing and industrialized countries are developing women's programs. Test cases on women's rights are being taken to court. A 1992 Botswana case involving a mother's right to convey her nationality to her children was won at least partially by invoking the convention as an international standard even though Botswana had not ratified it.[29] In 1992, a public accommodations case was won on the basis of Zambia's new constitution.

Yet, the extent to which the convention mandates change in the most basic legal and cultural assumptions about women—and the resistance to that change—is indicated by the nature and extent of reservations that were entered with ratifications.[30] The treaty carries the largest number of reservations of any international human rights instrument. Twenty ratifying countries entered over eighty reservations. Many reservations are to the nationality, employment, legal capacity, and family law articles, the contentious issues during the drafting and adoption of the convention. Nevertheless, the ever-increasing number of ratifications indicates that political regimes understand that women are a constituency whose concerns must be recognized.

The convention is both a revolutionary and an evolutionary document, revolutionary in the sense that its objective is equality between men and women; evolutionary in the sense that its language implies orderly change in laws, policies, and behavior. Full implementation of the convention's principles will take generations because its scope is unprecedented, ranging from family life to the appointment of women to international decision-making posts. This convention unites women across the traditional developing-versus-industrialized–country dichotomy and proves the 1975 Mexico City prediction that "in our times, women's role will increasingly emerge as a powerful revolutionary social force."[31] People working on convention implementation, just as their predecessors on CSW and in the Third Committee, see themselves as peers. They recognize common legal, economic, and social situations across what used to be seen as huge geographic, cultural, and intellectual divides.

The Convention on the Elimination of All Forms of Discrimination Against Women sets standards for development, defines women's rights as human rights, and demonstrates that abrogations of human rights are not limited to what governments do to its citizens but also include what citizens do to each other. By defining discrimination as "any distinction, exclusion or restriction . . . which has the effect or purpose of impairing or nullifying the recognition, enjoyment or exercise . . . of human rights and fundamental freedoms in the political, economic, social, cultural, civil or any other field," this convention, along with the International Convention on the Elimination of All Forms of Racial Discrimination, has put eliminating discrimination on the world agenda.

The political women within the UN who cared about guaranteeing women their human rights and fundamental freedoms accomplished their mission. A treaty is in place with ratification by two-thirds of the UN member states. Full implementation of the treaty will depend on whether women at the national level can be as effective as were the women within the UN.

NOTES

The author is grateful to Miho Omi of Japan, a graduate research assistant at the Humphrey Institute of Public Affairs, University of Minnesota, for extensive research and note checking for this chapter and to Marsha Freeman and Sharon Ladin, fellows at the Institute, for editorial comments and suggestions.

1. UN, *Report of the Economic and Social Council*, A/5606, (15 November 1963), 26. The sponsors of the resolution were: Afghanistan, Algeria, Argentina, Austria, Cameroon, Chile, Colombia, Czechoslovakia, Gabon, Guinea, Indonesia, Iran, Mali, Mexico, Mongolia, Morocco, Pakistan, Panama, the Philippines, Poland, Togo, and Venezuela.

2. For a description of the commission's work through International Women's Year, 1975, see Margaret Galey, "Promoting Nondiscrimination Against Women: The U.N. Commission on the Status of Women," *International Studies Quarterly* 23, no. 2 (June 1979): 273–302.

3. UN, *Draft Declaration on the Elimination of Discrimination Against Women: Memorandum by the Secretary General*, E/CN.6/426, 30 October 1964.

4. Ibid., 5–29. Industrialized countries that responded were Denmark, Finland, France, the Netherlands, Norway, Sweden, the United Kingdom, and the United States.

5. Ibid. Developing countries that responded were: Afghanistan, Argentina, Cambodia, Ecuador, India, Iraq, Madagascar, Nepal, Rwanda, Sudan, Syrian Arab Republic, Trinidad and Tobago, Turkey, and the United Arab Republic.

6. Ibid., 5.

7. UN, ECOSOC, 39th Session, Official Records, Supplement No. 7; CSW, *Report on the 18th Session* (1–10 March 1965), 23. Delegates from Austria, Colombia, Guinea, Iran, Mexico, the Philippines, and Poland were joined by volunteers from the Dominican Republic, France, Ghana, the Soviet Union and the United States.

8. At this international convention of the International Alliance of Women, the president reminded the delegates that the women's movement existed in every country and that its goals were equality, international understanding, and peace. In 1926, the issue of development had not yet been defined, but the phrase "international understanding" clearly is a harbinger of the concept of development. Arnold Whittick, *Woman Into Citizen* (London: Athenaeum, 1979), 92.

9. GA, 20th Session, *Report of Third Committee*, 11 November 1965.

10. GA, 20th Session, Official Records, 275.

11. Ibid., 282.

12. UN, ECOSOC, 42d Session, Official Records, Supplement No. 7 (E/4316), 36–37.

13. GA, 22d Session, Official Records, Supplement No. 16, A/6716 (December 1967), 35–37.

14. UN, ECOSOC, CSW, *International Instruments and National Standards Relating to the Status of Women: Study of Provisions in Existing Conventions That Relate to the Status of Women*, E/CN.6/552, (21 January 1972).

15. Ibid., *International Instruments and National Standards Relating to the Status of Women: Working Paper by the Secretary-General*, E/CN.6/573 (6 November 1973), 4.

16. Ibid., *The Role of Women in the Family: Status of Women and Family Planning*, E/CN.6/564, (28 December 1971). Helvi Sipila of Finland, a longtime CSW member, was the special rapporteur.

17. Ibid., *Consideration of Proposals Concerning a New Instrument or Instruments of International Law to Eliminate Discrimination Against Women: Report of the Working Group to the Commission on the Status of Women*, E/CN.6/574 (18 January 1974), 3. Leticia Shahani was the Philippines representative at this meeting; she later became UN Assistant Secretary-General for Social Development and Humanitarian Affairs and played a major role in preparations for the 1985 world conference on women.

18. UN, *Meeting in Mexico: Report of the World Conference of the International Women's Year* (New York: UN, 1976), 51.

19. UN, ECOSOC, CSW, E/5909, E/CN.6/608 (1977), 44.

20. UN, ECOSOC, E/5090, E/CN.6/608, 48.

21. GA, *Report of the Working Group of the Whole on the Drafting of the Convention on the Elimination of Discrimination Against Women. Note by the Secretary-General.* A/34/60 (2 March 1979); GA, *Report of the Working Group of the Whole on the Drafting of the Convention on the Elimination of Discrimination Against Women*, A/C.3/34/14 (30 November 1979).

22. Note by the SG, A/34/60 (2 March 1979), 31.

23. UN, GA, 34th Session, Official Records, Agenda Item 75, A/34/PV.107, (18 December 1979, 1996). Those abstaining were Brazil, Burma, China, Dominican Republic, Malawi, Mali, Morocco, Saudi Arabia, Senegal, Sri Lanka, Upper Volta, Venezuela, and Yemen.

24. UN, GA, Official Records, A/34/PV.107. Those abstaining were Bangladesh, Bra-

zil, Comoros, Djibouti, Haiti, Mali, Mauritania, Mexico, Morocco, Saudi Arabia, and Senegal.

25. The first twenty nations to ratify were Barbados, Byelorussia, Cape Verde, China, Cuba, Dominica, German Democratic Republic, Guyana, Haiti, Hungary, Mexico, Mongolia, Norway, Poland, Portugal, Rwanda, Saint Vincent and the Grenadines, Sweden, Ukraine, and the USSR (from status chart of ratifying countries, Division for the Advancement of Women, UN Vienna International Centre).

26. UN, *The Work of CEDAW*, vol 1, 1982–1985, ST/CSDHS/5 (1989), 3.

27. UN, CEDAW, 2d Session, CEDAW/C/7 (11 August 1983).

28. Interviews and correspondence with Isabel Plata of Colombia, Silvia Pimentel of Brazil, and Chaloka Beyani of Zambia. Sao Paulo State and numerous municipalities in the state have adopted a local convention based on the international treaty.

29. This case gained international attention as the Unity Dow case.

30. Rebecca J. Cook, "Reservations to the Convention on the Elimination of All Forms of Discrimination Against Women," *Virginia Journal of International Law* 30 (1990): 643–709.

31. "Introduction to the World Plan of Action" Paragraph 6, in *Meeting in Mexico* (New York: UN, 1976). "The World Plan of Action" is also available as UN Doc. E.CONF.66/34, *Report of the World Conference of the International Women's Year*.

7
The Politics of Women and Development

Margaret Snyder

The distinct though parallel subjects of women and of development began to merge on the United Nations (UN) agenda in 1970, when several factors converged to change the international community's perceptions of development. That confluence created the conceptual basis for the movement to link women and the development process.

Both the concept and the movement itself were further stimulated by a surge in research and data collection, by the momentum of three international UN conferences, and by the impact of the revolution in global communications. At first, however, the movement's potential for transforming societies was constrained by a lack of consensus on the relevance of macroeconomic and political factors to women. Additional constraints arose from the single-minded adoption of an integration theory and from women's steadfast adherence to a microresource mentality.

The achievements of women in both the developing and industrial countries were also seriously offset by the engulfing negative influences on global and national economies and by the politics of the 1970s and 1980s. Despite these international obstacles, however, the women at the grassroots and national levels in developing countries were able to act creatively, and their efforts were assisted at times by donor agencies. Using their solidarity organizations and their governments, women gained access to education, skills, and other resources, and demonstrated that they made a positive difference to development efforts.

Taken together, the experiences of the movement, the institutions that were put in place, and the common goals that evolved offered the potential for organizing a better world for people everywhere.

THE TURNING POINT: CONVERGENCE OF DEVELOPMENT AND WOMEN'S AGENDAS AND CREATION OF A MOVEMENT

Despite the concern for the welfare of women expressed by the Commission on the Status of Women (CSW), the Commission on Social Development (CSD), the UN International Children's Emergency Fund (UNICEF), and other agencies, the centrality of women to their nations' economic and social progress was, for a long time, neither fully understood nor acted upon.

In 1970, as alluded to above, four factors interfaced to create a new concept that merged women with development. First of all, there was disillusionment with the industrial-oriented development models of the 1960s. Second, that disenchantment coincided with the increase in developing nations' membership at the UN. Meanwhile, third, clear evidence began to emerge that pointed to women's centrality to economic and social progress. And finally, the women's movement in industrial countries was beginning to take shape. It was not long after those factors converged that the concept of women and development turned into a movement of its own.

The strategies set forth in the first UN Development Decade, the 1960s, assumed that adequate external investment would lead to economic development by boosting gross national product (GNP), whose benefits would "trickle down" to the people. Critics, especially UN Secretary-General (SG) U Thant (Burma), found such strategies wanting and in 1969 called for "integrated social and economic goals."[1]

Individual governments also acknowledged that modernization theory was largely ineffective and that its related programs worsened the situation of the poorest people. As a result, in adopting the International Development Strategy (IDS) for the Second Development Decade, the 1970s, the UN General Assembly (GA) redefined the ultimate purpose of development, namely, "to bring about sustained improvement in the well-being of the individual and to bestow benefits on all." This major reorientation of development goals enabled women as well as men to be seen as essential to the development process. In fact, the IDS specifically encouraged the "full integration of women in the total development effort."[2]

The new emphasis on people-centered development was quickened by the newly won independence of thirty-eight African, ten Asian, two West Asian, and four Caribbean countries and their subsequent representation at the UN in the 1950s and 1960s. The independence movements provided the impetus for women with rich experience as indigenous leaders in women's movements, and as partners with men in national liberation struggles, to debate the nature of their participation in their new nations. Representing their countries at the UN, they brought a fresh, grassroots approach, identifying women as providers of food, energy, and water and as the backbone of rural economies. Although anecdotal knowledge of women's economic activity, largely in peasant but also in "modern" societies, was plentiful, systematic data and research on their work in agriculture, trade, and commerce was scarce.

The information gap was filled by the timely publication of a classic text, *Women and Economic Development*, by Danish rural economist Ester Boserup; it caused a radical reordering of ideas about development.[3] Widely respected because of an earlier publication, *Conditions for Agricultural Growth*, Boserup gathered and analyzed data from official statistics and research to prepare her 1970 study. She offered clear evidence of women's crucial yet usually uncounted contributions to national economic productivity, and warned that "the whole process of growth" would be retarded if women were deprived of their productive functions. Boserup's thinking was revolutionary in the context of the largely welfare-driven development policies and the programs for maternal and child health, mother craft, and home craft that were being assisted at that time, for example by UNICEF.

Simultaneous with those new ideas, the feminist movement in the West was being revitalized with impetus from Betty Friedan's book *The Feminine Mystique*.[4] Even though the main focus of Northern feminism was Western culture, its activities fostered a readiness to support women's interests in other regions and the use of development funds in their behalf.

The decisions on the Second Development Decade and CSW's Programme of Concerted International Action for the Advancement of Women[5] (initiated in 1962 and completed when developing country representatives had increased from six to nineteen in 1970), set the stage for Boserup's broad influence. A first-ever interregional Meeting of Experts on the Integration of Women in Development was cosponsored at the UN by the CSW and CSD, which collaborated for the first time. The purpose of the historic 1972 meeting was to "advise on broad policy measures regarding women's role in economic and social development."[6]

Boserup prepared the working document for the meeting; it was chaired by Sir Arthur Lewis of Princeton University, also an experienced UN planner who was president of the Caribbean Development Bank at that time. The organizer was Aida Gindy (Egypt) the chief of the UN Social Affairs Section and a former staff member of the UN Economic Commission for Africa (ECA). Experts attending included Aziza Hussein (Egypt), Justice Annie Jiaggie (Ghana), Vida Tomsik (Yugoslavia), Leticia Shahani (Philippines), and Inga Thorsson (Sweden). Each of them played or would play a major role in the international women and development movement.

Meanwhile, the notion that women were key to the effectiveness of development efforts reached a mature stage at the ECA in Addis Ababa. The momentum of independence had already led to the establishment of the All Africa Women's Conference and organization of the first Kenya Women's Seminar by Margaret Kenyatta, both in 1962. The recommendations of African intergovernmental conferences sparked the Women and Development item of ECA's Work Programme for 1968–1969, which in turn led to the creation of a Women's Programme at the ECA Secretariat in 1972. To implement the program, two posts were established by ECA Executive Secretary Robert Gardener (Ghana) on the urging of James Riby-Williams (Ghana), director of the Human Resource Development Division. In 1974, ECA's Conference of Ministers approved the program[7] that became the African Training and Research Centre for Women (ATRCW) in 1975. Outreach to African women leaders and to governments in member states, coupled with the publication of pioneering documents made ECA/ATRCW a focus for research and for donor investment, and a model for other regions.[8]

Globally, the fledgling women and development movement in the UN system rode on the crest of population resources. Rafael Salas (Philippines), executive director of the United Nations Population Fund (UNFPA), used the finances that he controlled to underwrite posts for women and population activities in UNICEF, ECA, the Food and Agriculture Organization (FAO), and other agencies and to finance global and regional conferences. FAO's World Food Conference in 1974 also contributed to the movement in the UN system through resolutions recognizing women's economic activity in the food cycle and in family nutrition and in decisions on family size. Women's need for expanded access to training, technology, and markets was also affirmed.

Foreshadowing the multilateral initiatives, Sweden set the pace among the donor countries of the UN and the Organization for Economic Cooperation and Development (OECD) by enacting legislation in 1964 that mandated government support to women through its foreign assistance programs. Thorsson (Sweden), who later proposed the ECA posts, inspired that legislation after her own journey through Africa.[9]

Nearly a decade later, in 1973, the historic Percy Amendment to the United States Foreign Assistance Act, inspired by Mildred Marcy and Clara Beyer, aimed at a similar goal. Other OECD countries adopted legislation and assigned individuals or special units in their development cooperation ministries to implement it.

In 1975, the OECD Development Advisory Committee convened an expert group meeting on women and development, the first of a regular series of meetings that promoted cooperation among its members. Criteria for bilateral aid were adopted, such as that requiring women to be involved in preparing both women-specific and general development projects. Verifiable objectives were set and measures to overcome obstacles defined for all projects. (WID became a popular acronym meaning "the integration of women in development," as discussed below.)

Women moved quickly at Mexico City to institutionalize the movement then underway. They proposed to set up new organizations to be managed mostly by women themselves and to pressure existing development cooperation organizations to incorporate women's concerns in their programs. Dr. Shirley Summerskill (United Kingdom) offered financial assistance to establish a global intergovernmental fund to assist poor women, and Princess Ashraf (Iran) reinforced that pledge while adding contributions to two other new institutions, an international training and research institute and an Asian and Pacific regional center similar to ATRCW. Drafters of a resolution titled "Special Resources for the Integration of Women in Development," led by Terese Spens (United Kingdom), recognized that some government contributions to the International Women's Year (IWY) Trust Fund for the Conference would remain unspent. They therefore requested the SG to report to the GA on how the IWY Trust Fund, with additional finances to be contributed by governments, could best be administered. In response to that request and to the GA decision of 1985 to extend the IWY Trust Fund to cover the Decade, the SG presented the GA with his proposals for the Voluntary Fund for the UN Decade for Women (VFDW, renamed the UN Development Fund for Women—UNIFEM—in 1985).

Confirmed by the GA in December 1976,[10] VFDW's mandate was to strengthen technical cooperation activities, regional and international programs, research, data collection, analysis and communication, to implement the goals of the Decade for Women. The VFDW was to give special consideration to rural and poor urban women and to emphasize programs in the least-developed countries. A five-country intergovernmental consultative committee was appointed by the president of the GA to guide VFDW. Most of the early members—Mair (Jamaica), Shahani (Philippines), Balogun (Nigeria), and Spens (United Kingdom)—were already central figures in several women and development efforts. The consultative committee in turn urged the appointment of this writer, then at ECA/ATRCW, to initiate the activities of the fund.

The International Research and Training Institute for the Advancement of Women (INSTRAW) was the second institution to be established. A resolution at the Conference on IWY called for an expert group meeting to draft its terms of reference. The statutes, which were eventually approved in 1984, mandated INSTRAW to "undertake research and provide training to integrate and mobilize women in the development process . . . and to act as a catalyst in the promotion of the role of women in these areas."[11] Dunja Pasticci-Ferencic (Yugoslavia) was appointed first director, and Boserup (Denmark) became a member of the first advisory board. To ensure that women would themselves manage both new institutions, UNIFEM was eventually (1984) placed in autonomous association with the UN Development Programme (UNDP), while INSTRAW became autonomous within the UN. Both were to be financed on an annual basis by direct voluntary contributions from UN member states and by additional contributions from public donations, including nongovernmental organizations (NGOs).

Besides UNIFEM and INSTRAW, two global NGOs originated at Mexico City. The International Women's Tribune Centre (IWTC)—sparked by Mildred Persinger (United States) and Rosalind Harris (United States) and institutionalized by Anne Walker and Vicki Semler—grew out of NGO demands for a system to exchange information, strategies, and educational materials. The idea of Women's World Banking (WWB) arose at a rural development workshop of the American Association for the Advancement of Science and the UNDP cosponsored Seminar on Women in Development. Business woman Esther Ocloo (Ghana) spoke to the failure of banks to extend credit lines to women and stated firmly: "What we need is a women's bank." Her UN colleagues seconded the idea, and UN staffer Virginia Saurwein drafted a resolution entitled "Women and Credit," that provided the legislative backing for WWB, whose first president was Michaela Walsh.

The conference in Mexico did not limit itself to creating new women-specific institutions. Its World Plan of Action (WPA) also targeted and challenged existing multilateral and bilateral operational organizations, foundations, and other international financial institutions to place a high priority on giving women the skills, training, and opportunities necessary to improve their situation and enable them to participate fully and effectively in the total development effort.[12]

While there was agreement on special development activities, other discussions at Mexico reflected the tensions at the UN between the industrialized and the developing countries. The Group of 77 (G-77) developing countries held the position that issues like persisting imbalances in the global economy and the lack of democracy for large population groups (owing to factors that included apartheid, racism, and colonialism) had to be addressed. These factors not only constricted the overall development of low income countries, they said, but also imposed double burdens of exploitation on women. Therefore, international issues like the New International Economic Order were women's issues.[13] Industrial countries, in contrast, emphasized equality between men and women as the key issue for a long-disadvantaged group. Such divergent concepts of development priorities would cause confrontations at the 1980 conference in Copenhagen, but reach consensus at the Nairobi conference in 1985.

In summary, during the early 1970s and at the Conference on IWY in 1975, women entered the discussion on social and economic development in a major way. Their priorities established a fresh perspective on women as farmers, farm managers, and entrepreneurs and articulated fresh concerns such as women's need for credit and the importance of women-specific organizations. Their strength influenced the UN political agenda in at least four areas.

1. Women's economic as well as social contributions to their societies and nations were recognized, thus making economic development no longer just a male issue. Women's issues were "hard core economic ones" in the words of Asia's Noeleen Heyzer, who would become the director of UNIFEM in 1994.[14]
2. In the GA and the Economic and Social Council (ECOSOC), agenda items on women

expanded from human rights concerns to embrace and feature development. As a result, CSW and its secretariat were brought, albeit sometimes reluctantly, from issues that primarily affected individual women in industrial countries to those articulated by developing-country women, that is, poverty, productivity, and the global economy.

3. The identification of linkages between women's ability to progress and the degree of economic equity among nations added a new element to the women's movement that would persist and expand over time. This linkage, together with Boserup's emphasis on women's economic contributions, enlarged the scope of women's concerns once and for all.

4. From being merely a concept, women and development became a movement that was firmly established in an international action plan. Global institutions were created to utilize and expand the knowledge base and implement programs.

Table 7.1 is a comparative time line showing when key women and development actions were taken in the South, the North, and the UN since the early 1960s.

THE CONCEPT AND THE MOVEMENT: ISSUES EMERGE

The concept, program, and movement for women and development evolved in political and developmental fora during the "UN Decade for Women: Equality, Development and Peace, 1976–1985." Women and men discussed its complex dimensions. Differences of opinion centered around the microagenda, for example, equality of women versus macroeconomic/political issues affecting women. There were also divisions over how to interpret and proceed with the "integration" and "mainstreaming" of women in development.

The first issue was the highly political one that persisted after the Mexico City Conference; it concerned the parameters of the concept of women and development. Should women stop at gender equality or embrace national and international economic and political issues? That question came under the spotlight when efforts were made to relocate VFDW from New York to the Vienna International Centre where the Centre for Social Development and Humanitarian Affairs (CSDHA) had been relocated in 1978.[15]

After reviewing the VFDW objectives, its intergovernmental consultative committee determined that VFDW should relate to a New York–based development cooperation organization, like UNDP, rather than to one focused on women's equality, like CSDHA.

The Fund went forward and established an alliance with regional offices by underwriting two senior staff positions, each at the UN economic commissions in Bangkok, Addis Ababa, Santiago, and Beirut (the last, having vacant posts of its own, used the grant for one Egyptian woman for just a few months). Technical advisory systems for agriculture, credit, and rural technology were put in place with UNDP and UNICEF cooperation to provide the expertise that CSDHA could not offer.

Table 7.1
Where Did Women Accomplish It First?

WOMEN AND DEVELOPMENT: A COMPARATIVE TIME-LINE OF SOUTH, NORTH, AND UNITED NATIONS ACTION

Year	The South	The North	The United Nations
1962	1st Kenya Women's Seminar All Africa Women's Conference: 1st regional organization		
1963		*Feminine Mystique* written	
1964	East African Women's Seminar	Sweden: legislation mandates assistance to women	
1965			ECA study on women and development
1968		Western feminism movement launched	
1970		Ester Boserup writes *Women & Economic Development*	
1972			ECA: 1st regional UN Women's Programme UNHQ: 1st global meeting on women & development
1973	CARIWA: Caribbean Women's Organization	USA Legislation: the Percy Amendment mandates assistance to women	
1975			ECA: African Training & Research Centre for Women International Women's Year Conference, Mexico City UNIFEM legislation: 1st UN Development Fund for Women for Women INSTRAW legislation: 1st UN Research & Training Centre for Women
1976	Association of African Women for Research and Development (AAWORD)		
1978		Association for Women in Development (AWID) USA	
1979	1st global feminist meeting, Bankok		
1980			2nd global Women's Conference: Copenhagen
1982	Dakar Conference of women in the South		
1984	Development Alternatives with Women for a New Era (DAWN)		
1985			3rd global Women's Conference: Nairobi
1995			4th global Women's Conference: Beijing

Despite those achievements, the Austrian government and some UN officials continued to pressure for VFDW's transfer to Vienna. After a trade-off of votes between Security Council members on the subject of Secretary-General Waldheim's third term in office, the balance of favor shifted toward keeping VFDW at the UN. The GA formally voted for that arrangement, thus opting to support the broader concept of development over that of equality.

The debate continued, however. The dichotomy between the limited agenda of equality and macropolitical/economic issues was clearly evident in the U.S. decision to cease contributing to VFDW following the 1980 World Conference in Copenhagen. The final version of the Conference Programme of Action was adopted by majority vote. It called on every imaginable category of organization "to provide assistance in consultation and co-operation with the PLO." There were no specific requests directed to VFDW, or to any other fund for that matter. Astonishingly, however, VFDW was later singled out as a scapegoat by some American organizations. The Reagan administration requested that Congress cut its appropriation in half, from $1 million to $0.5 million. Congressman William Lehman of Florida succeeded in persuading Congress to delete its annual appropriation entirely, for two successive years (fiscal years 1982 and 1983).[16]

The consequences were severe; the early momentum of VFDW was extinguished, as Figure 7.1 demonstrates. The leadership of American women was lost. In 1984, under heavy pressure from women's organizations, the U.S. Congress restored the contribution, but put the level at $0.5 million. The object lesson was an ironic one; the same people who objected to the macropolitical/economic agenda vis-à-vis women and development ended up using that same agenda to penalize the only UN fund that assisted poor women. A further irony, less well known, was that the U.S. Agency for International Development (AID) gave $200,000 to support the Copenhagen Conference, while VFDW gave nothing at all.

Figure 7.2 shows how contributions to VFDW-UNIFEM—the majority of them from Western countries—were depressed for several years, until the relocation of VFDW/UNIFEM to association with UNDP and the consensus outcome of the Nairobi Conference (1985) restored UNIFEM to its favorable position. However, as seen in Figure 7.3, the United States not only failed to return to a leadership role but trailed far behind other, smaller countries.

The second issue of the concept and movement dealt with goals and strategies for "integrating women in development."[17] Many delegates, NGOs, and UN staff accepted the phrase with the expectation that the organizations they proposed to influence would automatically give women full access. To that end, they set about "integrating" women's concerns into the language, planning, and activities of the UN system.

In many fora, however, the term *integration* began to be challenged by women from the newly independent nations. Dr. Achola Pala (Kenya) set the tone of the opposition by pointing out that African women had always been economically active—hence, "integrated"—in both labor and market activities. Africa's

Figure 7.1
U.S. Contribution to VFDW/UNIFEM: 1978 to 1994

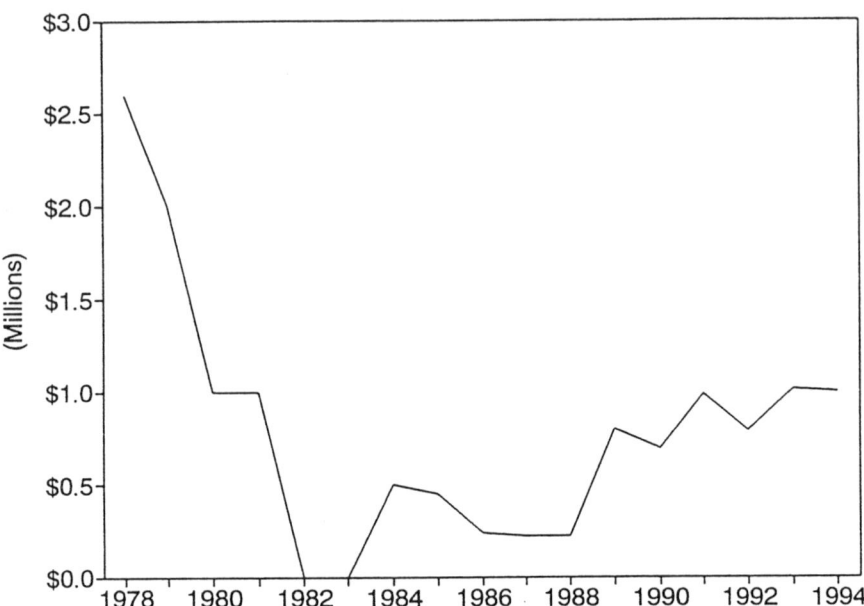

Source: Margaret Snyder, *Women, Poverty and Politics: A UN Fund for Women* (London: Zed Books, 1995).

dependency on external economies required examination, she said, and through that lens the problems of African women would be seen in proper perspective.[18] Professor Lycklama à Nijeholt (Netherlands) agreed with Pala and pointed to proof that women always contributed substantially to their societies.[19]

As such views accumulated, women asked: "Integration into what?" They saw their societies as basically flawed and put forth alternative approaches to development. One of the first was the 1982 "Dakar Declaration on Another Development with Women" that linked the success of development with structural transformation throughout societies, from household to international relations.[20] On behalf of a group led by Devaki Jain (India), called Development Alternatives with Women for a New Era (DAWN), Gita Sen (India) and Karen Grown (United States) articulated new goals and strategies for development, including the empowerment of women's organizations at all levels.

In the process of designing alternatives to the integration theory, the Dakar Declaration and DAWN began to merge the two seemingly opposing positions of the South and the North—*development* and *equality*—into a coherent whole. They spelled out the interrelationships between macroconcerns, for example, the

Figure 7.2
Total Contributions to VFDW/UNIFEM: 1978 to July 1994

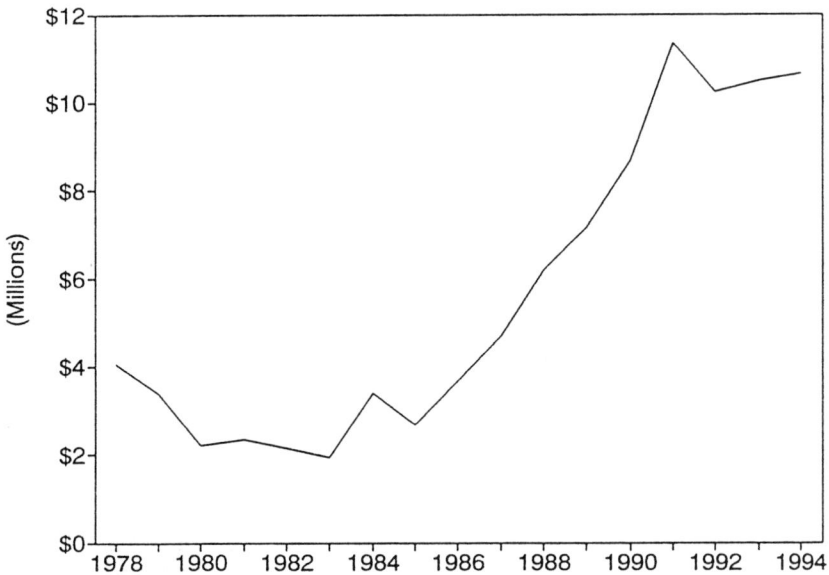

Source: Margaret Snyder, *Women, Poverty and Politics: A UN Fund for Women* (London: Zed Books, 1995).

global economy, and the issue of gender subordination. They went further: Starting from the vantage point of "poor and oppressed women"—and from that perspective all of the poor and oppressed—they concluded: "We cannot propose a social/political/economic programme for women alone. We need to develop one for society from women's perspectives." The world they wanted was one without inequalities based on class, gender, or race within or between countries. DAWN expressed the desire for a world where resources used for destruction would be diverted to relieve oppression inside and outside the home and where democracy meant that women would share in setting priorities and making decisions.[21] The women of DAWN thus envisioned a new world for everyone—men and women.

Despite the mounting skepticism about integration strategies and goals, the term *integration* remained a leading slogan in the Decade for Women and beyond. It was uncritically and almost exclusively employed by multi- and bilateral development cooperation agencies in the UN and by women themselves. The challenges posed by Pala, Lycklama, African Association of Women for Research and Development (AAWORD), DAWN, and others had apparently fallen on deaf ears.

The third related issue during the Decade involved institutions. Should resources and energies be concentrated on "mainstreaming" women into existing

Figure 7.3
1992 Contribution to UNIFEM Per Person: Norway, Netherlands, and the United States

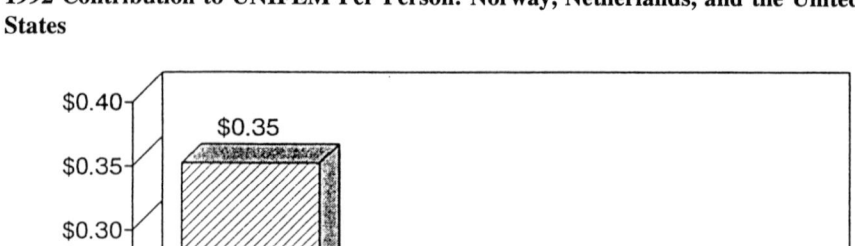

Source: Margaret Snyder, *Women, Poverty and Politics: A UN Fund for Women* (London: Zed Books, 1995).

organizations that men controlled or on distinct organizations and institutions, from grassroots to global levels, that had women members and managers? Was a two-stream approach necessary? The record of UNDP illustrates the complexity of the challenge in getting women's concerns institutionalized in large-scale bureaucracies.

Dr. Ulla Olin (Sweden) was a senior UNDP professional who dealt with women's concerns well before IWY. Olin produced two very forthright evaluations of the results of those efforts. The first, entitled *Rural Women's Participation in Development*,[22] concluded in 1980 that the results of UN agency efforts were scanty because the subject of rural women was generally overlooked in programs supporting popular participation.

Olin's follow-up Interorganizational Assessment of four countries—Rwanda, Democratic Yemen, Indonesia, and Haiti—analyzed all of the UN organizational support in each country. Its findings were even more discouraging than those of the previous study. Of $500 million in budgetary allocations in 1984 in the four countries, only about 13 percent was for "projects designed exclusively for women or designed to include women as well as men." The UNDP found those results "in some respects disappointing."[23] "Mainstreaming" continued to move at a snail's pace at the country level, where real results must be measured. The women's office was upgraded to a division for a few years after the appointment of a new WID officer, and among its activities were participation in reviews of all large-scale UNDP projects and the cosponsoring of a Top Management Seminar on Women and Development.

Even more challenging was the effort to assert women's influence on the Bretton Woods organizations (the World Bank, and the International Monetary Fund [IMF]), which were outside the purview of the GA. In 1980, IMF historian Dr. M. G. de Vries (Canada) tallied the costs to development when women were overlooked. She found that "inflation and measures designed to control it, had wider implications for the economic welfare of women than for men." Recession, "stagflation," unemployment, indebtedness, and excessive exchange rate fluctuations had similar differential impacts.[24] But despite those cold facts, the unwavering policy of the IMF was that "its responsibilities . . . did not allow for activities directed at particular population groups within member countries,"[25] even though the measures that it fostered had disparate effects on women and men. Only with the publication of *Adjustment with a Human Face*[26] seven years later were actions designed to alleviate the impact of adjustments on the poor, including a disproportionate number of women. Nonetheless, devastating effects have continued until now.

The World Bank, the largest multilateral lender—and, thus, a critical target for "mainstreaming" efforts—moved slightly faster than the IMF in setting systems to take account of women. Ex-UN staffer Gloria Scott (Jamaica) was appointed to the project policy department in 1977 as the World Bank's first WID officer. Unfortunately, the World Bank staff, trained in technical, economic, and financial analysis, were slow to accept WID; women continued to be considered mainly in their reproductive roles.

Under the leadership of Barbara Herz, Scott's successor, a program was built with external assistance initially from bilateral donors (the Netherlands, Norway, and Sweden) and UNDP. Yet at this writing, World Bank information is limited to stating what "gender-specific action and interaction" is contained in the approved documents on which project execution is based. I was told that no information is yet available on results of projects having that terminology. Furthermore, the poverty-enhancing elements of the economic adjustment policies recommended by the IMF and World Bank (which are most often conditional to loans and grants) offset any positive results of their "gender-specific" actions. There is no more controversial issue in the field of development assistance today.[27]

The Organization of Economic Cooperation and Development/Development Advisory Committee (OECD/DAC) Women in Development Committee produced guiding principles and a major study.[28]

The as-yet meagre results of efforts to influence large-scale development cooperation organizations lead us to consider the impact of distinct, women-managed funding organizations. The UNIFEM—the only women's fund in the multilateral system—undertook a comprehensive evaluation of its actual influence in developing countries, to provide a basis for GA decisions on its future after the Decade for Women. *Development Co-operation with Women: The Experience and Future Directions of the Fund,*[29] known as the Forward-looking Assessment, included thirty desk reviews and 42 field evaluations, totalling 21 percent of the fund's financial portfolio. The external evaluators found that "because of its interfacing role between women and development" UNIFEM was a "guardian as well as a vehicle of the potential explosion of talent that women signify."

The evaluation consequently stressed that "the Fund must grow" if the goals of women and development were to be realized. It set a two-pronged approach for the future. UNIFEM should direct support to innovative and experimental activities benefiting women and should act as a catalyst to ensure the appropriate involvement of women in mainstream development activities. That dual emphasis constituted UNIFEM's expanded mandate set by the GA in 1984.[30]

Ironically, while the importance of the economic empowerment of women at grassroots level through their ownership and control over resources became well understood during the Decade for Women, that awareness was not transferred to the level of global institutions. Small groups of women were left with the task of transforming vast UN bureaucracies. Strangely, despite the findings of the UNIFEM assessment that more women-specific resources were needed to leverage systemic change, few demands were made by women for real growth in their own new multilateral organizations. Instead, they adhered steadfastly to a microresource mentality vis-à-vis UNIFEM and INSTRAW, whose meagre resource bases placed severe limitations on financing of the growing number of requests from the field (see Figure 7.2 above). The institutions that women had enthusiastically created at the Mexico City Conference were expected to do too much for too many with too few staff and too little funding.

Like the questions raised by DAWN and AAWORD in the past, the issues raised or implied in the UNDP, IMF, OECD, and UNIFEM evaluations seemed to fall on deaf ears. The issues were not seriously debated in UN fora or, in fact, among women themselves. It is small wonder then that the SG, in his first semiannual report on the Decade, found that the impact of UN system efforts were inadequate.[31]

APPRAISING THE PROGRESS OF A DECADE

By the time of the Nairobi Conference, 1985, many development strategies had been successful despite negative economic forces and institutional lethargy.

—The concept of women and development had unmistakably matured. Supported by a wealth of practical experience, an enriched database, and feminist theories, the revised concept now incorporated both the macro and the micro aspects. The shattering effects of the worldwide recession, the costs of armaments, and the burdens of the debt crisis on developing nations (most harshly on women) were now widely acknowledged as impediments to women; earlier beliefs that economic growth would automatically benefit women were judged to be oversimplified. Equality, development, and peace were seen as indivisible.[32]

—Enormous strides were made in documenting and quantifying women's situation and activities. The (1985) *World Survey of the Role of Women in Development*[33] brought the UN system to bear on both developing and industrial countries. The venerable UN Statistical Office (UNSO) published the *Compendium of Statistics and Indicators on the Situation of Women* (1986) and *The World's Women: 1970–1990*.[34] Reflecting the newly acquired knowledge, the Nairobi Forward-looking Strategies for the Advancement of Women devoted an extensive section (140 paragraphs) in a major chapter to the subject of development.[35]

—A transnational view of trends influencing women's situations emerged. The movement's knowledge base was used to prove that certain trends observed on the national or regional level were actually global changes. One of the trends was the growing number of female-headed households. While acknowledging that the severe conditions in developing countries made women's lives a "matter of survival,"[36] the Nairobi conferees also came to the conclusion that from women's perspective few, if any, countries in the world could claim to be "developed."

—Institutionally, 90 percent of the UN's member states had set up "national machineries" mandated to promote women's concerns in governments. Ministries of women's affairs, women's bureaus, units in sectoral ministries, and women's wings in political parties were established. In response to the demands of women, who were suddenly perceived to be a political force, those entities were given broad mandates on the one hand, but slim resources on the other.

—Strategies and methodologies were devised to open women's access to resources. Appropriate technologies became available to lighten women's workloads and increase their productivity. Channels for multilateral financing were opened. Under UNIFEM's persistent pressure, UNDP's grant systems were transformed to allow revolving credit funds for community microenterprises, and direct support to NGOs rather than just to governments.

—Women's development organizations and grassroots solidarity groups proliferated during the Decade. Women opted to support each other's struggles to lift themselves and their families out of poverty, thereby demonstrating that women are often the most effective initiators of community-based activities. Examples of women's initiatives were visible everywhere:

- Although men participated, it was under the leadership of women that two offshoots of the National Council of Women of Kenya received substantial seed grants from UNIFEM. The Kenya Water for Health Organization (a nonprofit technical agency created by Margaret Mwangola) complemented the World Bank's water pump hardware

with training software for villagers in pump maintenance and sanitation practices. The Green Belt Movement, founded by Professor Wangari Maathai, had tree planting as its major activity and involved 50,000 participants with 1,500 tree nurseries.
- In Ahmedabad, India, Ela Bhatt and her colleagues established the Self-Employed Women's Association (SEWA) as a trade union that provided services for 30,000 members (now 55,000) through a bank owned by illiterate women themselves and through legal aid, productivity training, and maternity protection.[37]
- In Cartegena, Colombia, the Interamerican Commission on Women created a program with SENA, the National Training Institute in which women constituted a third of the trainees for microenterprise management. They negotiated with banks to loan the entrepreneurs start-up funding, which granted $17 for every $2 deposited as collateral by UNIFEM and UNICEF.[38] A credit project was also initially successful in China.[39]
- New groups like Grassroots Organizations Operating Together in Sisterhood, linking autonomous organizations globally, and the Women's Network were created at the Forum.

—Women's autonomous organizations were often essential to getting resources like training, credit, and labor-saving technologies and to controlling their labor product. Women also realized that time was needed to create mutual trust to support their solidarity organizations.

—The UN became the leading forum for advancing the global women and development concept and movement and for promoting collegial networks. Having created new UN institutions and having set goals for existing ones at Mexico City in 1975, delegates at Nairobi had proposed a broad-based system to assess periodically the progress of implementing their forward-looking strategies, including coordinating and monitoring UN system activities in the post–Decade for Women era. *The World Survey of the Role of Women in Development* would be published every five years as would a *System-Wide Medium-Term Plan*. The SG would present to the GA biennially a report on the *Effective Mobilization and Integration of Women in Development.*

While women debated the relative merits of equity, efficiency, antipoverty, welfare, and empowerment as goals of the Decade for Women, the phrase "gender and development" was introduced in the movement. It was put forward "as a socially constructed category carrying with it expectations and responsibilities that are not biologically determined."[40]

THE CONCEPT AND MOVEMENT AFTER THE DECADE: CHALLENGES AHEAD

In the years after the 1985 Conference, the world experienced a recession unprecedented since World War II. Faced with both a decline in their export income and the burden of debt, in addition to interest owed overseas, governments of most developing countries made severe cutbacks in public sector investments that impacted most heavily on women. The need for concessional development assistance from North to South to combat poverty and environmental damage continued to escalate, even as the monetary value of the aid fell.[41] The situation of the vast majority of women in developing countries worsened during this global economic downslide.

The tragedy is that, after nearly two decades of much-proclaimed mandates to "integrate women" as participants and beneficiaries of their programs, the facts about the effectiveness of many "mainstream" organizations are sobering.

- World Bank and the IMF structural adjustment and economic recovery programs sometimes claim, as in the case of Tanzania, "dramatically improved economic performance in all major sectors." Yet the World Bank states that in that country "the social sectors are in crisis"; malnutrition, malaria, and infectious diseases "continue to be severe and are on the rise"; and "water supply and sanitation services have not received sufficient support."[42]
- Ironically, the World Bank knows but does not act upon the fact that water is critical to freeing women's energy for child care, family production and income-earning activities. Because of this duplicity, the World Bank has been asked why its "handsome speeches accompany such scandalous practices."[43]
- A Norwegian evaluation stated that "information on how women have so far gained from NORAD programmes is poor and scanty, but what is available indicates rather few benefits for women in general."[44]
- In 1985, UNDP had 6 women Resident Representatives heading its developing country offices. In 1994, there were only 12 women of a total of 119! (Interestingly, 4 of the 12 were former UNIFEM workers.)[45]
- The Netherlands, a recognized leader in development theory, spoke bluntly: "Economic and political development processes have in general had no beneficial effect on the position of women."[46]

Much has been written to explain why, despite a "massive shift of rhetoric" toward women in UN and bilateral aid bureaucracies, the flow of real resources to women has been "noticeably less massive."[47] Bureaucracies' tendencies to clone rather than to transform traditional practices is one reason. Another is the minuscule size of women and development units charged with transforming vast bureaucracies. Monitoring of policy implementation is weak, and incentives for staff to carry out policies are all but nonexistent. Further, there is a dearth of feminist (male or female) staff at policy-making and higher professional levels.

Secretary-General Perez de Cuellar, in his 1991 *Report on the Effective Mobilization and Integration of Women in Development*,[48] confirmed the lack of progress, pointing out that the 1990 *International Development Strategy for the Fourth Development Decade* still "associates women's issues with vulnerability."[49] The importance of women to agriculture and food production is well recognized, he noted, but in other sectors, like entrepreneurship, informal sector employment, and labor-intensive manufacturing for export, women's work was overlooked. He said that there was a "feeble representation of women" in top positions in governments and in parliaments despite the importance of female leadership in community and grassroots organizations.[50] Women's representation in parliaments has plummeted from 15 percent in 1989 to 10 percent in 1994, the Interparliamentary Union reported to ECOSOC.

WOMEN AND DEVELOPMENT: THE OUTSTANDING AGENDA

The anniversary of IWY, in 1995, means that a quarter of a century has elapsed since the world's perception of the meaning and methods of development was radically reoriented. While excellent progress was made in several areas as the concept, program, and movement for women and development evolved, the goal of the Conference on IWY still remains on women's political agenda: "To define a society in which women participate in a real and full sense in economic, social and political life, and to devise strategies whereby such societies could develop."[51]

To achieve that goal, to achieve a sustainable development for people and the earth, some of the strategies of the past must be used, and some revised. I propose a five-point plan.

1. *A new world order that puts people first.* Women have taken issue with the type of structural adjustments imposed on poor countries by the IMF, but we have yet to challenge many of the everyday practices of the World Bank and other major development cooperation institutions, such as UNDP and the OECD/DAC bilateral aid agencies. Prodded by groups like DAWN, we can bring women's perspectives to bear on creating societies that benefit everyone—male and female. This calls for acknowledging that global economic and political forces impact right down to the individual household budget of people in both rich and poor countries.[52]

2. *A unified knowledge base for planning.* There remains a dichotomy between the knowledge base used in overall development planning and the now-extensive knowledge base that verifies women's actual economic activities and social responsibilities. Just as women's food cycle activities were incorporated in national plans during the past two decades, the new data and research findings must be used to dispel outdated concepts, such as the myth of the male breadwinner.

3. *A grassroots democratic process.* Women's rich experience with grassroots, self-reliant activities and with women's solidarity groups in the civil society is of special relevance and value in the 1990s. Major donors are becoming self-critical of their massive-scale projects and have a new respect for smaller-scale activities and NGOs. The wisdom of UNIFEM's 1984 mandate and the value of UNIFEM's experience is now more evident than ever. Development is different when women at the grassroots level are fully involved in setting priorities and disposing of income.

4. *Strong partnerships between grassroots and educated women.* The voices of grassroots women can gain strength from alliances with professional women, who are in turn enriched by such association. In addition, tripartite alliances among feminist politicians, NGO representatives, and UN bureaucrats can create strong constituencies

of NGOs and politicians outside the UN to pressure action within it.[53] We must come together to define mutual strategies with other groups that are marginalized by race or class or as people of the least-developed countries.

5. *Transformed institutions.* The history written in this chapter shouts out that hard-won GA resolutions and phrases in UN documents recognizing women's centrality to development can be instrumental but do not in and of themselves effect change. The nature of bureaucracies must be faced: They will proceed with hardly a ripple of change, except for recycling statements about women and development in project documentation. What is needed is structural transformation that goes beyond developing countries and engages all of the institutions that were established for development cooperation, that is, governmental, bilateral, and multilateral. Elements of change should include the following:

- "Mainstreaming" should be perceived as the long-range goal, achievable over time rather than immediately. The means to attain that goal must include ample and women-managed resources at every level, from global to household.

- The women and development movement needs a strong power center that may do for women what UNICEF has done for children and the United Nations Fund for Population Activities (UNFPA) for population issues. The UNIFEM/INSTRAW annual budget must begin to be commensurate with the tasks—about $400 million as a start. This is possible. For example, the United States, which made no contribution to UNFPA for several years, has committed $50 million in 1994. Much more could be committed to women.

- Women's capacities for exerting leverage in vast bureaucracies should be affirmed by adequate staffing and financing of women's units and "focal points" (bureaus, ministry desks, women's studies programs) in the UN, governments, and donor institutions. Expectations placed on women's offices to accomplish all things for all women must be lowered by assigning precise and realistic goals.

- A gender ratio in the range of 60 to 40 should be established in the staffs of the UN and other organizations. Performance incentives should be provided to all staff who carry out policies.

With those transformations, the women and development agenda must adopt the approach of DAWN and others and begin to look at societies everywhere from the perspectives of poor men and women. From those perspectives, other women, like those mentioned in this chapter, will emerge to face the political risks of promoting grassroots development. They will heed the wisdom of Professor Maathai, who says that the Green Belt Movement appears threatening to the status quo because "it is organizing ordinary people, poor people, and it is empowering them, telling them that they can cause positive change to their environment and that they can do it on their own."[54] The Forward-looking Assessment of UNIFEM speaks to the future: "The case for women and development, or for providing support to the 'poorest' of the poor, has not come to rest."[55]

NOTES

1. UN, *Note on Preparations for the Second Development Decade with Special Reference to the Social Aspects*, E/CN.5/438 (14 January 1969), pars. 11, 16, 18; ibid., E/CN.5/441 (17 February, 3 March 1969).
2. A/RES/2626 XXV. UN, 25th Session, Official Records, Supplement 28; and UN, CSW, 21st Session, Provisional Summary Record, E/CN.6/SR 535, 542 (7 February 1969).
3. Ester Boserup, *Women and Economic Development* (New York: St. Martin's Press, 1970).
4. Betty Friedan, *The Feminine Mystique* (New York: Norton, 1963).
5. A/RES/2626 XXV; A/RES/2716 XXV.
6. UN, *Integration of Women in Development: Report of the SG*, E/CN.5/481, 14 November 1972. Two years later, in 1974, American women discovered Boserup's volume when preparing a Society for International Development (SID)/WID bibliography. See Irene Tinker, *Persistent Inequalities* (New York: Oxford University Press, 1990), 30.
7. Conference of Ministers, UN Economic Commission in Africa (UNECA), Resolution 170, VIII, 1974. The Swedish International Development Authority (SIDA)-financed positions were filled by myself in 1971 and by Daria Tesha (Tanzania) in 1972.
8. For example, see Margaret Snyder and Mary Tadesse, *African Women and Development: A History* (London: Zed Books, 1995).
9. Karin Himmelstrand, "Can an Aid Bureaucracy Empower Women?" in *Women, International Development and Politics: The Bureaucratic Mire*, ed. Kathleen Staudt (Philadelphia: Temple University Press, 1990), 104.
10. A/RES/31/133.
11. A/RES/39/249. ECOSOC decided that UNIFEM and INSTRAW should merge; the structure was to be decided by the GA in 1994.
12. UN, *Report of the Conference on IWY* (New York: UN, 1975), 48–50; UN Res. 27, "Measures for the Integration of Women in Development."
13. See UN, Res. 3201 (S-VI) and 3202 (S-VI).
14. Noeleen Heyzer, ed., *Women Farmers and Rural Change in Asia: Towards Equal Access and Participation* (Kuala Lampur, Malaysia: Asia Pacific Development Centre, 1987).
15. The CSDHA and the Division for the Advancement of Women were returned to UN (NY) in 1993.
16. UN, *Report of the World Conference of the United Nations Decade for Women: Equality, Development and Peace* (New York: UN, 1980), pars. 223, 234, 244, and Resolution 42 (Voluntary Fund for the United Nation's Decade for Women). See also Carol Leimas, "A Success Story," *Graduate Woman*, the journal of the American Association of University Women (Washington, D.C., May-June 1983): 114–15; the relevant records of the U.S. Congress; and Church Center, *Global Negotiations Action Notes*, No. 15, (6 July 1981, Church Center, New York City). Senator Percy diverted some money to the U.S. Agency for International Development, which in turn provided it to UNDP to support some projects identified by VFDW when the U.S. contribution was suspended.
17. The phrase came into use in the UN about 1970.
18. Achola Pala, "Definitions of Women and Development: An African Perspective," *Signs* 3, no. 1 (Autumn 1977): 9–13.

19. G. Lycklama à Nijeholt, "The Fallacy of Integration: The UN Strategy of Integrating Women into Development Revisited," *Netherlands Review of Development Studies* 1 (1987): 23–37.

20. "Dakar Declaration on Another Development with Women," *Development Dialogue* 1–2 (1982), 13. See also *Developing Strategies for the Future: Feminist Perspectives* (New York: International Women's Tribune Centre, 1980).

21. Gita Sen and Karen Grown, *Development, Crises and Alternative Visions: Third World Women's Perspectives* (New York: Monthly Review Press, 1987), 79–80.

22. UNDP, *Women's Participation in Development*, Evaluation Study, no. 3, New York, June 1980.

23. UNDP, *Women's Participation in Development: An Inter-Organizational Assessment*, Evaluation Study, no. 13, New York, 1985. See also DP/1985/10, pars. 74, 109.

24. A/RES/35/82, footnote 72 quoting the January 1980 issue of *IMF Staff News*.

25. IMF, *IMF Survey: Supplement to the Fund* (September 1979), 1.

26. Giovanni A. Cornia et al., eds., *Adjustment with a Human Face: Protecting the Vulnerable and Promoting Growth* (Oxford: Clarendon Press, 1987).

27. World Bank, *Women and Development: A Progress Report on the World Bank Initiative* (Washington, D.C.: World Bank, 1990), 14. See also, discussions with Ellen Tillier, Human Resources Development and Operations Policy Office, the World Bank, Washington, 19 July 1994.

28. See Winifred Weeks-Vagliani, *The Integration of Women in Development Projects* (Paris: OECD, 1985). See also Kathleen Staudt, *Women, Foreign Assistance and Advocacy Administration* (New York: Praeger, 1985), 136–45, which reviews a report to Congress of 1982 that found just 4 percent of USAID assistance to be directed to women.

29. UN, *Development Co-operation with Women: The Experience and Future Directions of the Fund* (New York: UN, 1985), 4, 7. See also my history of UNIFEM entitled *Women, Poverty and Politics: A UN Fund for Women* (London: Zed Books, 1995).

30. A/RES/39/125.

31. A/35/82, 27 March 1980.

32. UN, *The Nairobi Forward-looking Strategies for the Advancement of Women* (New York: UN, 1986), par. 103.

33. UN, *World Survey of the Role of Women in Development*, ST/CSDHA/6, New York, 1985.

34. UN, *Compendium of Statistics and Indicators on the Situation of Women* (New York: UN, 1990); see also UN, *The World's Women, 1970–1990* (New York: UN, 1991).

35. UN, *Nairobi Forward-looking Strategies*.

36. UN, *Role of Women in Development*, par. 104.

37. Self-Employed Women's Association, *Annual Report*, 1989, 1993.

38. UNIFEM, unpublished report of Perdita Huston and discussions with Lola Rocha.

39. UNIFEM, *Reports from the Field: China* (New York: UNIFEM, 1988). Regrettably, that factory ran into difficulty and, as of 1994, is very small.

40. See Eva Rathberger, "Operationalizing Gender and Development," Association for Women and Development (Washington, D.C.: Association for Women in Development, 1991).

41. United Nations Department of Public Information, *UN World Economics Survey* (New York: UN, 1992), 8.

42. World Bank, *Adjustment in Africa: Lessons from Country Case Studies* (Washington, D.C.: World Bank, 1994), 352–426.

43. Pierre Galand, "Enough," *South Letter* (Geneva, Summer 1994).
44. Royal Ministry of Foreign Affairs, *Evaluation Report 3.91* (Oslo, 1991), 11.
45. Telephone information from UNDP personnel office, July 1994.
46. Ministry of Foreign Affairs, *A World of Difference: A New Framework for Development Cooperation in the 1990s* (The Hague, Netherlands: Ministry of Foreign Affairs, 1991), 203–4.
47. Robert Chambers, *Rural Development: Putting the Last First* (London: Longmans, 1983), 80.
48. A/46/464, 10 October 1991.
49. A/RES/48/199, Annex.
50. Interparliamentary Union Address to ECOSOC, July 1994; UN, *The World's Women: Trends and Statistics, 1970–1990* (New York: UN, 1991), 35.
51. UN, *Report of IWY*, 16.
52. Margaret Snyder, "Gender and the Food Regime: Some Transnational and Human Issues," *Transnational Law and Contemporary Problems* 1 (1991): 469–505.
53. Kathleen Staudt, ed., *Women, International Development and Politics* (Philadelphia, Pa.: Temple University Press, 1990), 304.
54. Wangari Maathai, interviewed by Daphne Topouris in "Empowering the Grassroots," *Africa Report* 35, no. 5 (The African-American Institute) (November–December 1990): 31.
55. UN, *Development Co-operation with Women*, 187.

8
Equality for Women in the United Nations Secretariat

Kristen Timothy

In the interwar years there was a widely shared perception that diplomacy was "men's business." A characteristic expression of this attitude was a statement from a distinguished British diplomat, Sir Harold Nicholson. Noting three specifically feminine qualities—namely, zeal, sympathy, and intuition—he argued that these were dangerous in international affairs unless kept under the firmest control. The ideal diplomat needed "male" qualities such as "impartiality and imperturbability: a diplomat needed to be a trifle inhuman."[1]

This point of view was carried over into the United Nations (UN). Although governments voted for women's rights in creating the UN Charter, their actions reflected the extent of discrimination practiced at home. Senior management within the UN (all male) was most reluctant to change accepted ways to allow women to invade a traditionally male preserve.

The UN Secretariat continues to be a multicultural environment where political influence plays a critical role and daily attitudes and practices reflect gender biases and political agendas at home.

Trygve Lie (Norway), the first Secretary-General (SG), while known to be sympathetic to having competent women in senior positions, was expected to ensure that the staff was drawn from all member states. Article 101 of the UN Charter requires the SG, in appointing staff, to seek the highest standard of efficiency, competence, and integrity but, at the same time, to pay due regard to equitable geographical distribution. Trygve Lie prepared a formula based on the assessed contribution paid by each member state. No criteria were included in the formula for gender equality nor, for that matter, for merit. In making appointments, it has been said, he and many of his successors have allowed nationality to take precedence over both.[2]

GEOGRAPHICAL REPRESENTATION

While the egalitarian principle of Article 8 of the UN Charter[3] gives support to the rights of women to participate equally in the UN, Article 101 has proved to be a hindrance. It has been used repeatedly to explain the low percentage of women on the staff. Personnel directors have often argued that it is not due to discrimination but to the overriding need to satisfy member states' demands that their nationals receive staff posts—the majority of those proposed being male.

Claire Hedervary, one-time deputy director in the Division for Political Affairs and later Belgian representative on the Fifth Committee (budget and finance), argued that the geographical representation requirement has meant a "double whammy" for women. According to the formula, efforts have to be made to recruit from countries that are still underrepresented, like the Comoros, Belize, and Fiji. When female candidates are not available because of a shortfall of trained women in those countries, it is then claimed that women candidates cannot be found. At the same time, qualified female candidates are disqualified because they come from overrepresented countries. Men, on the other hand, from these countries are still being hired on the ground that their skills cannot be found elsewhere.[4] Other factors also figure. One is the extent of patronage and cronyism. A number of nations lobby to secure positions for their nationals. Diplomats are known to seek opportunities for relatives or friends to spend time at the UN, especially at New York, Geneva, or Vienna. Some governments also want to dispose of troublesome but important persons by interring them in the Secretariat. Very few women have been nominated this way since few have the necessary standing in the old boy's network.

STATUTORY DISCRIMINATION

Discrimination takes other forms as well. Administrative rules and regulations governing staff allowances, benefits, and conditions of employment have been patently discriminatory. For example, as late as 1953, the rules on staff benefits assumed that a married male staff member was "head of the household." Married female staff were automatically classified as dependents. Moreover, females were not entitled to a child allowance unless they could prove that they had been widowed, divorced, or separated with custody of their children. They were entitled to such benefits available to male staff only if the husband could be proved to be unemployed or fully dependent for support.

Pension regulations were another example of inequity. Married women staff were automatically excluded from coverage. The assumption was that they were taken care of by their husbands. The regulations explicitly treated females as "not men."[5] Nor were the husbands of women employees eligible for their working wives' pensions in case of death. In 1954, after intense lobbying by women staff and some national delegations, these regulations were finally revised to allow widowers to benefit from their wives' pensions. There was a caveat, however. A widower had to be found totally and permanently incapable of providing for his own support at the time of his wife's death. Other major changes in gender biased staff rules and pensions regulations were not made until the UN Decade for Women (1976–1985).

THE FIRST TWENTY-FIVE YEARS

In the early days of the UN, women professionals were (and still are) few in number. Most women served as secretaries and clerks or had similar low-paying jobs. Despite a realization that they were far from achieving equality with men, women accepted their situation. They had joined the UN full of idealism and dedication. They considered it a privilege to be part of the effort for international peace. Their attitudes and expectations largely reflected the position of women in the mid-1940s—in the workplace, in politics, and diplomacy.

Political pressure for women's employment and equal treatment in the UN first came from the Commission on the Status of Women (CSW). It urged the SG to hire and promote qualified women to senior management positions. Jessie Street, delegate from Australia, and Isabel Urdaneta (Venezuela), both active at the UN Charter Conference, attended the first sessions of the CSW and lobbied for a woman to head the Status of Women Section of the Division of Human Rights, a middle-management position.[6] The first one appointed was Amanda Labarca (Chile), followed by Lakshmi Menon (India), both from developing countries which had also been active in the founding of the UN.

In 1949, the United States' CSW member, Dorothy Kenyon, proposed the first study on the levels and percentages of positions occupied by women in the UN. The results confirmed the fact that most women were serving in general service jobs (1,270 women compared to 621 men). Only 393 women held professional jobs out of a total of 1,678, of which only eleven women were in senior management. The study also showed that women accounted for only 23 of 588 delegates from fifty-nine countries at the fourth session of the GA. Four of these women headed delegations (Canada, Chile, India, and United States) and eight served as alternates (Sweden, Belgium, Denmark, Mexico, Netherlands, Norway, United Kingdom, and United States). The rest were advisors.[7]

As a result of the study, CSW and women's international nongovernmental organizations (NGOs) urged the SG, Dag Hammerskjold, to appoint more women to senior jobs and eliminate gender discrimination in UN rules and regulations.[8] Hammerskjold replied to CSW in 1954 that women's emancipation had not progressed far enough to find women qualified for UN jobs,[9] this despite the fact that women had become lawyers, doctors, and university educators.

THE 1970s—ADVOCACY FROM WITHIN

In the 1970s, women staff began to see the historical, structural, and linguistic grounding of their subjugation. They understood that both the structure and process characterized by patterns of dominance and subordination were antithetical to their instincts for caretaking, nurturance, empathy, and connectedness.[10] This experience shed light on the nature of bureaucratic domination, while women's experience as caretakers offered a vision of a nonbureaucratic collective life. The feminist case against bureaucracy is constructed out of concrete and shared experience, not a romantic vision of precapitalist life or an abstract ideal of "human nature."[11] The effect of this awareness within the Secretariat resulted in a feminist discourse that opposed bureaucratic practices that had marginalized women. The drive for women's equality within the UN bureaucracy became increasingly influenced by the growing number of women's organizations that were springing up around the world. Women's movements in various countries added their pressure for putting women staff on an equal footing with male colleagues. At the same time, strides were being made in establishing a global principle of gender equality.

The CSW was also making its impact felt. For the first time, its recommendations on staffing were seriously considered, although they were watered down by the insistence of the UN Economic and Social Council (ECOSOC) and the UN General Assembly (GA) that nationality and merit be given equal weight with gender.[12] An ad hoc group was formed in the Secretariat to lobby for gender equality, led by Patricia Tsien, a staff member in the Political Affairs, Trusteeship, and Decolonization Department.[13]

At its first meeting on 6 April 1971, the ad hoc group decided to focus on discriminatory rules and regulations. Initially, it supported the appeal of Silvia Mullan (Translation Section) challenging Staff Rule 107.5, under which her husband, not being her dependent, was ineligible to accompany her on home leave at UN expense, a benefit available to male staff for their wives. The Administrative Tribunal set up in 1949 to review staff complaints rejected the appeal, but in so doing issued a landmark ruling in 1972, which states that "by making a distinction between wife and husband in connection with home leave travel expenses, the rules made a distinction by reason of sex between staff members contrary to the principle in Article 8 of the Charter.[14]

Meanwhile, the staff union that took up issues related to the whole Secretariat staff, called for eliminating all discriminatory conditions of service based on sex. The ad hoc group helped the union to identify these provisions and proposed specific revisions relating to home leave, official travel, and repatriation grants. Pension fund regulations were similarly targeted.

Opposing the bureaucracy was not easy. The system for redressing grievances is largely controlled by the UN administration. The staff union has negotiating power but little more. The elaborate machinery for airing staff grievances, of which the administrative tribunal is one, is largely advisory and decisions of grievance bodies are often delayed or bypassed by the administration.

Diana Boernstein, a lawyer and feminist activist who worked with the grievance procedure of the UN for a number of years, wrote that most UN administrative decisions were made collectively. Many grievances resulted not from a specific administrative action but from a series of actions or inactions over the years that left women in a disadvantageous position in relation to men. Time limits for challenging a decision—and especially the problem of evidence—often quelled initiatives. In the latter regard, "Evidence in a bureaucracy was not fingerprints or smoking guns, but bits of paper: memos, form letters, written documents." Nobody at the UN wrote contentious things in memos. All were bureaucrats—"the bland leading the bland."[15] Proving discriminatory intent from a form letter regretting that your promotion was not successful, was very difficult. It had nothing to do with gender. "It was because poor Mabel was simply not up to snuff, she could not cut the mustard. She was stupid or incompetent; too aggressive or too passive; too fat or too thin. And, as the coup de grace, they might say: confidentially, other women don't like her."[16] Boernstein also asserted that women who filed gender discrimination cases faced massive and humiliating retaliation. She concluded that bringing a sex discrimination case was an intolerable burden that took more courage than most had. Thus, few such cases were brought before UN grievance panels.

Members of the ad hoc group agitated for discussion by policy makers of the situation of women in the UN. In 1972, the UN Institute for Training and Research (UNITAR) convened a colloquium for senior UN officials at Schloss Hernstein in Austria. Among the twenty-five participants, half were women and included Margaret Bruce (United Kingdom), Division of Human Rights, and Patricia Tsien from the ad hoc group. The colloquium made recommendations on rules and regulations, recruitment, placement, assignment, conditions of work, and separation from service for women.

The background report for the colloquium described the situation of women in the Secretariat with data on staffing by gender, based on a new computerized personnel roster. It helped analyze ways to improve the recruitment, placement, and assignment of women. For instance, the report documented the fact that the higher the level, the smaller the percentage of women professionals in the UN. In 1971, only 17 percent of professional staff (subject to geographical distribution), including those at the middle-management level (D-1, D-2)[17] were women. Most women occupied posts at the lowest professional levels (P-1–P-4). In addition, the data refuted the traditional view that women dropped out after a few years of a UN staff career. Moreover, after twenty years, 40 percent of men but only 30 percent women had reached the P-5 level; 15 percent of men and 2 percent of women had reached the D-1 level; and 1 percent of men and no women were found at the D-2 level.[18]

The colloquium also endorsed the target advocated by the ad hoc group for 25 percent professional women on the UN staff. It called for affirmative action (preferential treatment) for women to reach higher levels and equal opportunities for women staff to show their management potential, including assignment to field (country level) offices. The colloquium was a watershed in the efforts of the ad hoc group. The data demonstrated that the old tired arguments against women were no longer sufficient to explain the discriminatory practices in the Secretariat. The data also enabled the ad hoc group to lobby more convincingly and raise consciousness about the status of women both in the UN Secretariat and in other parts of the system. The colloquium was a watershed in these efforts.

Meanwhile, the Joint Inspection Unit (JIU), an independent body created by the GA to audit UN management practices, corroborated the Hernstein report in 1971. It depicted a pyramid where the proportion of women grew slimmer at higher levels and disappeared at the D-2 level.[19]

A modest change for the better came in 1972 when the new SG, Kurt Waldheim (Austria) appointed the first woman Assistant Secretary-General (ASG). He chose Helvi Sipila (Finland) to head the Centre for Social Development and Humanitarian Affairs. According to Waldheim's aides, Sipila's selection was linked to his wish to appoint a Finn to compensate for the defeat of the Finnish contender for the post of SG. A lawyer and Finland's first female judge, Sipila had a record of service as chair of the CSW from 1968 to 1972 and of the GA's Third Committee at the time of Waldheim's election, a long association with international NGOs, and networks of contacts that made her politically acceptable. Initially, her portfolio consisted of "Social Development" to which the section on "Women's Status from the Division of Human Rights" was added. Once appointed, Sipila used her position effectively to publicize the UN's role in promoting women's rights around the globe.

Prior to this time, several women, including Dame Mary Smeaton (United Kingdom), Julia Henderson (United States), Inga Thorsson (Sweden), and Margaret Bruce (United Kingdom) had been well positioned for an ASG post but had been passed over either on grounds of nationality or because of inhibitions about promoting women.

A full-scale survey conducted by the JIU in 1977 drew attention to the invisible barrier, or glass ceiling, beginning for women at the P-4 level. It also documented the fact that the few women who had broken the barrier and moved to levels above P-4 were much older than their male counterparts and had served the organization much longer.[20] It concluded that there was need for support from senior management to solve gender discrimination and stressed the need for availability of mentors (usually sympathetic males) to help women climb the organizational ladder.

The JIU also considered issues of dual career couples and how to make the UN system more attractive to women. It found that women in accepting a UN position considered conditions of service such as the availability of child-care, maternity leave, spousal employment opportunities, and flexible hours or part-time work. It concluded that the Secretariat should consider liberalizing policies in these areas. But it also recognized that women, more than men, had to make hard choices between family and career. While men tended to separate career and family, women with children were trying to combine both.

Examples from the handful of successful UN women illustrate the conflict between home and job. Margaret J. Anstee (United Kingdom), who was the first woman to be Undersecretary-General (USG) in the UN, did not believe she would have had a successful career in the UN had she married. She noted in an interview: "One didn't necessarily take a deliberate decision in regard to marriage, but all the time one made unconscious choices because of the interest of the job or whatever. And even when the rules were made a bit more flexible than when I was starting my career in 1952, women still faced harder choices between professional and personal goals than their male counterparts."[21] Anstee did not consider herself a token woman. She was simply a woman doing what in the past had been a man's job.[22]

Leticia Shahani (Philippines), a member of CSW before becoming head of the UN Centre for Social Development and Humanitarian Affairs as an ASG, advised that women who wanted to establish themselves were urged to delay marriage.

Lucille Mair (Jamaica), SG of the 1980 Copenhagen Conference on Women and the International Conference on the Question of Palestine maintained that personal life and personal attachments were never allowed to infringe on her professional life. Mair was a single parent during much of her career.

Most advocates for change in the UN have focused on the plight of professional women. But the majority of women staff are in the General Service (GS) category. In many cases, these women, while qualified for professional posts, are anxious to work for the UN for various reasons and, thus, accept clerical positions. For non-Americans working in New York, this often has been a way to get a work permit in the United States. Others simply have not realized their potential and have settled for clerical jobs in what promises to be an interesting environment with people from different nations dealing with world affairs. Still others hope to advance to the professional category. Some GS staff have been promoted to the professional level at the end of their careers because of long service and experience. This has "aged" the so-called junior professional levels (P-1, P-2). But a majority of women remain GS staff and suffer great frustration at their lack of advancement.

In 1979, an examination was introduced for GS staff to gain access to professional jobs. The majority who took the examination were women. As a result, between two to five GS women advanced yearly to junior professional posts. Overall, the exams benefited the advancement of GS women, bringing them into the professional ranks through competitive rather than political channels.

As part of the growing discourse of opposition within the UN bureaucracy, the ad hoc group, on International Women's Day, 8 March 1975, presented the

SG with a petition signed by over 2,000 staff members. The petition generated greater awareness of gender issues in the UN administration and the wider UN community.[23] It also led to the formation of a subcommittee on women of the Joint Advisory Committee (JAC).[24] Such a committee had been proposed in the CSW by Australia, Norway, and the United States to advise executive heads of UN entities on promoting equitable representation of women.[25]

Christine Stettner Rollet (France), one-time president of the ad hoc group, helped to establish the JAC subcommittee to legitimize opposition to the antifeminist bureaucracy. Gloria Scott (Jamaica), later head of the first Women in Development unit at the World Bank, served as the subcommittee's first chair. Members included a number of activist women in the Secretariat who attempted to work from inside the bureaucracy to bring the gender issue squarely before the UN administration.

Despite their organized efforts within the Secretariat, women still face barriers to advancement. One reason for their being frequently passed over for promotion in the UN may be their reluctance to play by the rules of the game.[26] While it is no secret that women want to change the system, the question is can they both "make it" and "change it"? Women's entering the higher realms of Secretariat politics holds promise of changing the very nature of politics. But UN politics are believed to be a man's game. Any woman who wants to reach the top has to play the game.

Another feature of the UN's male-defined organizational culture is discriminatory language. Feminists have pointed to language as a symbol and tool of male dominance, whereby labels for positions of authority tend to be masculine.

As feminist consciousness has increased both among the staff and in groups associated with the UN, collective pressure has been brought to bear. After considerable debate, the gender-free term *work months* was introduced to replace *man months*. After a rather difficult debate among female as well as male staff from different cultures, the term *Ms.* was introduced. Today, Ms. is largely accepted in correspondence and debates. An even more difficult but related practice was the use of the term, *chairman*. The CSW members began to use the gender-free term *chairperson* in the 1970s. In 1977, in commemorating International Women's Day, the SG, at the instigation of women staff, issued a bulletin reminding staff of their obligations to respect—in their attitudes, behavior, and language—the equality of their colleagues regardless of sex. It stated: "The need to follow the principles of common courtesy between people regardless of rank should be self-evident. However, especially in a large organization . . . which has a well-defined hierarchical structure, that need is sometimes overlooked. Such violations of courtesy most affect women staff members as a consequence of the fact that at present most of them are in lower grades than their male colleagues."[27]

The necessity of such a circular indicated not only the existence of gender insensitivity but also the interface between class and gender—both subjects of whispered complaints and fears of repercussion. Addressing these concerns in a formal way was a major step forward.

Two years later, the USG for Administration and Management issued a sequel to the 1977 circular. Prompted by the ad hoc group, which sought to engage the SG's commitment to the women's cause, the circular again raised the issue of gender-free language—the use of the pronouns *he* and *she*, of *chairman* and of the title *Ms*. It reminded staff of their obligation to respect the equality of their colleagues regardless of sex. It also discussed stereotyping, noting that women should not be expected automatically to perform traditionally female tasks, such as fetching coffee, when these tasks were not part of their official duties. Such tasks, it stated, should be voluntary and considered a courtesy.[28]

Davidson Nicol, former Director of UNITAR, characterized the UN's attitude toward women to be like the colonial ruler's view of his subjects: "Like the colonized, they lacked initiative, although professionally competent; they were unreliable, unpredictable and sometimes irrational and untruthful; they lacked punctuality and imagination and could not be depended on in a crisis; they endangered the safety and good running of the organization; they needed many years of training before they could be expected to hold high positions."[29]

Prior to 1980, the ad hoc group had surveyed the incidence of sexual harassment. It reported that women feared exposing male attitudes—a fear that often put them off guard and seriously affected their performance. The survey also revealed complaints by men about women's use of their femininity to seek advantages. It wasn't until much later that a strong administrative instruction on sexual harassment was issued.

THE 1980s—TARGETING EQUALITY

In the 1980s, the UN conferences on women and the UN Decade for Women challenged the UN to practice what its Charter and resolutions preached. Some members of the ad hoc group advocated affirmative action to enable women in the UN to exercise more clout than they had in the past.

Women in the UN themselves stepped up efforts to acquire influence and power. The Staff Council elected its first female president, Suzanna Johnston (United States). The SG appointed two women, each with more than thirty year's service, to ASG posts: Leila Doss (Egypt) and Alice Weil (United States). The GA approved a high-level coordinator for the Improvement of the Status of Women.

The idea of a high-level coordinator had been informally proposed by the ad hoc group at the Copenhagen Conference and was endorsed.[30] But no action was taken until December 1984 when the GA approved the proposal[31] and the SG selected Ms. Mercedes Pulido de Briceno (Venezuela) from a list of candidates proposed by the ad hoc group and representatives of member states. Pulido de Briceno was then Venezuela's minister for social affairs and a member of the Venezuelan president's cabinet.

In November 1985, Pulido presented to the GA the first action program to overcome obstacles to gender equality in the Secretariat, with ways to incorporate affirmative action into Secretariat policy making.[32] The next year she reported on the implementation of the action plan.[33]

Member states welcomed the plan, but the ad hoc group called the report a "veil of vague generalities woven together by strands of hope for the future and tears of regret." Despite these measures, there had been a net loss of women in the professional category. The ad hoc group then offered its proposals for career development, including an open system of vacancy announcements and improved data on promotion opportunities.[34]

In June 1988, the coordinator's office was disbanded. The SG and the GA had ignored ECOSOC's request to maintain the office, citing shortage of funds. The ad hoc group failed to defend the coordinator, as many felt that she had not pushed through their promotions.

Pulido de Briceno, who returned to Venezuela and ran successfully for the senate there, believed the recruitment freeze and the UN's financial crisis at the end of 1986 had blocked all possibilities for recruiting women at higher levels. She also cited stereotyping and prejudice: "We found people wouldn't take a decision in favour of a woman because they feared the reaction that would follow."[35] During her term, thirty men were recruited on an exceptional basis at P-5 and above and only two women.

In an attempt at affirmative action, the Office of Personnel in February 1987 issued guidelines for the "Appointment and Promotion" bodies, calling for greater flexibility in applying the rules of seniority when considering women for promotion by allowing their cumulative seniority to be counted as compensation for an earlier period of career stagnation.[36] The guidelines however, were issued too late. The GA was in the process of approving a reform package, including a vacancy management system, to respond to the UN's financial crisis and demands of major donors. The United States had called for an overall reduction of Secretariat staff by 15 percent. The UN administration then used the financial crisis as an excuse for dragging its feet on hiring and promoting women. The ad hoc group cancelled its traditional International Women's Day celebration on March 8 in protest, announcing that it would mark Women's Day only when it was satisfied with action taken.

Meanwhile, the GA target to have 25 percent professional women by 1980 was not met.[37] In 1985, the GA set the goal of 30 percent of women in professional posts by 1990.[38] The next year, senior recruitment officers from the personnel offices of the UN and its agencies unexpectedly concluded that geographical restrictions would need to be lifted or exceptions granted. They also identified the key element in the successful enhancement of women's status to be the demonstrable commitment by the executive head supported by senior management but proposed little to make senior officers accountable for affirmative action.[39]

By 1987, the percentage of professional women was 25.7, and by 1989 it was

26.9 percent (679 out of 2,523 professional jobs). Yet, between July 1988 and June 1989, 98 men and only 36 women were appointed.[40] In 1989, 9 women[41] and 126 men occupied senior management jobs.

In 1989, with one year remaining to achieve the new 30 percent target, the administration reestablished a focal point on women in the UN Secretariat. Suzan Habachy, a long-time staff member, was appointed and the steering committee set up under Pulido de Briceno was revived. Personnel officers valiantly met with UN delegations to solicit female candidates for posts, especially in such areas as economics where women were grossly underrepresented, and asked department heads to designate focal points to pinpoint the main obstacles to recruiting and promoting women in each department.

AFFIRMATIVE ACTION IN THE 1990s AND BEYOND

In 1990, with some easing of the financial crisis, the UN administration renewed its efforts to reach the 30 percent target. It had succeeded in raising the percentage between 1989 and 1990 by 1.5 percent, the most significant annual increase since 1986. Moreover, an activist woman was promoted to D-2 to head the Recruitment Division in the Personnel Office. Angela King (Jamaica), a long-standing member of the ad hoc group, targeted those regions with the lowest percentage of women, trying to match the geographical quotas with the low showing in proposing women candidates from Africa, Eastern Europe, and the Middle East—areas with poor records for female participation in diplomacy and international affairs. The Office of Personnel issued instructions to all heads of departments calling for special emergency measures to attain the 30 percent target and to increase the number of women in senior management. It proposed that 50 percent of vacant jobs be earmarked for women, that some women on temporary assignments be converted to regular budget assignments, and that certain women be extended beyond the statutory retirement age of sixty. It stated that "the criteria for advancement should stress performance and potential and not simply nominal qualifications and seniority in grade."[42]

In response, male staff members wrote to the Personnel Office to complain about reverse discrimination from the concrete affirmative action measures that had at last been introduced. This male backlash against the relative success achieved in redressing the long years of discrimination against women was counteracted by Kofi Annan, head of the Office of Personnel, who responded that the objective was not merely to give women preferential treatment, but to make a deliberate attempt to correct an imbalance.[43]

In 1990, the president and several members of the newly named Group on Equal Rights for Women (formerly the ad hoc group), met with SG de Cuellar and then with members of the CSW and the GA to rethink the strategy for achieving the ephemeral 30 percent target and establish new targets for 1995 and beyond. As a result, the GA in 1990 called for increasing the percentage of professional women staff to 35 by 1995 and increasing women in jobs at the

D-1 level and above.[44] Subsequently, de Cuellar established the most radical policy to date to remove gender imbalance in the Secretariat. He specified that where the percentage of women did not conform to 35 percent overall and 25 percent at P-5 and above, vacancies were in all cases to be filled by a female candidate if there was at least one female candidate whose qualifications matched all requirements for the vacancy. Positions were to remain vacant until all efforts had been made to find a suitable woman. Notably, his instruction made no mention of geographical distribution.

Growing solidarity among women in the Secretariat, made so difficult over the years by the heated competition for token positions, emerged in tandem with the concrete targets for women's advancement. A number of women staff finally rose up the ladder through persistence and success at playing the bureaucratic game. Another group of women, who "grew up" with feminism, was working to oppose the bureaucracy of inequality, and to support its members for advancement. Overall, more women held positions of responsibility. Thus, a critical mass had emerged that was having a profound effect on male attitudes and on motivating female solidarity. Despite the glacial pace of their advancement, women understood that they had a better chance if they pulled together and collectively demanded better treatment.

In 1991 for the first time, two women candidates were considered to succeed Perez de Cuellar as SG: Prime Ministers Margaret Thatcher (United Kingdom) and Gro Harland Brundtland (Norway). Some thought the election of a female SG could signal better prospects for women in the UN. Others took a cynical view that electing a woman as SG spelled a decline in the UN's prestige. Neither woman was elected; but in the same year in a surprising move, the Japanese government proposed a woman, Sadako Ogata, to head the UN High Commissioner for Refugees and in return offered to contribute several million dollars to refugee activities. Dr. Nafis Sadik (Pakistan), who had come up through the ranks, was confirmed as head of the UN Fund for Population Activities.

The election in 1992 of a new SG, Boutros Boutros-Ghali (Egypt), dampened women's hopes. Taking office in the post–cold war era, he promised the big powers that he would introduce major reforms and streamline the UN. In his first days in office, he dismissed over twelve top officials, displacing two women then serving as USGs, Therese Sevigny and Margaret Anstee, and made it clear to the women's lobby that he could not actively support their agenda while reducing staff overall. Eight months later, after seeing the significant contribution being made by women to often dangerous peacekeeping operations—for example, in the Middle East, where 37 percent of the UN Relief and Works Agency staff were women[45]—and under continuing pressure from delegates and staff, the SG proposed to redress male bias in the Secretariat and bring about parity in senior management jobs by 1995 when the UN convened a global conference on women. He also appointed two women to high posts, Catherine Bertini (United States), World Food Programme, and Elizabeth Dowdeswell (Canada), UN Environment Programme. But the proportion of women in the highest echelons of the UN does not increase in a permanent way—indeed, it regularly goes backward. For example, there was one woman (and fourteen men) at the level of ASG in June 1993, while there were two women in this position in 1983. Even when achieving high positions in the UN, women tend to be placed in positions in social fields or administration rather than in more prestigious and powerful political areas.

In 1994, the JIU prepared another analysis of the status of women in the Secretariat. Author Erica-Irene Daes introduced the study by noting that "women in the UN are dissatisfied with the painfully slow progress; some male staff fear being pushed aside by ambitious new hiring and promotion targets and many decision makers dislike being reminded of the seemingly endless piece of unfinished business." She points out that whereas nine out of fifty-seven D-2 posts were filled by women as of 30 June 1993, only one out of fourteen ASGs and three out of eighteen USGs were women. The overall percentage of women professionals was 31.3 percent, up from 28.3 percent in 1990 and 26.6 percent in 1988.[46]

Achieving equality for women inside the UN requires commitment from senior managers who must be held accountable for hiring and promoting more women, and from member states who must be willing to propose qualified women to fill vacancies. In some cases, member states will also have to allow affirmative action to override strict adherence to geographic representation if the gender imbalance which has existed for over forty years is to be at last redressed. Despite twenty years of official recognition that the low representation of women in the UN is a serious issue for the organization, the rate of progress in professional posts was as of 1994 still approximately 1 percent growth a year overall and half that rate in the senior levels (D-1, D-2, and above).

Practical strategies are needed to achieve the goals of equal participation and transformation. Measures to increase the proportion of women in policy positions must be more closely monitored and senior managers must be held accountable for recruiting and promoting women. Human resource management strategies must be modernized, including the introduction of a succession plan requiring that women also be groomed for senior positions. The organizational culture should be studied to determine what types of organizational behavior contribute to discrimination against women in competition for senior positions. These may range from assumptions about women being best in supportive functions to use of weak language to describe women's performance. For example, a woman may be praised for being a team player, while a man may be said to show leadership ability—differences of perception that slow women's advancement into management and decision-making jobs.

Member states also need to recognize their own responsibility to increase women's participation in the Secretariat through their influence over the staff nomination process. They might, for example, withhold dues if targets for women in professional posts are not met.

Responsibility for the unequal participation of women in the UN rests both with member states, which play a very significant role in the composition of the Secretariat, and with the Secretariat's own management. The commemoration in 1995 of the fiftieth anniversary of the UN brought calls for reform and for a new vision. Increasing the participation of women in the UN is one aspect of the effort to secure the UN's future and increase its accountability and effectiveness. Gender equality has, however, been largely ignored in implementing programs for reform. Achievement of equality for women in the UN before the twenty-first century is therefore likely to remain an illusive goal.

NOTES

The views expressed in this chapter are those of the author and not of the UN.

1. *Spectator* (London), 23 January 1942, cited in Carol Miller, "Conflicting Perceptions of the Role of Women in International Politics during the Inter-war Years," paper presented at the Joint Annual Convention of the British ISA, London, 1989, photocopy.

2. Theodor Meron, *The United Nations Secretariat, the Rules and the Practice* (Boston: Lexington Books, 1977), 12, 25.

3. Article 8 states: "The United Nations shall place no restrictions on the eligibility of men and women to participate in any capacity and under conditions of equality in its principal and subsidiary organs."

4. UN, *Ad Hoc Group on Equal Rights for Women, Strategies for Success*, ed. Leslie Parker (Vienna: UN, 1986).

5. Leslie Parker, *Women in the United Nations (1945–1988)* (Vienna: Group on Equal Rights for Women, 1988), 4–5.

6. UN, *ECOSOC Report on the First Session of the Commission on the Status of Women*, E/281/Rev.1 (1947), 11–12.

7. UN, *Participation of Women in the Work of the United Nations*, E/CN.6/132, 1950.

8. UN, "Status of Women," *United Nations Review*, 3, no. 10 (April 1957), 5.

9. UN, CSW, 8th Session, Report, E/2571 (April 1954), 17.

10. See, for example, Kathy Ferguson, *The Feminist Case Against Bureaucracy* (Philadelphia: Temple University Press, 1984).

11. Ibid., 26.

12. See, for example, UN, GA, Res. 2715 (XXV), 1970.

13. UN, *Strategies for Success*, 9.

14. Administrative Tribunal of the UN, Judgement No. 162, AT/DEC/114–166 (1974), 387–94.

15. Diana Boernstein, "Enforcing Justice for Women in the UN," *Staff News* (April 1986): 3.

16. Ibid.

17. Professional levels are graded P-1–P-5. After level 5, staff move to middle management, D-1 and D-2. The next level is Assistant Secretary-General (ASG), then Undersecretary-General (USG). These senior jobs are largely obtained through political appointment. Candidates often come from outside.

18. Alexander Szalai, "The Situation of Women in the United Nations," *UNITAR Report*, no. 18 (1973), 15–16.

19. UN, JIU, *Personnel Problems in the United Nations*, JIU/REP/71/7 (1971), pt. 1, 41–42; pt. 2, 348.

20. UN, JIU, *Women in the Professional Category and Above in the UN System*, JIU/77/7-A/33/105 (1977), 43.

21. Ad Hoc Group on Equal Rights for Women, "The Most Successful Woman in the UN," *Equal Time*, 7, no. 4 (January 1979), 4.

22. Ibid.

23. UN, "Back to Normal," *Secretariat News* 31, no. 1 (January 1976), 8–11.

24. The JAC, established under Staff Regulation 8.2, advised the SG on personnel policies and general questions of staff welfare. It was composed of representatives of the SG and of the staff union.

25. UN, CSW, Resolution IX, 29 January 1974.

26. In 1974 Dr. Miriam Seborer (United States) resigned as acting director of the UN Medical Service after holding the title for six months. Despite her credentials, she was not appointed allegedly because she had been at the UN for only two years and had not learned the tactics for surviving in the bureaucracy and had been accused of refusing unjustified requests for drug prescriptions from several UN officials (*Washington Post*, 3 March 1974, B2).

27. UN, "Guidelines for Promoting the Equal Treatment of Men and Women in the Secretariat," SG's Bulletin, ST/SGB/154, 1977.

28. UN, "Guidelines for promoting the equal treatment of men and women in the Secretariat," Information Circular, ST/IC/79/17, 1979.

29. Davidson Nicol, "Reflections," *UNITAR News* 7, no. 1 (1975): 3–4.

30. UN, *Report on the World Conference of the UN Decade for Women: Equality, Development, and Peace* (New York: UN, 1980).

31. UN, GA, Res. 39/245, 1985.

32. UN, *Improvement of the Status of Women in the Secretariat*, A/C.5/40/30 (1985), 11.

33. UN, *Implementation of the Action Programme for the Improvement of the Status of Women in the Secretariat*, A/C.5/41/18 (1986), 1.

34. UN, *Strategies for Success*, 116–23.

35. Ad Hoc Group on Equal Rights for Women, "Women Working for the UN: Interview with Mercedes Pulido de Briceno, *Equal Time* (November 1988): 24.

36. UN, *Status of Women in the Professional Category and Above: Second Progress Report*, A/37/469 (1987), 21.

37. UN, *Improvement of the Status of Women in Secretariat*, A/C.5/42/24 (1987), 6.

38. UN, *Report on the World Conference to Review and Appraise the Achievements of the UN Decade for Women: Equality, Development, and Peace* (New York: UN, 1985).

39. UN, *Strategies for Success*, 107.

40. UN, *Improvement of the Status of Women in Secretariat*, A/C.5/44/17 (1989), 3.

41. They were nationals of Algeria, Japan, France, United Kingdom, Canada, Jamaica, and the United States.

42. Kofi Annan (director of Department of Human Resources), "Special Emergency Measures To Attain the Target of 30 Percent Women on Posts Subject to Geographical Distribution and Measures To Increase the Number of Women in the Secretariat on Higher Level Posts," memo to all heads of departments, 23 January 1990.

43. UN, "Profile: Kofi Annan, UN Personnel Chief," *Secretariat News* 43, no. 5 (June 1987): 9.

44. UN, GA, Res. 45/125, 14 December 1990.

45. Gayle Kirshenbaum, "Inside the World's Largest Men's Club," *Ms. Magazine* 3, no. 2 (1992): 16–19.

46. UN, JIU, *Advancement of the Status of Women in the UN Secretariat in an Era of Human Resources Management and Accountability: A New Beginning?* JIU/REP/94/3 (1994), iii. See Table 8.1 on next page.

Table 8.1
Number and Percentage of Women in Posts Subject to Geographical Distribution (as of 30 June 1988, 1990, and 1993)

Position/Level	30 June 1988		30 June 1990		30 June 1993	
	Number	Percentage	Number	Percentage	Number	Percentage
USG	2	7.7	2	7.7	3	14.3
ASG	1	5.3	0	0	1	6.7
D-2	5	5.7	8	10.1	9	13.6
D-1	19	8.6	16	6.8	31	12.8
P-5	59	12.4	73	15.8	103	21.7
P-4	162	23.3	180	26.7	203	30.5
P-3	251	39.0	261	39.0	396	37.7
P-2	137	43.2	175	45.8	237	46.9
P-1	27	73.0	10	62.5	6	60.0
Total	667	26.6	725	28.3	804	31.3

Source: UN, JIU, *Advancement of the Status of Women in the UN Secretariat in an Era of Human Resources Management and Accountability: A New Beginning?* JIU/REP/94/3 (1994), iii.

9
Women's International Nongovernmental Organizations at the United Nations

Carolyn M. Stephenson

International Women's Year (IWY) and the United Nations (UN) Decade for Women have been, in a sense, both creatures of, and creator of, the international women's movement. Nongovernmental organizations (NGOs) in turn were a necessary, if not sufficient, part of the development of a women's agenda in the UN from the start. It would be remiss not to focus specifically on NGOs. Two distinct generations of women's organizations contributed to these developments. The women's movement that began as early as the 1830s produced, by the start of the UN, roughly twenty-five women's international nongovernmental organizations (WINGOs); and by IWY in 1975, roughly fifty.

In the early 1970s, a new feminist movement developed as a significant social and political factor, generating new theories of power and social change. While some feminists continued to hold "realist" theories of power and influence, seeking to be part of conventional male power structures, by the end of the decade new feminist theories had developed. Not only was sisterhood powerful, but there was a different sort of power. Based in the unity of a social movement of the less privileged, this was power *with* rather than power *over*, or *con*structive power rather than *de*structive power.[1] While the new feminist movement of the 1970s set the stage for worldwide attention to women, it was the older women's NGOs that actually pushed for IWY.

A note of caution is necessary. In certain parts of the feminist literature, there is a presumption that NGOs, and especially women's NGOs, speak for the less privileged. Social movements and NGOs are often held up as the way to restore democracy to bureaucratized state systems, the voice of the people in a landscape of money and governmental power.[2] While that potential is there, the opposite potential is there also. Most NGOs, in membership or headquarters, reflect rather than counteract the prevailing hegemonic structures of the world system, coming primarily from rich Western nations.

INTERNATIONAL NONGOVERNMENTAL ORGANIZATIONS AND THE DEVELOPMENT OF THE NGO/UN CONSULTATIVE PROCESS

International *nongovernmental* organizations (called INGOs, or NGOs for short), in contrast to intergovernmental organizations (IGOs) like the UN, are those that are created in other ways than by agreement of governments and that generally are composed of private individuals or other associations rather than governments. The NGOs, which are formal organizations, are also contrasted with *social movements*. This distinction became especially important in the context of the UN Decade for Women, where NGOs and the feminist movement played important, but different, roles that sometimes led to conflict between them.

Generally the term *NGOs* is taken to mean *international* nongovernmental organizations, especially those that have consultative status with the Economic and Social Council (ECOSOC). This is particularly important in the area of women, because the work of the Commission on the Status of Women (CSW) falls within the purview of ECOSOC. It is ECOSOC status that determines access to the basic work of the UN including the General Assembly (GA) Decade, for Women conferences.

While NGOs worked with the League of Nations, it was in the UN Charter that the relationship was formalized. In the U.S. delegation to the San Francisco Conference were consultants who were representatives of forty-two national organizations, including five women's organizations.[3] The American NGO consultants led the United States to support what became Article 71.[4] Thus, Article 71 of the UN Charter came to read: "The Economic and Social Council may make suitable arrangements for consultation with non-governmental organizations which are concerned with matters within its competence. Such arrangements may be made with international organizations and, where appropriate, with national organizations after consultation with the Member of the United Nations concerned."

At its 19 March 1947 session, ECOSOC's Committee on Arrangements for Consultation with NGOs admitted thirteen women's organizations to consultative status.[5]

Many of the NGOs banded together in the Conference of Nongovernmental Organizations in consultative status with ECOSOC (CONGO) by the late 1940s.

The CONGO has been described as a trade union of the NGOs, which exists primarily to protect the rights of NGOs with consultative status. Roughly one-fifth of the NGOs with consultative status are members, currently about 200. They have tended to be among the more conservative members of the NGO community and, like the UN, to set considerable store in precedent. Thus, when CONGO was asked to run its first NGO Forum at the Stockholm environment conference in 1972, it was unable to do so because many of its Geneva member organizations insisted that there was no precedent. Since then, CONGO has run many successful forums, beginning when Rosalind Harris, as president of CONGO, persuaded its board to run the "Tribune" at the World Population Conference in 1974.

Women's organizations, like others, were buffeted about by cold war politics in the UN. The Women's International Democratic Federation, an Eastern European bloc headquartered organization that had initially been granted consultative status, lost that status in 1954 and regained it in 1967, with strong support from other women's NGOs.

Current arrangements for consultative status are provided for under Resolution 1296 of the 44th Session of ECOSOC adopted on 23 May 1968.[6] The resolution distinguishes between Category I and II and Roster NGOs. Category I NGOs must be able to make "marked and sustained contributions" to the fields with which ECOSOC is concerned and must also be representative of "major segments of population in a large number of countries." Category II organizations must have a special competence in, and be internationally known within, a few fields that ECOSOC covers. Roster organizations, on the other hand, need only make "occasional and useful contributions" to the work of ECOSOC or other UN bodies. Resolution 1296 also provides that all NGOs may send representative observers to ECOSOC meetings and may receive documentation. Categories I and II may also submit written statements for circulation to member states. Category I organizations may also propose agenda items and may, in certain cases, make oral interventions.[7]

A more flexible process of consultation began in connection with the 1992 "Earth Summit" Conference in Rio, with more NGOs admitted for a time to consultation with the new Commission on Sustainable Development (CSD). This led to a two-year review process (to be completed in late 1995) over whether 1,296 rules or Rio rules would predominate. Conclusions from a January 1995 NGO committee meeting went to the July ECOSOC meeting and then to the fall 1995 GA session for approval. Meanwhile, somewhat more flexibility was introduced into the application process for the September 1995 Beijing Women's Conference, for which the due date for NGO applications was set for 13 January 1995. As of late 1994, about 960 NGOs were in consultative status, in addition to 550 more that were provisionally included on the roster by virtue of their CSD status. Moreover, the UN Department of Public Information listed 1,400 NGOs, of which about 700 were in ECOSOC consultative status.

WOMEN'S INTERNATIONAL NONGOVERNMENTAL ORGANIZATIONS

One of the most significant effects of the UN Decade for Women was cross-fertilization between women's NGOs and social movements, the founding of new women's NGOs, and the development of international networks of women that began to coalesce by the end of the Decade for Women into an international movement.

Elise Boulding identified forty-seven women's NGOs just prior to the start of the Decade for Women. While the largest number of organizations formed prior to 1915 was religious, the largest number formed from 1916 to 1970 was professional. All of those organizations with over sixty sections were formed before the UN, while only one formed after 1946 had even fifty sections. Clearly, it takes time to become truly international.

Boulding raises the issue of whether NGOs form an elite that is essentially colonialist. She concludes that women's NGOs do not constitute an elite but are rather "an elite of the powerless" that can help to redistribute global power. However, her data show that the largest number of branches and headquarters were in Europe and North America.[8] Less than 10 percent of headquarters were in the developing countries, echoing the pattern of other NGOs and IGOs. Of the thirty women's NGOs formed between 1980 and 1989, however, over half were based in the Third World.

A total of thirty-three women's NGOs had some form of IGO consultative status at the start of the Decade for Women, with a smaller number having this status with ECOSOC itself. By 1989, there were fifty women's NGOs in consultative status with ECOSOC. These NGOs included only a small proportion of all the women's organizations in the world and even a smaller proportion of the women's organizations that participated in the various NGO forums associated with the UN women's conferences. The result was that there were two tiers of women's organizations associated with the Decade for Women. Women's NGOs with consultative status had observer delegates to the actual UN conferences, while others, which necessarily included most of the newer feminist organizations created since the early 1970s, were only able to attend the non-governmental forums, which any individual could also attend. This led to both cooperative and conflictual dynamics within the organizational community of women, as well as between women and the UN. By 1995, consultative status was achieved by both.

NONGOVERNMENTAL ORGANIZATIONS AND THE DECADE FOR WOMEN: BACKGROUND

The NGOs contributed significantly to the series of large ad hoc or megaconferences that characterized UN politics during the decade of the 1970s, beginning with the UN Conference on the Human Environment (UNCHE) in

Stockholm in 1972. The rising level of consciousness on environmental issues meant that the Swedish government was suddenly faced with the prospect of hundreds of environmental organizations and activists coming to Stockholm to make their ideas known to the UN and to the world public. Sweden asked CONGO to help it in organizing a forum outside of the formal UN conference structure. While CONGO could not agree to run it, a parallel nongovernmental forum was set up, like subsequent forums, with no official channel to the UN conference. Thus, the precedent was set for the pattern that was to be followed in the UN women's conferences and others. More conferences and CONGO-arranged forums followed, with NGO participation ranging from a high of 253 NGOs at the 1972 Stockholm Conference on the Human Environment to a low of 44 at the 1977 Desertification Conference.

The UN population and food conferences in 1974 were consciousness-raising and training opportunities for women's NGOs, which had pressed for increases in numbers of women delegates. Women especially noted the relationships between population, development, and food supply, and highlighted the connections between the status of women and population growth, which the draft World Population Plan of Action hardly mentioned. The politics of the NGO community, reflecting East-West, North-South, and other tensions, often echoed governmental politics, but the fact that most NGOs had international constituencies often allowed them to play a facilitating role between governments and to assure that women's rights and perspectives did not get lost amidst other international issues.

One central observer remembered an instance of particular NGO effectiveness. At the Water Conference at Mar del Plata (Argentina) most of the discussion had to do with the provision of water for business and large-scale agriculture. Women's organizations, five of which were represented by women in the water field, turned the agenda around, adding social issues of health and sanitation and succeeding in getting a resolution on water that related to small farmers, most of whom are women.[9] Success and sufficient expertise to participate in the debate may be related.

THE DECADE CONFERENCES: UN AND NONGOVERNMENTAL

The NGOs played key roles in both the official UN conferences and the forums organized by CONGO in consultative status with ECOSOC and were open to anyone who registered. In the former case, the role was primarily lobbying governments, while in the latter it was more of a networking and educational role. There was more of everything as the Decade for Women progressed, more nations represented at the conferences, more UN agencies and NGOs, more resolutions, more participants from more nations at the forums, and more panels and workshops. NGOs at the conferences increased from 113 in Mexico City to 134 in Copenhagen to 163 in Nairobi. The numbers of forum participants increased from 7,200 to 13,500 by 1985.

Geographical representation and the increase in sophistication of women at both the conferences and forums increased through the Decade for Women. The largest numbers at the Mexico City Tribune were from Mexico (about 2,000), the United States, Japan, and the rest of Latin America. In the Copenhagen forum, there were roughly 3,000 from Denmark, 2,000 from the rest of Europe, 1,000 from North America, and almost 1,000 from Asia and the Pacific. Over the decade there was both wider geographical representation and some decrease in American influence. Women at both conferences and forums were political, economic, social, and intellectual leaders in diverse countries and situations. The forums reflected both the diversity and increased sophistication of the women's movement.

Mexico City, 1975

On 28 April 1975, ECOSOC authorized the UN Secretary-General (SG) to invite to Mexico City as observers NGOs in consultative status. The 154 NGOs that had indicated interest in attending were invited to be represented by not more than two observers.[10] Rule 54 of the Provisional Rules of Procedure provided that "upon invitation of the presiding officer and approval of the body concerned," observers could make oral statements on questions "in which they have a special competence," and written statements "on subjects on which they have a special competence and which are related to the work of the Conference."[11]

Of the 154 organizations invited to participate, 114 registered, sending a total of 192 individual observers to the Mexico City Conference.[12] Some organized well in advance of the conference and submitted statements on various topics ranging from justice for rural women to women's participation in strengthening international peace, or from family planning as a human right to greater precision in provisions for review and appraisal of activities, including yearly reporting.[13] One NGO report on the conference noted that statements had little effect unless NGOs had followed through with specific ideas in the preparatory committee, because of the volume of resolutions and amendments being considered by the conference.[14] The lateness of the opportunity to speak in the general debate had less effect since many delegates had gone on to working meetings or simply did not bother to attend for NGO statements. This pattern has been typical of subsequent UN conferences as well.

The Mexico City Tribune operated with very different rules and practices. Either tribune registration or IWY conference identification was required for admission to sessions. No formal statement was allowed to come forth as a tribune position, but groups could make and request signatures for statements. Tribune sessions were designed so that at least half of the time was available for audience discussion.[15]

The tribune's opening plenary at 6 P.M. on 19 June began with the sound of the marimba—by an all-male band—and a speech by Senora Echeverria, First Lady of Mexico, before those 2,400 of the participants who could get into the auditorium.[16] The remainder of the tribune's formal program consisted of twenty panel sessions, with simultaneous interpretation. Panels covered the following subjects: building human community, women across cultures, Third World craftswomen and development, attitude formation and socialization processes, law and the status of women, agriculture and rural development, health and nutrition, education, women at work, women and environment, urbanization, population and planned parenthood, women in public life, the family, and peace and disarmament, running from 10 A.M. to 1 P.M. and 3 to 6 P.M.

Every morning at 8 A.M. the tribune Organizing Committee met to assign additional rooms for the next day and to deal with emergencies. At 9 A.M. there was a briefing on the proceedings of the UN World Conference. Beginning on 24 June, the tribune also held an informal press briefing every day at 1:30 P.M. This became an important source of information on changes in the tribune program, which by that time had "grown like Topsy." The tribune Press Information Office also put out mimeographed summaries of each of the panels, and *Xilonen*, the daily newspaper partly in English and partly in Spanish.

There was an air of informality and festivity to the Mexico City Tribune, which was intentional on the part of tribune director Marcia Bravo. It is almost impossible to capture the fullness of the additional events scheduled by the Tribune Committee, let alone the unscheduled happenings, exhibits, dancing, singing, praying, and talking. Several events organized by others are of special import however.

An "Encounter for Journalists," sponsored by the UN Center for Economic and Social Information, ran from 16 to 18 June to acquaint journalists with the themes of the Conference prior to its opening. Some of those attending, including Gloria Steinem, calling themselves the Feminist Caucus of International Women's Year, drew up a working document of a feminist manifesto, which was criticized by Germaine Greer (author of the landmark *Female Eunich*) in the next day's *Xilonen* as premature at this stage of the meeting, insufficiently attentive to the diversity and criticisms of feminist views, and not sufficiently hard-headed.[17] Eventually, the Feminist Caucus merged with a larger and also impromptu group, Global Speakout, which had broken into working committees to examine and contribute to the World Plan. This became the nucleus for the statement issued by the "United Women of the Tribune."

The American Association for the Advancement of Science, together with the UN Institute for Training and Research and the UN Development Program, organized a seminar on Women and Development from 16 to 18 June. Roughly sixty source persons from fifty countries worked to bridge the gap between research and action and make recommendations for the World Plan of Action. The 99 participants were divided into health, education, food and small technology, women's professional organizations, and urban living workshops. One important outcome of this seminar and the discussions on women and development that continued throughout the tribune was the eventual advent of Women's World Banking, which later became an NGO in consultative status with ECOSOC. Two important books on women and development, by Tinker and Bo-Bramson and by Buvinic, resulted from the seminar.[18]

Each night at 6:30 P.M., the NGO committee ran a special briefing and strategy meeting for NGOs in consultative status at the Melia Purrua Hidalgo Hotel near the center of Mexico City, away from both the tribune and the conference. The high level of sophistication and knowledge among some of these women long involved in the traditionally volunteer sort of organizations was aptly demonstrated at these briefings. The gap between these women (primarily American) and American feminists was even greater than that between American and Latin American feminists. Yet these women were the ones who set up the Mexico City Tribune and provided opportunities or information to women trying to affect the international political process. Because of differences in age and approach, each group regarded the other warily, yet one NGO briefing session (23 June) was the source of much information for the feminist group, which included Betty Friedan (of *Feminine Mystique* fame), and NGOs overturned much of their own program to satisfy this need.

At the briefings, much discussion focused on the role of women in development and the effects of development on the status of women. Specific examples of development aid that worsened the position of women were given by NGOs at the briefing meeting Friday, 27 June. They spoke of the Singer sewing machines sent to Africa and used by men while women worked in the fields, and of agricultural development courses given to men in countries where women do the agricultural work.

Many of the women who came to the Mexico City Tribune had no conception of what the procedures of an international conference were, expecting to have an effect on the conference, to be heard by the world, and to talk to each other. Attempts at the tribune to influence the conference resulted in two additional documents. On 26 June, a "Call to Action on Women, Food and Population within a Development Strategy," signed by over 600 women from 83 countries, was presented to the SG of the Conference, Helvi Sipila.[19]

Perhaps the most interesting, and certainly the most controversial, document that came out of the tribune was the unauthorized 26 or 34 pages of suggested revisions to the World Plan of Action. Drafted in informal working groups, and somewhat ambiguously approved in a 25 June meeting of the roughly 1,800 "women of the Tribune," the document was presented to Helvi Sipila in her office at 10:15 A.M. on 26 June by fifteen women. The main document proposed paragraph by paragraph changes to the World Plan, including a woman's right to control her own body, and a UN Office for Women's Concerns at the undersecretary level. Some of these appeared in the Declaration of Mexico, an official conference document hammered out by a drafting committee chaired by Leticia Shahani, later to become a leader of the Nairobi conference. Appended to both documents were English translations of three pages of Latin American concerns, including those over cultural dependency, rights to sex education and reproductive freedom, political prisoners, the strengthening of the family, and the socialization of housework, among others. It concluded: "We aim at carrying out our struggle side by side with men."[20]

The level of frustration over the lack of communication between tribune and conference was noted at the beginning of the document itself. Betty Friedan, a prominent participant, had threatened to lead a demonstration of 500 women at the conference but was persuaded not to do so.

The day after Mrs. Sipila came to the Tribune to explain that there was no channel for presentation of the proposals to the official conference, a press conference called by the group to publicize the proposals broke up in the face of what many thought were deliberate outside attempts at disruption.[21] Conflict broke out over the demands of some Latin American women that their ideas had not been incorporated. Both conference and tribune were underfunded, and one of the results of this was that there was no provision for interpretation for other than the regular panels at the tribune. This led to separate English and Spanish amendments to the World Plan, and apparently only those in English had been submitted to Mrs. Sipila. This roughly one hour of conflict over the microphone was well covered by news media as an example of infighting among women. It was one of two short instances of such conflict.

In 1975 in Mexico City, peace—the third theme of IWY—was conspicuously absent from the discussion. Not only did the themes of equality, development, and peace receive unequal attention, but they were not related to the degree that they could have been. Equality and development were related in the confrontation of women and nations over whether economic development is a prerequisite to the improvement of the status of women. Peace did not receive much emphasis in either conference or tribune; and when it did receive attention, it was attention to wars in specific nations rather than to women.

Some NGO preconference activities did focus on peace. In May 1975, the Women's International League for Peace and Freedom (WILPF) and the Women's International Democratic Federation (WIDF) cosponsored a seminar in New York. Entitled "Women of the World United for Peace and Disarmament and its Social Consequences," the seminar brought together 250 women from twenty-seven countries. The seminar marked the first time since 1959 that an official Cuban representative was allowed to attend a nondiplomatic function in the United States.[22] While WILPF and WIDF did continue to cooperate across cold war lines at the Mexico City conferences, their ability to raise the issue of peace was only barely visible.

While individuals did not speak for their countries at the tribune, there were still national and regional differences. Rounaq Jahan of the Society for International Development said: " 'development' was the major issue for Asians and Africans, 'imperialism' was the major issue for Latin Americans, and 'sexism' was the major issue for the Western countries."[23]

Perhaps the most important outcome of the Mexico City Tribune was the continuation of the organizational infrastructure that had set up the tribune and the international communication that continued as a result. The International Women's Tribune Centre, Inc. (IWTC), located near the UN in New York City, provided a resource center (country profiles, a project data bank, skills archives) and liaison services between NGOs, governments, the UN, and women (primarily in the Third World), as well as technical assistance and training in collaborative projects, media and library techniques, proposal writing and project development.[24] Newsletters, the *IWTC Newsletter* (later *The Tribune*, in English), *La Tribune* (French), and *La Tribuna* (Spanish) were produced quarterly and were sent free to Third World women and at low cost to others. Building on the list of 6,000 official registrants (i.e., excluding the 1,200 Mexican walk-in registrants) from the IWY Tribune, the IWTC facilitated the development of communication and networking among women worldwide and provided programs at later forums.

Copenhagen, 1980

At Copenhagen, as at Mexico City, the official conference was held at a location (the Bella Centre), different from the NGO Forum, which was centered at the Amager University Centre. The forum ran only for the first part of the conference, from 14 to 24 July, while the conference itself ran from 14 to 30 July. One hundred and thirty-four NGOs registered for observer status at the conference. Fifty-three NGOs submitted written statements to the UN Mid-Decade Conference for Women, roughly fivefold the number submitted in Mexico City. Of these statements, twenty were submitted by women's organizations and thirty-three by other NGOs, on topics ranging from a report of an organization's own regional seminars, the condition of Palestinian Arab women in the administered territories, the status of older women, women and community development, education for peace against the arms race, refugee women, "the heroic women of Namibia and South Africa," indigenous women, and equal employment in the UN.[25]

One reflection of the long-standing cooperation between NGOs, women in the UN Secretariat, and women on delegations was the increased references to NGOs that appeared in the final report of the conference. The major reference was a two-page section of the Programme of Action at the national level entitled "National Strategies for Accelerating the Full Participation of Women in Economic and Social Development."[26] Paragraphs 100 to 104 focused on the role of NGOs, recommending mutual cooperation between governments and NGOs, while Paragraph 105 focused on grassroots organizations.

By the time of the Copenhagen Mid-Decade Conference, much of the leadership had shifted to Europe. Edith Ballantyne of WILPF, headquartered in Geneva, was president of CONGO. Elizabeth Palmer, a former general secretary of the World Young Women's Christian Association (WYWCA), also based in

Geneva, was the convenor of the CONGO Planning Committee of the Mid-Decade Forum itself. The cocoordinators of the NGO Forum were Hilda Rwabazaire Paqui and Marianne Huggard of the United Kingdom. Ballantyne had been in charge of the international office of WILPF from the early 1970s, and in 1976 became the first representative of a peace organization to head CONGO. Her role meant an increased presence for WILPF and for peace issues—ranging from issues of colonialism and apartheid through those of war—at the Copenhagen Forum.[27]

The CONGO had established the planning committee for the forum by May 1979. Thirty-four organizational members of CONGO, 18 of which were women's organizations, worked with Convenor Elizabeth Palmer to integrate a broad geographic perspective in the planning and to develop programs, media contacts, and a forum newspaper. Two 1980 consultations in New York and Geneva agreed that this forum should be action oriented, with plans for follow-up, but that there should be opportunities for informal gatherings and events.[28]

The NGO Forum began with an opening ceremony at 10 A.M. July 14 and proceeded to include eighteen substantive panels on the themes of equality, development, peace, education, health, employment, as well as racism (including apartheid), sexism, the family, refugees and migrants. Speakers came from every continent, with the largest numbers, fourteen each, from Western Europe and Africa.

The logistics of the Copenhagen conferences were again significant. Not only was the conference at some distance from the forum, but this time the forum itself was spread out. The formal panels were at the Royal School of Librarianship in an auditorium that could hold only a small proportion of forum participants. Briefings on the conference, from 9 to 9:50 A.M. and from 1:30 to 2:20 P.M., were also held here. The school was somewhat removed from other forum activities such as "Vivencia!" and the international exhibit of women's books at the Amager University Centre and the International Festival of Women Artists at the Ny Carlsberg Glyptotek Museum and elsewhere. The lack of any central gathering place, coupled with political conflict over issues such as Palestine and South Africa contributed to a sense of fragmentation in this meeting.

These other activities, while fragmented, created a sense of decentralized vitality in and around the forum. But the forum activity called "Vivencia!" was the centerpiece for most participants. Based on the Spanish word that means "an experience that becomes part of life," Vivencia! was a more informal program of over 370 events, displays, exhibits, meetings, performances; over 130 films and slide shows; and workshops on project design, funding, mass media, and feminism—all of which took place around the formal program.[29] It was a colorful and noisy place, in which one could easily get lost and in which there was constant meeting, organizing, and networking activity. Angry groups of men, women, and children from liberation movements paraded through the halls periodically with music and speeches. A march led by Domitila, a woman trade union leader from Bolivia who had been brought by tribune leaders for the formal panels, left from here for the Bella Centre.[30]

The International Festival of Women Artists was quieter but even more dispersed. Directed by Susan Schwalb in New York and Annelise Hansen of the Danish Council of Women in Copenhagen, it included panels, workshops, slide shows, exhibits of old and new women's art in at least four museums and four private galleries, as well as films, music, theater, dance, comedy, and mime. A photographic exhibit on "Women in Copenhagen, 1880–1940" was staged at the Town Museum and at the Bella Centre in cooperation with Unesco. A craft exhibit and sale, featuring artwork of Third World women, was another important addition.[31]

Feminist writers have noted that the issue of the equality of women, supposedly the main focus of the Decade for Women, had received short shrift in the Mexico City Conference and was treated only marginally better at the Copenhagen Conference.[32] In both forums, on the other hand, equality was a main focus of discussion. The change from 1975 to 1980 was the realization that equality was broader than just the Western feminist conception of women's rights. National liberation (or national development) and women's liberation were seen to be related, but with national liberation and development by no means seen as sufficient for women's liberation. Forum panels focused on the effects of multinational corporations on women's lives, on child care, on foreign aid, on women and technology, as well as a woman's rights related to her own body, and on women's studies, banking systems, and on research institutes. Many panels focused on the achievement of equality for women in the areas of health, education, and employment—the three subthemes of the 1980 Conference.

Emphasis on development continued in the Copenhagen Forum. The highly visible leaders of the newer women's rights movement in the United States, who pushed a Western brand of feminism at the World Conference in Mexico City, had by Copenhagen, become both more sophisticated in international politics and more cognizant of the needs and demands of women in other parts of the world and joined others in workshops on development, providing a real dialogue between "first" and "third" worlds on issues related to women. These panels were a concrete illustration of the cross-fertilization and synthesis that had begun in Mexico City between "first"- and "third"-world feminism.

Peace, the third theme of the decade, also began to be considered in 1980, both in discussion at the forum and the conference and in the Programme of Action, largely through the actions of NGOs. At the opening of the conference, Lucille Mair, secretary-general of the conference, spoke of the problem of the use of scarce resources for war. A delegation of Nordic Women for Peace presented to UN SG Kurt Waldheim petitions signed by 500,000 women demanding an end to the arms race.

The joint statement made to the UN Conference Plenary on 24 July 1980 by Edith Ballantyne, head of CONGO, on behalf of the forty-five NGOs that had asked to speak, reaffirmed the goals of the Decade for Women and urged that "governments recognize that present military expenditures are incompatible with these goals." The NGOs urged that peace be restored to equal emphasis with the other two goals of the decade. They stated that "peace is more than the absence of war; it must also be the presence of economic, social and political justice."[33]

At the forum there were plenary panels on peace each day. In addition, the World Peace Council, WIDF, WILPF, and the newly formed Scandinavian action group, Women for Peace, ran ongoing series of panels on strategies for ending the arms race, the relationship between women, peace, and the mass media, the problem that national heroes have more often been heroes of war than of peace, the relationship between nuclear power and nuclear weapons, and disarmament education. While the issue of peace was now included, the *process* itself was far from peaceful. Attempts to achieve consensus at the conference were unsuccessful.

Nairobi, 1985

Consensus was more in evidence at the Nairobi Conference. During the February–March 1984 session of the CSW, which was acting as the preparatory body for the World Conference, seventeen NGOs submitted a statement commending the preparatory body on its use of consensus and urged delegates to continue "that same spirit of consensus."[34] They emphasized implementation of the subthemes of education, employment, and health, urging highest priority for rural women's health, food and water supply, as well as for the elimination of illiteracy, the needs of refugees and migrant women and children, older women, and children and youth, and for accelerating the participation of women in public life.

The Nairobi Forum '85 was again organized by CONGO, with a planning committee of 60 international NGOs, along with a Kenyan NGO Committee. Dame Nita Barrow served as convenor, and Virginia Hazzard as coordinator of Forum '85. The Kenyan NGO Committee was chaired by Dr. Eddah Gachukia. The CONGO Planning Committee sponsored NGO meetings before the regional UN preparatory meetings in Tokyo in March, Arusha in October, Havana in November, and Baghdad in December 1984, where they authored recommendations to bring to the attention of the meetings. The NGOs also participated in these meetings as observers. At the NGO Pre-Conference Consultation in Vienna in October 1984, ninety-one NGOs attended workshops on equality, development, peace, health, education, employment, elderly women, refugees, migrants, women in emergency situations, and the media, in addition to a panel on young women and girls.[35]

The NGOs cooperated on two questionnaires. A UN questionnaire to governments was also circulated to relevant NGOs, receiving twenty-six replies. The Planning Committee also circulated a five-page survey with the help of volunteer women researchers from the Women's Anthropology Conference. Replies of seventy-two national and sixty-five international NGOs confirmed those of the UN questionnaire, highlighting equality of opportunity in education, health, and employment, with progress seen most in education and least in health.[36]

Forum '85 opened at 10 A.M. on 10 July 1985 at the Kenyatta International Conference Centre, where the UN conference would start on 15 July; and on the next day, the forum moved to the University of Nairobi to run through 19 July. This time, the two sites were accessible to each other by means of a Kenyan government-provided bus service. This time, translation in Arabic, English, French, Spanish, and Swahili would be provided for the main Forum sessions.[37] Once again the NGO Planning Committee published a daily newspaper.

The forum was the largest international meeting of women ever held, with over 13,500 in attendance, far more than had been expected. The result was a housing crunch, especially during the days of overlap between forum and conference. On 8 July, NGO women in first-, second-, and third-class hotels were told by the Kenyan government that they would have to vacate by 12 July so that governmental delegates, also numbering more than expected, could move in. After much heated discussion, combined with nonviolent action and skilled negotiation, agreement was reached on 13 July between women, the hotels, and the Kenyan government that they would stay in their rooms and triple up so that extra rooms would be freed for the additional government delegates.[38] It was an interesting exercise in women's exertion of a new sort of power.

The majority of forum activities took place at the University of Nairobi, where the Planning Committee coordinated plenary sessions in the areas of equality, development, peace, health, education, employment, youth, aging, migrants, refugees, women in emergency situations, and media, and where hundreds of other sessions were organized by NGOs and women's groups from around the world. Craft demonstrations and music were located in the grassy area in the center of the university. A crafts marketplace was organized by Maendeleo ya Wanawake, the Women's Bureau of Kenya, and the Kenya External Trade Authority. Child care and development activities were coordinated by the Kenya NGO Organizing Committee, as were field trips to village projects. A ten-day International Women's Film Festival at the Kenya National Theater took place with only one major incident over the Kenyan government's requirement that they be able to censor each film. A five-day seminar for Third World women, the "Third World Forum on Women, Law and Development," was sponsored by the Overseas Education Fund of Washington, D.C. The International Women's Studies Institute in Kenya provided training and support for 26 women, who were half Western and half African, over four weeks, to report on the sessions of the Forum. Karibu, a Women's Centre for Women of All Faiths, was organized by the World Council of Churches, Church Women United, and the All-Africa Council of Churches, in a nearby church.[39]

The fact that the final conference of the Decade for Women was held in Africa further helped to highlight the relationship between women and development.

Similarly, the holding of the conference in Nairobi, site of the UN Environment Program (UNEP), brought to the agenda the triple relationship between women, environment, and development. The Environment Liaison Centre in Nairobi, with 231 members in sixty-six countries, put on a "Women, Environment and Development" program from 15 to 19 July, including plenaries and four workshops on women and water management, forests, energy, and sustainable agriculture.[40] The NGOs and environmental movements put on a "Tech and Tools" exhibit, coordinated by the International Women's Tribune Centre, which included a variety of practical technologies, such as solar cookstoves, which could benefit women. Their workshops and exhibits ranged from computers, to building low-cost duplicating machines, to the jam and jelly business, to building energy and environment networks.[41] African NGOs took us on trips to the countryside to witness tree-planting farms and multiple-cropping techniques developed and carried out by women. All of this brought an air of practical reality to the panels and lectures sponsored by NGOs and others. One new NGO in particular, DAWN (Development Alternatives for Women in a New Era), which had only been formed in 1984, put on a large number of outstanding panels that questioned many of the traditional assumptions of development theory. This was also true of the Trickle Up Program—a New York–based program oriented to small-scale development aid and particularly focused on women—which had grown from almost nothing to a major endeavor from its birth in 1979. The focus on women and development had come of age.

In the Nairobi forum, peace as an issue became equal to that of the other two themes of the Decade for Women. The result was visible and concrete. A blue-and-white–striped tent stood at the corner of the grassy courtyard inside the entrance to the University of Nairobi campus, where Forum '85 was held. Under the bright blue banner proclaiming "Peace Tent," women congregated from morning to evening. At one side was a handmade globe, the height of a human being, that became completely covered with signatures and comments.

Forum panels and workshops on the peace theme ranged from strategies for ending the arms race, to peace education, disarmament education, the relationship between disarmament and development, a Palestinian-Israeli dialogue, a U.S.–Soviet dialogue, to race issues, to more theoretical discussions on the relationship of women to peace, and whether women's view of peace is distinctly different from men's. In the peace tent, operated primarily by the newly formed Feminist International for Peace and Food and by WILPF, one of the oldest women's peace organizations (1915), the dialogues continued daily on all of these issues, with the tent almost always hot, packed, and the scene of stimulating discussions. Organizers, though they faced disagreements, managed to preserve an atmosphere of open debate and a spirit of reconciliation. This was in noticeable contrast to Mexico City and Copenhagen, where much of the debate on peace issues had broken down into vitriolic misunderstandings. The underlying sense was that the women's movement had matured over the course of the Decade for Women.

One hundred sixty-three NGO representatives went on to monitor and lobby the UN Conference itself as observers, with delegations ranging in size from one to twelve members. Fifty-nine written statements were offered by NGOs, with twenty authored in whole or in part by women's organizations. These ranged from the effects of racism and militarism on women, to women entrepreneurs in India, to African traditional practices, and women and the household.[42]

There were references to NGOs in at least forty-three paragraphs of the Forward-looking Strategies (FLS) adopted by the conference. In the summary of the general debate, Paragraph 97 noted that many countries referred to the valuable contribution of NGOs, stressing their contributions in such community activities as maternal and child care, vocational training for the disabled, and social services for the aged, and emphasized the need for strengthened cooperation.[43] When the GA took note of the report of the conference and endorsed the FLS on 13 December 1985, it urged not only governments and IGOs but also NGOs, to give high priority to the FLS. The NGOs mattered, even to governments.

Women's NGOs have continued to be active in the UN context. While there was no world conference in 1990, the NGOs in consultative status with ECOSOC organized a two-day consultation on 22 and 23 February 1990 in Vienna in conjunction with the 34th session of CSW. They agreed to organize the NGO Forum at the 1995 World Conference on the Status of Women and joint work between NGOs and UN professionals in Vienna on creative styles of problem solving before then. An NGO committee was set up long before the UN apparatus for Beijing was in place, with cooperation between CONGO and other organizations, headed by a Thai woman, but organized primarily in the church building across the street from the UN in New York. The NGO planning for the 1995 Beijing Conference was ahead of either the UN or governments. Perhaps even more important, the development of a Women's Caucus has resulted in significant impact in bringing women's perspectives into other UN conferences, such as the 1992 Rio de Janiero "Earth Summit" and the September 1994 Cairo Population and Development Conference.

CONCLUSIONS: EVALUATING THE NGO ROLE

The NGOs have played two significant roles in the development of women's rights through the UN. First, they have organized and educated to create the constituency that put the issue on the table. We began by saying that the UN Decade for Women has been, in a sense, both a creature of, and creator of, the international women's movement. To be more accurate, both national women's movements and international NGOs played a central role in the creation of IWY and the Decade for Women. The UN conference—and especially the forums accompanying them—were in turn largely responsible for the development of both an international women's movement and the more formal governmental and nongovernmental infrastructure that could begin to serve as the basis of an international women's regime. The NGOs were responsible for setting up the forums that allowed thousands of women to come together in Mexico City, Copenhagen, and Nairobi, interactions that allowed for the exchange of varied conceptions of women's goals and how to achieve them. The cross-fertilization of ideas, which appeared largely as conflict in Mexico City and Copenhagen, resulted in a new, more international, women's movement by the time of the Nairobi conference.

Second, NGOs played key lobbying and monitoring roles, first helping to initiate the UN conferences on women, then putting pressure on UN member governments at the conferences to come up with documents clearly directed at improving the status and participation of women and, in turn, utilizing those documents as leverage to get countries to change their own laws and structures relating to women. While it would be extremely difficult to separate the effects of women's movements and NGOs from that of the UN itself, or from the actions of nation-states, it is safe to say that without WINGOs most of the progress on women's issues in and around the UN would not have taken place.

NOTES

1. For an earlier examination of the politics of women, peace, and power at the Mexico City and Copenhagen conferences, see C. M. Stephenson, "Feminism, Pacifism, Nationalism and the UN Decade for Women," *Women's Studies International Forum* 5, no. 3 (1982), reprinted in Judith Stiehm, ed., *Women and Men's Wars* (Elmsford, N.Y.: Pergamon, 1983).

2. See, for example, Elise Boulding, *Women in the Twentieth Century World* (New York: John Wiley, 1977), 165–218.

3. *Charter of the United Nations, Report to the President on the Results of the San Francisco Conference by the Chairman of the United States Delegation, the Secretary of State*, Department of State Publication 2349, Conference Series 71 (June 1945), 262–66. The women's organizations included American Association of University Women, General Federation of Women's Clubs, National Federation of Business and Professional Women's Clubs, National League of Women Voters, Women's Action Committee for Victory and Lasting Peace.

4. Ruth Russell, *History of the United Nations Charter* (Washington, D.C.: Brookings Institution, 1958), 798–802. See also *Report to the President*, 120–21; Dorothy B. Robins, *Experiment in Democracy* (New York: Parkside Press, 1971), 34–56, Appendix XIII.

5. UN, ECOSOC, Official Records, Second Year, Summary Record of the 74th Meeting, Lake Success, New York, 19 March 1947.

6. UN, *Report of the Council Committee on Non-Governmental Organizations*, E/4485 (6 May 1968); UN, ECOSOC, Official Records, 44th Session, 517th to 524th Meetings, 20–27 May 1968.

7. Category I and II may both make oral statements in the commissions. Because of this, and because fewer NGOs attend the commissions regularly, they may have more effect there.

8. Boulding, *Women*, 195–96, 202, Table 9.1.

9. Interview with Virginia Saurwein (former chief of NGO Section, UN Department of International Economic and Social Affairs, from late 1975 through June 1988), 22 January 1991.

10. UN, GA, 30th Session, *Report of the Secretary-General: Measures and Activities Undertaken in Connexion with the International Women's Year*, A/10263 (October 1975), 105.

11. World Conference of IWY, Provisional Rules of Procedure of the Conference, E/CONF.66/2 (1975), p. 17.

12. UN, GA, 30th Session, A/10263.

13. UN, E/CONF.66/NGO, 4, 5, 8, 10–27 June 1975.

14. Harold Wilkinson, "Women in Mexico City, 1975," (July 1975), 3–4, 10, mimeographed.

15. International Women's Tribune, "Guidelines for Conduct of IWY Tribune Sessions," June 1975, mimeographed.

16. *Xilonen*, 20 June 1975, 1.

17. *Xilonen*, 20 June 1975, 4.

18. *IWY Bulletin* no. 5 (May 1975): 29. See also Irene Tinker and Michelle Bo Bramsen, *Women and World Development* (Washington, D.C.: Overseas Development Council, 1976); Mayra Buvinic, *Women and World Development: An Annotated Bibliography* (Washington, D.C.: Overseas Development Council, 1976).

19. "Call to Action Presented to Helvi Sipila," UN press release, 27 June 1975, mimeographed; "Notice to Media," UN press release, 24 June 1975, mimeographed; "List of Signers of a Call to Action," UN press release, 9 June 1975, mimeographed.

20. American Embassy, Mexico City, "Suggested Revisions to the UN World Plan of Action for International Women's Year," undated mimeograph. See also 26-page version by Tribune Press Information Office, Mexico City.

21. *Xilonen*, 30 June 1975, 1; 1 July 1975, 1.

22. Catherine Foster, *Women for All Seasons: The Story of the Women's International League for Peace and Freedom* (Athens: University of Georgia Press, 1989), 76.

23. *International Development Review* (1975), 40.

24. "International Women's Tribune Centre," c. 1980, undated brochure.

25. UN, *Report of the Conference of the UN Decade for Women* (Annex, "Submissions by Non-Governmental Organizations," A/CONF.94/NGO/1-53), A/CONF.94/35 (14–30 July 1980), 235–38.

26. UN, *Report of the Conference of the UN Decade for Women*, 25–26.

27. Foster, *Women for All Seasons*, 60, 77–79.

28. CONGO, Planning Committee, *NGO Activities at the World Conference of the UN Decade for Women*. "NGO Forum Draft Schedule of Panels and Speakers as of 8 July," c. 1980, undated mimeo.

29. *International Women's Tribune Centre Newsletter*, no. 11 (1st Quarter 1980): 10–12.

30. Her full name was Domitila Barrios de Chungara. She spoke on the Forum Employment panel. See also Domitila Barrios de Chungara with Moema Viezzer, *Let Me Speak! Testimony of Domitila, A Woman of the Bolivian Mines* (New York: Monthly Review Press, 1978).

31. *International Women's Tribune Centre Newsletter*, no. 11 (1st Quarter 1980): 13; ibid., no. 13 (2nd Quarter 1980): 32.

32. Irene Tinker, "A Feminist View of Copenhagen," *Signs* 6, no 3 (1981): 531, 535.

33. *Statement of the Non-Governmental Organizations to the World Conference of the UN Decade for Women*, A/CONF.94/NGO/36, 24 July 1980.

34. Commission on the Status of Women, Acting as the Preparatory Body for the World Conference to Review and Appraise the Achievements of the UN Decade for Women, Second Session, *Statement Submitted by the International Council of Women et al.*, Vienna, 27 February–7 March 1984. GA, Document, A/CONF.116/PC/NGO/13, 23 February 1984.

35. UN, SG, *The Participation of Non-Governmental Organizations in the United Nations Decade for Women*, A/CONF.116/14 (22 May 1985), 6.

36. Ibid.

37. Nita Barrow, "The NGO Decade Forum," *Africa Report* 30, no. 2 (The African-American Institute) (March–April 1985): 9–12. See also interview with Rosalind Harris, New York City, 19 June 1991: Arabic translation at the Forum was paid by the Iraqis; the Kenyans also paid for a translator.

38. Compiled from personal notes and from "Women Fight Eviction Order," *Forum '85* (10 July 1985): 12; "Guests' Hotel Row Resolved," *Daily Nation*, 13 July 1985, 1, 12; "Forum Sisters Agree to Share Hotel Rooms," *Forum '85* (15 July 1985): 5.

39. *Daily Nation*, 13 July 1985, 6, 9; IWTC, *Women and Development Quarterly Newsletter* 30 (1st Quarter 1985): 22–25.

40. *Forum '85* (15 July 1985): 3.

41. *Forum '85*, 12 July 1985.

42. Statements submitted by NGOs are listed by number and first organizational author only in Annex III of UN, *Report of the World Conference to Review and Appraise the Achievements of the United Nations Decade for Women*, A/CONF.116/28/Rev. 1, (Nairobi, 15–26 July 1985), 303–4.

43. Ibid., para. 97, 112.

10
Specialized Agencies and the World Bank

Anne Winslow

Surrounding the all-purpose United Nations (UN)—the matrix of the UN system—is a cluster of specialized agencies and other bodies dealing with particular aspects of global problems. Only three agencies had given even the faintest recognition in their constitutions to the rights of women. The World Health Organization (WHO) merely referred to the promotion of "maternal and child health and welfare." The UN Educational, Scientific and Cultural Organization (Unesco) borrowed a UN formula "without distinction of race, sex, language or religion" and continued with a call for "universal respect . . . for the human rights" and for "the ideal of equality of educational opportunity."

Only the International Labor Organization (ILO), in its statement of objectives, affirmed the "principle that men and women should receive equal remuneration for work of equal value." Other provisions called for the participation of women in the inspection system and of at least one woman advisor when an issue involving women was under discussion and, finally, that "a certain number of the staff should be women." This was the only agency that mentioned the word *women* in connection with the staff.

The pump that primed the efforts to give women visibility was the Resolution of the UN General Assembly (GA) proclaiming 1975 "International Women's Year" and calling for an international conference to be held in Mexico City. Subsequently, a "Decade for Women" was proclaimed, calling for the integration of women as full and equal partners with men in the total development effort and the elimination of discrimination on the grounds of sex.

How the UN itself responded to this call for action is the subject of other chapters in this volume. The present one concerns the role of the specialized agencies and the International Bank for Reconstruction and Development (World Bank). Four of these—the three mentioned above (WHO, Unesco, ILO), the Food and Agriculture Organization (FAO) and the World Bank are dealt with here, in the order of their founding, because they employ over 80 percent of the total international staff outside of the UN and an even larger percentage of the female staff.[1]

Like the UN, the specialized agencies have a body consisting of all the member states that acts on matters referred to it by subordinate organs, an intergovernmental executive organ that oversees the operations of the organization (names vary) and an agency head who carries overall responsibility for the execution of the institution's mandate, and an international staff pledged to loyalty to the agency and not to any national government. Most of the specialized agencies have formalized relations with appropriate nongovernmental organizations (NGOs). Although the basic pattern was established by a provision in the UN Charter for "suitable arrangements," the subsequent elaboration of rules and procedures differed widely in the various agencies.

Both the agencies and the World Bank are linked to the UN by special agreements that, in general, provide for consultation, exchange of information, and, in the case of the agencies, for participation in common services.

THE EARLY YEARS

Women as a subject of concern was slow to percolate the consciousness of the agencies. Changes came very, very slowly. The decades of the 1950s and 1960s saw a trickle here and a trickle there. The UN Development Program (UNDP), which evolved from earlier arrangements made in 1949, is the main arm of a combined operation bringing together the competencies of the UN and the associated agencies in a partnership effort in the field of technical assistance. It has also created a central fund for the allocation of resources. Its early program of assistance to women concentrated on such subjects as domestic science, home economics, and dressmaking. It explained that the "emphasis given to developing training and education for girls and women . . . would appear to be linked to the traditional division of the labor market into male and female sectors, as well as customs, traditions and attitudes regarding women's role and responsibilities."[2]

Even Unesco, one of the earliest activist organizations on behalf of women, listed only four studies before 1960 and only forty-eight more prior to 1970.[3] The ILO initially placed its emphasis on women as mothers and as the frailer sex, although measures for the legal protection of working women soon followed. The WHO was primarily concerned with maternal and child health. The

FAO's contribution to women's issues was almost entirely in the area of home economics. The World Bank was happily oblivious to women as a subject for its first quarter century.

ILO

The ILO, dedicated to the achievement of social justice, is a unique organization and its effect on women has been shaped by a number of special conditions. It has the only tripartite structure—government representatives (the usual form of participation) and also representatives from employer and labor groups who are an integral part of the decision-making process. In principle, this should have enhanced opportunities for women's participation. It obviously did to a certain extent; but employer groups have only recently included women in their ranks, and trade unions were less than enthusiastic about equality for women despite pressures from organizations of working women.

The ILO's thirty-year emphasis on the protection of women split the ranks. As early as 1923, the British National Council of Women maintained that protection should be based on the nature of the job and not on sex. Later, a woman delegate to an ILO conference objected to what she called "discrimination against men." If an occupation was too hazardous for women it was too hazardous for men (pregnant women excepted). It was also claimed that protective legislation might cause employers to limit the employment of women and that limitations on night work might bar women from working hours more consonant with their family obligations.

Here there was a marked difference of opinion between women in the industrialized world and those in developing countries. A number of working women in the latter feared the removal of safeguards that might leave them without redress, particularly where unions were weak or nonexistent and where employers were all powerful and sometimes prone to abuse their female staff sexually.

However, even before ILO began to turn its attention to broader issues involving women, some steps in that direction had already been taken. A recommendation (1923) and a convention (1947) provided that the labor inspectorate should include women as well as men with the same powers and duties and the same opportunities for promotion. Women inspectors had been on the scene for a number of years, and they were well represented at ILO conferences. To them goes much of the credit for this provision. A recommendation for the application of sickness insurance to women (1927) and another dealing with benefits for widows and children (1933) were also adopted.

The real precursor of what was to come was a resolution introduced in 1937 by two U.S. delegates—one male and one female. It called on governments to reexamine the status of women with respect to "their political rights and opportunities, economic conditions, and protection from economic exploitation."[4] In 1964, it held a conference on the employment and working conditions of African women.

FAO

The FAO has the loveliest location of any of the specialized agencies—beside the Baths of Caracalla in Rome. With a staff of approximately 7,000, including the World Food Programme, it is second in size only to the UN. Its mandate is to raise levels of nutrition and standards of living; improve the production, processing, marketing and distribution of all food and agricultural products from farms, forests and fisheries; promote rural development and improve the living conditions of rural populations.

Despite the fact that women as major growers, processors, and distributors of food were a logical target, FAO paid little attention to them between 1946 and 1975, save in the field of home economics. Four activities, somewhat broader in scope, occurred in 1974. The first was an investigation of the extent of women's participation in rural programs, constraints on their participation, and the development of programs for future activities. The second and third, both in 1974, were FAO's World Food Conference and the World Conference on Agricultural Education, organized jointly with ILO and Unesco. The latter emphasized the growing importance of the role of women in economic and social life in general and in the development process in particular. Proposals included involvement of women in decision making in the areas of food production and nutrition policies; full access to all medical and social services; education and training on a par with men in food production, agricultural technology, marketing and distribution techniques, and consumer credit; equal rights and responsibilities for both sexes to allow women to take part in the battle against hunger. The fourth was a one-week seminar in Cairo, held in collaboration with the League of Arab States, the Economic Commission for Western Asia and the UN International Children's Emergency Fund (UNICEF), on the role of women in integrated rural development, with emphasis on population problems.

Unesco

Unesco has the broadest mandate of any of the specialized agencies. Its concerns range from the eradication of illiteracy to the promotion of science to the rescue of Egyptian temples when the Aswan Dam flooded the Nile. In regard to women, it has been unswerving in its efforts to abolish discrimination in education. In 1949, it convened a Committee of Experts to discuss the obstacles to women's equal access to education. In 1960, a convention and recommendation against discrimination in education was adopted. A long-term program for the equal access of girls and women to education, science and culture started in 1965–1966.[5]

In the 1950s, it dealt with the education of women for citizenship, the participation of women in political life, and the status of women in South Asia—the forerunner of a whole series of similar studies in various countries of the world. In the 1960s, it looked at the question of women in society. During the

1970s, a considerable amount of attention was devoted to women in the media and the stereotypes projected by the male controllers, the role of women in promoting peace, the plight of the woman breadwinner, and the need for educational and vocational guidance.

WHO

At the first meeting of its conference in 1948, WHO decided that initially it would deal with the following subjects: malaria, tuberculosis, venereal disease, maternity and child welfare, nutrition and environmental sanitation. Of most concern to women was the substantial number of model maternity and child welfare centers that had been set up in a number of countries by 1953. These were designed to demonstrate positive steps that could be taken to lower the incidence of material mortality and morbidity as well as infant mortality. However, in those early years WHO had a tendency to lump women with the elderly or infirm.

In a 1990 review of the history of WHO's involvement with women's programs, the Executive Board confessed that "before 1976, the start of the United Nations Decade for women, with the goals of equality, development and peace, there was little recognition, documentation or concern about the roles women play in social and economic development, nor of the relationship between these roles and their status and health."[6]

World Bank

The World Bank was established at the 1945 Bretton Woods Conference. Its founders were primarily concerned with the need to provide loans to restore the devastated areas in Europe, but the devastation in other parts of the world and the problems of development soon led to operations across the globe.

The World Bank was particularly slow in directing its attention to women. In a burst of frankness, it declared that it "had not totally ignored women's roles as both producers and consumers . . . but for a broad range of traditional projects, specific attention to the role of women had not seemed necessary."[7]

The real push started in the 1970s, impelled by two very different influences. One was the increasingly vocal and determined activities by women in their own countries. The other was the UN GA's adoption of the Strategy for the Second UN Development Decade. The latter brought into sharp focus the obvious fact that real development could not take place without women. However, the idea of women-in-development had not, as a rule, entered the institutional bloodstream; thus, programs for women tended to be added at some stage of the process like a series of Band-Aids. Another handicap was that women's contribution to development tended to be seen in purely economic terms with emphasis on the control of fertility or the contribution of women's labor.

While programs for women increased, programs with women made little headway. Even when sincere efforts were made at headquarters, they tended to be stymied in the field by staff who, by training, inclination, and time constraints, took the old familiar road. Thus, women became the object of an exercise rather than a partner in its implementation.

In the following sections we look briefly at how women have fared in recent years in the various organizations.

THE DECADE FOR WOMEN AND THE YEARS AFTER

The objectives of the Decade for Women—equality, development, and peace—gradually filtered into the bloodstream of the specialized agencies and the World Bank. Not unexpectedly—given the speed of action in national governments—responses gained momentum after the end of the Decade for Women.

ILO

From 1975, ILO's legislative activities increasingly emphasized issues relating to equality. In 1975, the conference adopted a convention extending the concept of equality with respect not only to employment and training but to society as a whole. A Declaration and Resolution Concerning a Plan of Action designed to promote equality of opportunity and treatment for women workers was submitted to the 1975 Mexico City Conference. Some 75 women participated in the committee that drafted the declaration. The vice-chairman was Ethel Chipchase, M.B.E., the last of the old-time British Labor leaders.

In 1981, a convention was adopted providing for maternity leave and extended child-rearing leave for *either* parent and for the development or promotion of child care and family services and facilities. In preparation for the 1985 Nairobi Conference, the ILO Conference adopted an omnibus Resolution on Equal Opportunities and Equal Treatment for Men and Women in Employment. Other instruments dealt with social security, collective bargaining, employment policies and conditions in the workplace.

In the area of technical cooperation, efforts became more women centered. In the 1980s, UNDP funded the creation of a Skills Training Unit for rural women in Nigeria, designed to increase their production of processed, farm, semiagricultural and craft products; a program in El Salvador to establish five "mothers' clubs" to provide social services, such as day care centers and communal kitchens; a program in Mexico to facilitate the design, planning, and implementation of rural development programs.[8] Other ILO programs included technical, managerial, or vocational skill development, as well as training and advisory services. Projects ranged from the introduction of improved ovens for smoking fish and the use of tools to the encouragement of handicrafts. This last once again divided women in the industrialized world from those in developing countries. Western feminists complained that ILO was perpetuating the old tradition of immuring women in the home instead of bringing them into the modern world. This attitude was often resented by women from developing countries. They agreed on the ultimate objective but, as one woman said, "We must begin by putting a woman into a sewing cooperative and not a leadership position when she does not know how to read and write."[9]

Women experts have so far played only a limited role in ILO's field programs, although there was a modest rise in the percentages—5.1 in 1985, 5.7 in 1987, and 6.4 in 1988. There was also a disappointing record of participation by women in ILO's regional meetings, designed to bring to local populations the experience and objectives of the organization. To increase the participation of women, greater emphasis was placed on seminars and workshops with more limited and concrete agendas. This is another facet of the effort to deal with the practical problems of women in place of the more theoretical schemes of headquarters. Particular attention was directed to the implications for women of technological change. Machines had taken over many of the lower-paying jobs in which women predominated, and women lacked the training to compete with men in the new technologies.

In all of the ILO activities women have played a part—sometimes as members of delegations (government, employer, or worker); as members of NGOs; or as the staff responsible for implementing programs, shaping them, or initiating proposals. Their role has varied over the years, varied geographically and varied according to the capacity of the individual. Twenty-three women out of a total of 269 participants attended the 1919 conference, none of them delegates. In 1993, there were over 300 women out of a total of over 2,200, and there were 51 delegates. The largest percentage of the latter represented government—16.9 percent. Workers came second (12.5 percent), and employers third (9.1 percent) (although this figure has been increasing).[10] The substantially larger number of women is more the consequence of the inclusion of a large number of newly independent states than of the expanded role for women. By 1993, however, over 5,000 women representatives had participated in ILO conferences. This provided women with a platform for the expression of their own ideas, exposure to the concerns of other women, and the solidarity of shared problems and methods of dealing with them. On the basis of percentages, however, the record was not brilliant, hovering around 10 percent.

Initially, the most dynamic women were the trade unionists, outnumbering employers by a substantial margin. One example, indicative of the quality of these women, was Margaret Bondfield (United Kingdom), the first woman chairman of the British Trades Union Congress, elected to Parliament in 1924 and appointed Minister of Labour. In later years, however, leadership shifted, to a large extent, to women employers. This was partly because in the industrialized countries working women felt less need of international support—although they still had plenty of battles at home—while labor unions were few and far between in the developing countries that provided the bulk of the membership. Women employers, moreover, were beginning to appear in the latter regions.

It is not surprising that the largest number of women, participating in the conferences, came from the industrialized West, particularly the Nordic countries with their long history of social legislation.[11] Next came France, the United Kingdom, and the United States. A number of countries had only token representation of women, and a few never sent a single one.

In addition to participating in delegations, women also played a role as Visiting Ministers.[12] Here Finland led by a substantial margin since its minister of social affairs was almost always a woman. It was followed by Sweden, which had the rare distinction of providing one of the only two women to serve as president of the conference—Frances Perkins of the United States in 1941 and Anna-Greta Leijon in 1984. In the 1980s, there was a remarkably wide geographic range of Visiting Ministers. There were seven from African countries, three from Central and Latin America, one from Asia as well as a number from Canada, Europe, and the United States.

For many years ILO's Governing Body was basically a male preserve. Until the 1980s, only a handful of women breached the barriers. These included women such as Violet Carrothers (Canada), authority on labor legislation, Frieda Miller (United States), who served as industrial commissioner for New York State, and Gertrude Stemberg, a Netherlands government official.

The real breakthrough came when a Mexican woman, Aida Gonzales Martinez, was elected chairman of the Governing Body in 1982, the only woman to hold that post in over seventy years. She owed her election to an unusual coalition—Latin American representatives and the African group as a whole. Since then, women have played a much bigger role on the Governing Body and, almost without exception, have held influential posts at home.

FAO

In its report to the Mexico City Conference, FAO listed the desiderata that were to govern its future programs. These included: raising the visibility of women; freeing rural women from being a "cheap, easily discardable labour force"; weighing the impact of given actions on women; and helping women to "accept the rural environment as an integral part of their contribution to development."[13]

In the intervening years, FAO carried out a number of projects relating to women both by itself and in cooperation with UNDP. The latter included participation of women in the fruit and vegetable productive process in Guinea-Bissau, assistance to the Nigerian government in setting up a Home Economics Division, and in Syria the training of field extension workers in new agricultural practices and technologies. FAO itself carried out studies on such subjects as women's participation in household production and in the labor market, marketing in given economic systems, rural-urban linkages, and the role of women in energy technology dissemination. Programs were designed, according to FAO, "to incorporate women as beneficiaries and participants in all technical co-operation, training and advisory services."[14]

Despite administration lethargy, professional staff managed to carry out a number of useful projects, most of them initiated in the 1980s. One target was to upgrade traditional food processing without resorting to expensive technology. From 1986, staff members helped to train women (selected by local women's groups) to be rural development promoters. In Zimbabwe in 1988, a group of women was given a two-year training course on crop selection, methods of planting and cultivation, bookkeeping, and so forth. Those who mastered the required skills became eligible for credit. In a number of other countries, programs were conducted on different aspects of food and milk processing. The 1988–1989 budget, while still allocating a substantial place to home economics, put major emphasis on a program on Women in Food Production and Food Security and one on Strengthening Policy, Planning and National Machinery for Women in Development.

The FAO programs were less effective than they might have been because of what appeared to be a lack of commitment on the part of the administration to the principles enunciated by the FAO Conference in 1975. Illustrative of this attitude is a fact reported in a World Bank study relating to a joint World Bank/FAO program in Northern Sierra Leone in 1979.[15] Although female rice farmers played a predominant role, accounting for some 80 percent of total production, they were totally ignored. Another problem was the ambivalent attitude toward the mix of simple technologies and of modernization. For example, small-scale fishing was "well integrated into marketing and distribution channels which are highly efficient and managed in many countries by women."[16] Modernization meant fewer jobs, requiring skills that most women lacked.

Unesco

Unesco, like its sister agencies, was profoundly influenced by the Decade for Women. Increasingly, emphasis was put on projects tailored to the needs of women. In the 1980s, it considered the role of women in liberation movements and the effects on them of their participation. The "invisible women" and the "conspiracy to conceal" women's essential contribution to economic life was another theme. In 1980, an international conference was held on the situation of women in technical and vocational education and a seminar on methods of opening up to women vocational training in jobs traditionally occupied by men. A symposium of experts was held on the changing roles of men and women in private and public life, women in literature, the arts and science. Stress was also laid on strengthening women's organizations and movements.

In 1989, Unesco hosted an international symposium on access by women to salaried employment as a source of social change and its effects on women's participation in social life. In April 1991, a group of international experts met to discuss means of "Protecting Women's Human Rights from Sexual Exploitation, Violence and Prostitution." The report pointed out the widespread traffic in Asian women stemming from the war in Vietnam and the large-scale organization of prostitution through sex tourism. A 1986 report on prostitution asserted that prostitution was "the result of the subordination of women in all societies and of the balance of power between the sexes."[17] The report concluded with a series of recommendations regarding practical steps and further research.

The record of Unesco concerning women is mixed. At its 1989 conference there were almost 400 women in delegations—more than 20 percent of the total. This was well above any of the other agencies. It has engaged in a number of imaginative programs, but participation by women shrank in a number of areas during the 1980s. Attendance at meetings held in the field dropped from 26.5 percent in 1986 to 18.2 percent two years later. Western Europe and North America provided the largest share of the women (those least in need), and Asia and the Pacific the smallest—29.8 percent compared to 12.3 percent. There was a similar drop in fellowships awarded to women—from 25 percent to 17 percent. There were no women in 40 percent of the field programs. Some of the decline may have been attributable to budgetary stringencies (the result of the withdrawals of the United Kingdom and the United States). However, it also seems to prove the adage that when funds are tight women are the first to suffer.

The medium-term plan for 1984–1989 included, for the first time, a chapter on the Status of Women; the 1990–1995 plan incorporates women under the heading labelled "Transverse Themes." This, Unesco stated, meant that the role of women would find a place in all major program areas and would be centrally coordinated and stimulated. In April 1994, Unesco established a Consultative Committee on Women. Its mandate was "to provide a fresh approach to Unesco's work relating to women and gender issues" and to "give advice concerning the elaboration of a new policy and strategy."[18]

WHO

The response of WHO to the Decade for Women, although belated, was serious. The years between 1976 and 1980 were a period of policy developments, while the next five years saw an emphasis on the creation of mechanisms within the organizations and within countries for "promotion, planning and coordination of action."[19] In 1985, the World Health Assembly had noted the "close relationship between equal rights for men and women and the participation of women in health activities and in the promotion of health for all, particularly as decision makers." In 1989, it launched its first program targeting women in the health field as workers. The assembly spoke of the "crucial role" of women in development, of the need to insure that "a woman's perspective" was reflected in policies and programs affecting the health of women. States were asked to "encourage and support the appointment of nursing/midwifery personnel in senior leadership and management positions" and to facilitate their participation in planning and implementing the country's health activities.[20]

A number of programs, both national and international, were subsequently undertaken. These programs suggest that some influence was being felt. The Ministry of Health of Nepal carried out a study of country health resources involving ministries and women's organizations. Other projects involved women, health, and development in India, Chad, and Ghana. The WHO launched programs to promote health care through women's functional literacy and carried out studies to identify women's organizations with potential for assisting in maternal and child health programs and family planning.

While women, for the most part, were restricted to middle-level jobs, there were some signs of progress if participation in World Health Assemblies afforded any criterion. In 1946, not a single delegation was headed by a woman, and the record for all male participation would have been unbroken save for the United States. It provided one female delegate and three female advisors. By 1990, twelve delegations were headed by women. Although this represented only 7.6 percent of all the delegations (and a drop from 17 delegations in 1986), it did demonstrate that at least some women had reached a top policy-making position. The geographic spread of these delegations was worth noting: three from Europe; two from Latin America; five from Africa, New Zealand, and Saint Kitts and Nevis. The total number of women delegates, alternates, or advisors amounted to 18.8 percent.

World Bank

Verbal acknowledgment by the World Bank of the objectives of the Decade for Women came at the outset, including a somewhat token appointment of an advisor on women in development. Credit for later developments, however, goes to a less unsympathetic administration and, especially, to vigorous and dynamic Barbara Herz, who came to her post in 1985, starting what was virtually a one-woman operation. By 1991, she had not only nine higher-level staff at headquarters but also regional coordinators. There was also a staff member who worked part-time on Women in Development issues in each of the nineteen country departments. The Women in Development Division (WID) was, potentially, in a position to influence policy because it received copies of all projects coming before the directors and could make comments and recommendations thereon.

The official reports of the World Bank looked as if Herz were being very successful. Between 1988 and 1991, World Bank operations with gender-specific elements relating to women, it was stated, rose from 11 percent to some 40 percent—a rather surprising record for a banking institution not notable for its concern with women. Forty-four percent of education projects approved in fiscal 1989 proposed action to improve female education. Ten out of eleven projects dealing with population, health, and nutrition and twenty-two out of fifty-three projects in agriculture addressed women's needs. All such activities, according to the World Bank's philosophy, were directed to the development of an integrated approach helpful to men as well as to women.[21]

In the field of education, World Bank–financed projects included more local schools nearer to pupils' homes (a matter of particular importance for girls), cheaper textbooks, priority for girls in boarding and lower secondary schools, and expansion of technical and industrial institutions and programs. In the areas of health, population, and nutrition, emphasis was placed on strengthening diagnosis and treatment of maternal and child health problems, family planning, and the mobilization and coordination of governmental and nongovernmental resources in which women play a leading role in designing and delivering family planning services.

A Woman in Agriculture program (WIA), part of WID, was established to identify women farmers' specific constraints and needs, prepare extension service advice to meet those needs, and modify services to reach women more effectively. Aside from training and processing technology geared to female farmers, attention was directed to the problem of credit. In a number of countries, women had no legal title to land or other assets for use as collateral for loans.

In China, one project involved training and deployment of 245 female extension workers and 20,000 female village technicians to improve access by women to veterinary and extension services. In Nigeria, retrained experts addressed the technical needs of female farmers, encouraged labor-saving devices, including improved tools and implements, and provided credit through the Cooperative Financing Agencies.

These are exemplary projects. Moreover, before embarking on them, thorough research is carried out. The WID has a number of substantial studies to its credit. One, for example, on the role of women in economic development in Kenya, covers such subjects as population pressure and strategies for smallholders; women's growing responsibility for farming; productivity; poverty and gender; agricultural extension and credit; the types of further research needed; as well as recommendations regarding feasible courses for governmental action. If other intergovernmental organizations had prepared the ground so well, many fewer errors would have been made.

Despite all this, the results leave something to be desired. The structural adjustment and economic recovery programs that have often been the condition for World Bank support have come under heavy criticism because they affect most severely women and girls. It is women who are the first to be dismissed when employment is retrenched, and it is little girls who are kept at home when school fees are imposed. It is emphasis on tools made for and adapted to men and capital investments that obliterated programs to improve the lot of working women.[22]

NONGOVERNMENTAL ORGANIZATIONS

As intergovernmental bodies have seen budgets frozen or reduced, while the scope of their activities has expanded, they have become increasingly dependent on NGOs for the execution of programs. Another influence has been the growing emphasis on projects tailored to local interests. Here, those NGOs with local branches have a substantial advantage.

The constitution of Unesco provides that member states should make arrangements for "associating its principal bodies interested in educational, scientific and cultural matters" with Unesco's work. Provision was later made for a special and more intimate relationship with those NGOs which had passed through a period of initiation and had been approved. Such NGOs were invited by the Director-General "to advise him regularly on the preparation and execution of Unesco's programme and to participate in Unesco's activities."[23]

In 1984, Unesco held its first collective consultation of international NGOs on problems of literacy—the majority of the participants were women. Between 1987 and 1989, ten grants to NGOs were made by Unesco to carry out programs within its mandate relating to women.[24] These programs included training seminars, workshops and roundtables, studies and publications.

No other specialized agency had any such provisions in its constitution. When ILO was under the League of Nations, it benefited from an early act of the League authorizing the inclusion of representatives of organizations in some of the advisory committees of the assembly. The relationships established at that time became formalized after World War II. The FAO also made its own arrangements, which evolved slowly over time, and so did WHO.

Some of the World Bank's best programs stem from a fruitful partnership among an intergovernmental organization, national governments, and NGOs. In Kenya, for example, over 16,200 women's groups were registered with the government and were thus eligible for assistance. The Ministry of Water Development shared its responsibilities with a local NGO, Kenya Water for Health Organization (KWAHO), in recognition of the fact that women are responsible for finding water and thus have a stake in the maintenance of the system. With the assistance of KWAHO extension teams, women in one district had majority representation on the well committee responsible for the organization and management of water supplies, local administration, finance, and revenue collection.

Three NGOs played a key role in the Kenyan government's program for maternal and child health and family planning. The Family Planning Association of Kenya contributed about 27 percent of all family planning services in the country. The Christian Health Association of Kenya coordinated the health care services provided by Protestant churches and gave both preventive and curative care. Kenya African National Union (KANU)/Maendeleo ya Wanawake, the oldest and largest of the NGOs, worked in five main areas: leadership development, maternal and child health and family planning, nutrition, environment and income generation.

A World Bank report, justifying its support, stated that such services appeared to "increase impact substantially ... with only a modest increase in program cost" and often achieved twice the national levels in the area of family planning.[25]

STAFF

The problems that women's staff face in the specialized agencies and the World Bank are similar to those in the UN (see chapter 8). Within these broad parameters, however, treatment of women has varied according to the attitude of the chief administrative officer, the strength displayed by organized women staff members, and, to a limited extent, the verbal prodding of governments.[26]

In 1971, the ILO Governing Body, influenced by its women members, had begun to press for a greater role for women. It called upon the administration to provide statistical information showing the distribution of professional staff by function and grade, place of assignment, category and type of contract with respect to age, sex, and grade.

Administrative response, however, was rather lethargic. On the eve of the Mexico City Conference, the ILO director-general had appointed a working party on equality of opportunity and treatment of women staff—membership equally divided between representatives of the administration and the staff. The working party recommended, inter alia, a thirty percent target for professional women within ten years, measures to improve recruitment of women, career development programs, and an increase in the number of women in high-level, decision-making posts. These recommendations were given due consideration, but there the matter ended.

In 1981, a joint subcommittee was established under the chairmanship of Antoinette Waelbroeck Beguin, recently raised to the level of Assistant Director-General of the ILO. The recommendations followed along the same general lines and were approved in principle by the Director-General but never fully implemented.

By 1985, an increasingly restless staff began to take matters into their own hands. An ad hoc group of women was set up and shortly transformed into the Action Group for Equality. Its aim was to provide an independent, informal network for contacts among women staff and to concentrate on "practical, self-help measures." It called for "immediate appointment at the directorate level of a person responsible for developing, implementing and monitoring a concrete program of action for equality of opportunity and treatment in the ILO."[27]

Subsequently, a representative of the staff union pointed out to the ILO Governing Body that the percentage of professional women was only 17.7, alleging that the fault lay with the lack of staff training—only two-tenths of 1 percent compared to a recommended level of 2 percent. Finally, the administration took a few measures, albeit with seeming reluctance. In 1989, it adopted a policy allowing P-1 to P-3 posts to be filled by qualified female candidates without competition. The Director-General also appointed a woman as Deputy Director-General (the first in the UN system) in charge of the $125 million technical cooperation program. She was Mary Chinery-Hesse from Ghana who had risen to be a principal secretary in her government's Ministry of Finance and Economic Planning. Despite supportive attitudes by most managers, there were, as of 31 December 1993, only two women D-2s (twenty men) and seven D-1s (sixty-one men). In 1993, an informal gathering in honor of the women participants at the International Labor Conference was convened by Ms. Chinery-Hesse. Discussions focused on the need for positive action measures, including temporary quotas, training, support measures, and child care facilities. The need was felt to continue sensitizing the ILO's constituents on the importance of women's participation in ILO meetings and activities.[28]

The FAO Conference was slow to express itself but its unease at the position of women staff members finally became manifest in 1987. It asked the Director-General to include in the Plan of Action a staff training program on how to integrate women in development issues. Two years later, it recommended full integration of women in the work of the staff relating to development concerns. It declared that the "highest priority" was to be given to training FAO staff on women in development and to the increased access of women to professional posts in FAO in order to reach the UN target.[29] Unlike the other agencies, FAO never established a target for the employment of professional women or a "focal point" to stimulate attention to women. Instead, it created an Inter-Divisional Working Group on Women in Development, a cumbersome institutional device too dilute to have any real impact. One inhibiting factor on staff pressure in FAO is that, unlike other agencies, there are three staff unions—one for professionals, one for field staff, and one for general services. Such a tripartite arrangement tends to splinter staff and make collective action virtually impossible. Moreover, FAO had no independent and active woman's group.

The cavalier attitude of the Director-General seemed to change in response to pressures from women's organizations and female members of FAO delegations. In his 1990 report he announced the establishment of a "comprehensive training programme" for staff on women in development designed to create an awareness and sensitivity to gender issues and to provide FAO staff with the skills and tools required to include women in the design, implementation, monitoring and evaluation of programs and projects. An FAO brochure on the Plan of Action concluded that what had been transpiring "signals a unique time in the history of FAO where there is greater understanding and willingness to make changes."[30] By 1992, the organization had three women D-1s and 1 D-2, some evidence of improvement.

One of the earliest governmental calls for action regarding women staff members in the agencies had come from the German member of the Unesco Board, Mme. Schlueter-Hermkes. In 1957, she introduced a resolution, subsequently adopted, stating that the proportion of women in the professional category was very small, particularly at the upper levels, and that the disparity between men and women had been increasing. Therefore, with due respect for geographic representation, preference should be given to female candidates until adequate representation had been achieved. When this resolution was introduced there was no woman above a P-5 and only one at that level.[31]

The Unesco administration also showed a considerable lack of enthusiasm for questions relating to women staff members. In 1984, the Director-General appointed a mediator to report directly to him any case of discrimination or sexual harassment. A coordinating unit for activities relating to the status of women was also established within the Bureau of Studies and Programming. It consisted of one professional and one "associate expert." Four years later, a coordinator for programs relating to women's issues was named and in the Personnel Department an internal committee on improving the status of women was set up.

An experimental program for the years 1986–1987 was developed with funds provided jointly with the government of Norway (many of the innovative programs for women receive funds from governments). It was designed to raise consciousness regarding the status of women in the organization. Seminars were held on women in development within the context of orientation courses for new staff members to sensitize them to the problems of women. However, as of 1991, none of these courses had been opened by the Director-General which would have given them standing and been evidence that he was serious when he declared that the organization was "duty bound to put more resolutely into practice the principle of equality between men and women of its Secretariat." One 1990 action gave some indication of the possibility of better things to come. The Director-General announced the creation, on an experimental basis for one year, of an ad hoc working group on equal opportunities for women in Unesco's Secretariat.[32] The most positive initiative and leadership was unquestionably provided by WHO. In 1974, the Director-General created the office of Ombudsman and the following year the post of Program Manager for Staff Development. While neither of these steps targeted women especially, they showed a concern for staff that included women. Other measures soon followed that were directed specifically at women.

In 1983, the Director-General appointed a former chairman of the board, Dr. Maureen Law, to "review the recruitment of professional women into the Organization and to make recommendations as to how the Organization might effectively increase the number of women recruited." An eleven-member ad hoc working group on the employment of women was set up as a steering committee consisting of representatives of senior management, personnel, and two governments. The Law report recommended, inter alia, that managers be given greater flexibility to hire women from certain overrepresented countries until a 30 percent target had been achieved; that exceptions be made to the geographic representation provision for three years, if this seemed to be achieving the objective of recruiting more women; and that there be established a period of perhaps two years during which managers might receive reimbursement of part, perhaps half, of the cost of employing women as consultants or temporary advisors.[33]

The International Civil Service Commission, in 1986, called a memorandum from the director-general of WHO, addressed to all directors and program managers, "an excellent example of commitment from the top."[34] The memorandum requested information on a regular basis on the attendance of women in the work of expert panels, steering committees, consultations, and other technical groups on reporting forms provided. It also requested that managers be given flexibility in recruiting women into geographically counted posts and that women be given priority over men. As of 1992, WHO topped the list of specialized agencies with four D-2s (9 percent) and nine D-1s (7 percent).

The World Bank Group Staff Association, established in 1972, had been vigorously espousing the cause of equal employment for women and men since its inception. While there had been progress—25 percent of higher-level staff were women by 1988—it had been uneven and disappointing. In a December 1989 report, the Staff Association declared that "long-standing and powerful attitudes and actions militate against women holding management and other senior positions in the Bank." On the bottom rung of the professional staff—young professionals and research assistants—was clustered 62 percent of the female staff. At the key professional level this dropped to 26 percent, and at the division head and senior advisor level it fell to 5 percent.

The report highlighted the critical influence of management. The one area in which women were relatively well represented was in finance—9 percent at the senior or director level and 25 percent at the level of division chief. This was attributed to the "active approach by the Finance Complex to attract competent women." It was also pointed out that the Finance Complex had "more measurable results by which to judge performance—leaving less room for subjective criteria."

One roadblock identified by the report was caused by the networks that "played a major role in excluding women from the development and selection process for managers." Networks gave premiums to common heritage, schooling, experience. Much informal networking occurred over lunch or drinks, from which women were excluded because of the danger of speculation about a liaison, if a man asked a female staff member to lunch or for a drink.[35]

To improve the situation, the report made a series of recommendations that included appointment of the first female department director in operations, early identification of women with high potential to be given growth opportunities, a mission leadership role for women as well as authority to substitute for absent bosses, openings to women at the grade just below division chief of the divisional managers development program, incentives to managers to recruit women, expansion of the part-time employment policy to meet the demands of parenting, and lessened reluctance to send women into the field. "Even in those countries where local women have difficulties, Bank female staff can be effective since they are seen as a 'third' gender."

The response of top management is an indication of the effectiveness of a strong staff association, especially when coupled with an administration prepared to listen sympathetically. When the recommendations came to the World Bank's president's attention, he and his senior staff quickly initiated a twelve-point action program.

Subsequently, two women were included in all selection panels. Most personnel officers had prepared lists and profiles of upper-level women to assess career development programs and advancement prospects. Personnel's Recruitment Division established an advisory group to help identify strong women candidates for key professional posts and above. Increased attention was being given to gender issues in management training courses.[36] Nevertheless, in 1991, the Staff Association declared that a number of key issues were still unresolved and called for "fundamental changes" in some areas and "further study and definition" in others.[37]

REFLECTIONS

The Decade for Women had a major impact, but its effect was slow in coming. Although equality is still on the far horizon, the percentage of professional women has risen in both the agencies and the World Bank. Most were, as of 1994, at least aspiring to the 35 percent figure that the UN had established for itself. While few women reached positions of real influence, the appointment in ILO of Chinery-Hesse as deputy director-general was a welcome sign. With the exception of WHO, however, it must be admitted that most of the administrations have excelled in foot-dragging. This is not entirely their fault. The key problem lies with the governments. While they have repeatedly uttered the most commendable statements and urged the organizations to hire more women in higher posts, their actions have seldom reflected these statements. Calls to governments to propose more women candidates seem to fall on deaf ears. At a meeting of WHO's executive board in 1990, there was the usual demand that the Director-General do more for the cause of women. When he looked around the table at the thirteen government representatives, he saw only men.

NOTES

1. The other specialized agencies, considerably smaller in size, are International Civil Aviation Organization, International Maritime Organization, International Telecommunication Union, United Nations Industrial Development Organization, Universal Postal Union, World Intellectual Property Organization, World Meteorological Organization, and the International Atomic Agency.

2. Cited by Dinah Shelton in VII *Revue des Droits de L'Homme* 51 (1975): 62.

3. Unesco, *The Status of Women: Annotated Bibliography* (Paris: Unesco, 1991).

4. Carol Riegelman Lubin and Anne Winslow, *Social Justice for Women: The International Labor Organization and Women* (Durham, N.C.: Duke University Press, 1990), 48.

5. For a discussion of women's programs prior to Mexico City, see UN Institute for Training and Research (UNITAR), Fadia Nasr, and Marcel Nguema-Mba, *Women and Development: The Role of the United Nations System*, Mexico, 16–18 June 1975.

6. WHO, Executive Board, Verbatim Records, EB 87/22 (1990), par. 1.

7. World Bank, *The Integration of Women into the Development Process* (Washington, D.C.: International Bank for Reconstruction and Development, 1975), 1.

8. For this and subsequent UNDP references, see UN, *UNDP Women in Development: Project Achievement Reports* (1989).

9. Cited in Lubin and Winslow, *Social Justice for Women*, 131.

10. Informal Gathering in Honor of the Women Participants at the International Labor Conference, 80th Session, ILO 80/WP.1 (1993), 5.

11. For an analysis of the Nordic countries' efforts to promote the advancement of women in the UN system, see Study Commissioned by the Nordic UN Project, *The Role of the Nordic Countries to Promote Efforts by the UN System for the Advancement of Women*, Report No. 16, 1990.

12. A "Visiting Minister" is a minister of government or equivalent who may, and usually does, participate in the Plenary Debate of the Conference but who is not a member of the delegation and does not vote.

13. UN, *World Conference of the International Women's Year*, E/CONF. 66/BP/11, (24 March 1975), 17.

14. UN, Doc. E/1989/16 (15 March 1989), par. 135; see also ibid., pars. 28, 55, 64, 76.

15. Katrine A. Saito and C. Jean Weidemann, *Agricultural Extension for Women Farmers in Africa*, World Bank Discussion Papers, No. 103 (October 1990), 16.

16. Patrick McCully, "FAO and Fisheries Development," *The Ecologist* 21, no. 2 (March–April 1991), 77–80.

17. Kathleen Barry and Barbara Good, Coordinators, *Protecting Women's Human Rights from Sexual Exploitation, Violence and Prostitution: An International Meeting of Experts*. Pennsylvania State University, University Park, Pennsylvania, and Capitol Hill, Washington, D.C., 8–10 April 1991 and 11 April 1991. See also Unesco, International Meeting of Experts on the Social and Cultural Causes of Prostitution and Strategies for the Struggle against Procuring and Sexual Exploitation of Women, Madrid, Spain, 18–21 March 1986.

18. Unesco, CAB-94/CONF. 001/2, Paris, 19 April 1994.

19. WHO, Executive Board 87/22, 6 December 1990.

20. World Health Assembly, 38.27, May 1985.

21. World Bank, *Women in Development: A Progress Report on the World Bank Initiative* (Washington, D.C.: World Bank, 1990).

22. On 6 September 1994, some thirty-five well-known NGOs announced the creation of "The 50 Years Is Enough Campaign." The group maintained that the World Bank and the International Monetary Fund had "been promoting and financing inequitable and unstainable development that has created poverty while destroying the environment." They were also charged with "profoundly undemocratic" procedures, having "consistently denied citizens information about, and involvement in, major decisions affecting their respective societies" (Washington, D.C., mimeographed).

23. Directives concerning Unesco's relations with international nongovernmental organizations, 1966.

24. World Federation of Unesco Clubs, Centres, and so forth; World Council of Churches; International Federation for Parent Education; Associated Countrywomen of the World; International Council of Women (two projects); International Federation of University Women; World Conference of Organizations of the Teaching Profession; United Schools International; Mediterranean Women's Studies.

25. World Bank, *Kenya: The Role of Women in Economic Development* (Washington, D.C.: World Bank 1989), 79.

26. For a comparative table of the status of women in the UN and the specialized agencies, see Table 10.1, p.175.
27. Cited in Lubin and Winslow, *Social Justice for Women*, 223.
28. Informal Gathering in Honor of Women Participants, ILO 80/WP.1 (1993), 2.
29. FAO, *Report of the Twenty-Sixth Session of the Conference*, Resolution No. 7/89 and Annex D6, 1989.
30. FAO, *Women in Agricultural Development: FAO's Plan of Action* (Rome: FAO, 1990), 41. As of 1992, there was 1 D-2 (2 percent) and 3 D-1s (also 2 percent).
31. Unesco, Executive Board EX/37 (1957), 17–18.
32. Ibid., Administrative Circular No. 1757, 1990.
33. Maureen Law, *Report Presented to the Director-General of the World Health Organization*, Geneva, 1985.
34. International Civil Service Commission, *Recruitment Policy: Report on Progress Made Since the Twenty-second Session in Undertaking Special Measures for the Recruitment of Women*, ICSC/24/R.13, (June 1986), 5.
35. World Bank Group Staff Association, *Technical Report: Report on Status of Higher-Level Women in the World Bank Group* (1989), Chairman's Introduction, 2, 7; Annex 2, 2.
36. The ad hoc task force issued a report that reviewed developments during 1990 and made recommendations for further action. See World Bank Group Staff Association, *Report of the Ad Hoc Task Force on the Status of Women in Professional and Higher Categories*, October 1990, Mimeo.
37. World Bank Group Staff Association, Bulletin, 5 March 1991.

Table 10.1
Grade Distribution by Sex at Headquarters and Other Established Offices as at 31 December 1992, Showing Female Staff as a Percentage of the Total in Each Grade

	P1				P2				P3				P4				P5				D1				D2				Ungraded		
	M	F	M+F	%	M	F	M+F	%	M	F	M+F	%	M	F	M+F	%	M	F	M+F	%	M	F	M+F	%	M	F	M+F	%	M	F	M+F	%
UN	19	43	62	69	306	253	559	45	717	414	1131	37	767	361	1128	32	544	149	693	22	247	31	278	11	90	12	102	12	48	1	49	2
UNDP	51	44	95	46	145	144	289	50	139	123	262	47	190	90	280	32	241	73	314	23	139	13	152	9	62	7	69	10	10	2	12	17
UNHCR	8	22	30	73	39	70	109	64	72	29	101	29	107	33	140	24	73	15	88	17	26	2	28	7	11		11		1	1	2	50
UNICEF	3	5	8	63	20	32	52	62	43	44	87	51	59	53	112	47	59	28	87	32	29	6	35	17	9	1	10	10	3	1	4	25
UNITAR					5	2	7	29					1	1	2	50	1		1		2		2									
UNRWA					7	8	15	53	30	8	38	21	48	3	51	6	22	1	23	4	7	2	9	22	3		3		2		2	
ITC					2	4	6	67	7	5	12	42	22	6	28	21	16	1	17	6	3		3		1		1					
ICSC					2	3	5	60	1		1		4	3	7	43	2		2		3	1	3	33	1		1					
ICJ					4	4	4	100	4		4		5	1	6	17					1		1		1		1		1	1		
UNU					2	2	2	100	2	1	3	33	4		4		7		7		4		4		1		1		2		2	
ILO	5	2	7	29	15	17	32	53	85	64	149	43	147	69	216	32	194	16	210	8	49	7	56	13	20	2	22	9	11	1	12	8
ICAT					4	3	7	43	10	9	19	47	16	3	19	16	8		8		1		1		1		1					
FAO					85	69	154	45	148	90	238	38	355	65	420	15	318	25	343	7	151	3	154	2	52	1	53	2	14		14	
WFP					6	8	14	57	35	14	49	29	34	9	43	21	27	3	30	10	16	2	18	11	6		6		1	1	2	50
UNESCO	15	10	25	40	62	68	130	52	98	85	183	46	176	60	236	25	212	31	243	13	58	9	67	13	21	1	22	5	10	1	11	9
WHO	3	6	9	67	34	28	62	45	88	80	168	48	169	81	250	32	365	68	433	16	121	9	130	7	42	4	46	9	14		14	
PAHO	6	8	14	57	12	11	23	48	10	20	30	67	22	13	35	37	68	8	76	11	4	1	5	20	2		2		2		2	
ICAO	3		3		16	22	38	58	51	19	70	27	108	13	121	11	49	6	55	11	17		17		4		4		2		2	
UPU	1		1		4		4		24	10	34	29	22	4	26	15	9		9		6		6		3		3		2		2	
ITU					11	6	17	35	45	16	61	26	79	13	92	14	74	2	76	3	23	1	24	4					9		9	
WMO		1	1	100	2		2		4	11	15	73	42	14	56	25	41	2	43	5	7		7		9	1	10	10	3		3	
IMO					6	5	11	45	7	7	14	50	20	13	33	39	29	1	30	3	10	1	11	9	6		6		1		1	
WIPO					4	5	9	56	20	10	30	33	32	12	44	27	25	2	27	7	18	1	19	5	5		5		4		4	
IFAD		1	1	100	6	4	10	40	7	12	19	63	26	4	30	13	36	5	41	12	4	1	5	20	8		8		3		3	
UNIDO					18	16	34	47	59	31	90	34	103	37	140	26	86	9	95	9	29		29		4	1	5	20	6		6	
IAEA	5		5		33	20	53	38	150	45	195	23	209	20	229	9	165	11	176	6	25	3	28	11	8		8		5		5	
GATT					3	6	9	67	30	18	48	38	32	19	51	37	26	10	36	28	14		14		7		7		3		3	
Totals	119	142	261	54	845	810	1655	49	1886	1165	3051	38	2799	1000	3799	26	2697	466	3163	15	1013	93	1106	8	376	30	406	7	157	8	165	5

Report of the United Nations Secretary-General.

11
Conclusion

At least it can be said that the "invisible" woman is no longer invisible. It did not happen quickly. A female representative taking her place at the League of Nations Political Committee was politely asked if she had lost her way. Some thirty years later, the UN Secretary-General, Dag Hammarskjold, declared that women's emancipation had not progressed far enough to find women qualified for UN jobs. Equality there is not even today, either in the developed or the developing world, but changes have taken place, faster in certain areas than in others.

The origins of the current stage for women's equality can be traced back, in Europe and the United States, to the eighteenth century. In 1792, Mary Wollstonecraft published a book entitled *Vindication of the Rights of Women*, a feminist declaration of independence and assertion for her own sex of the doctrine of inalienable human rights, a thesis that is still relevant today. In the next century, individual women joined together to create local and national societies to press for women's suffrage, the adoption of temperance, and other social measures. This was soon followed by a series of conferences and the creation of international organizations—an International Women's Rights Conference; the Women's Christian Temperance Union (with the motto, "Do everything"); the World Young Women's Christian Association, the International Council of

Women, led by U.S. suffrage leaders Elizabeth Cady Stanton and Susan B. Anthony; and a number of other organizations.

Meetings of the Pan American Union, early in the twentieth century, gave women the opportunity to be initiated in broad political arenas and to learn the arts of negotiation.

The advent of the League of Nations (LN) began to widen the canvas to include women in other parts of the world, women from many countries with widely varied interests. It gave them not only an institutional focus but entrée to a platform on which all the political, economic, and social concerns were aired. Even during the LN's organizational phase, women's delegations had been formed by the International Alliance for Women and others to lobby for women's rights. Although many of their requests were ignored, they did manage to get into the LN's Covenant an article opening all positions in the League, including the Secretariat, equally to men and women.

The creation of the United Nations (UN) in the 1940s and its historic assertion of the "equal rights of men and women" brought new opportunities. It extended and reenforced the LN's provision regarding women. "The United Nations shall place no restrictions on the eligibility of men and women to participate in any capacity and under conditions of equality in its principal and subsidiary organs" (Article 8). It provided for a formal relationship between the UN and nongovernmental organizations (NGOs)—which included many women—and gave formal recognition to human rights by creating a statutory commission. It gave women constitutional legal leverage. The UN also provided new impetus for achieving women's rights and an enormous broadening of the geographic scope of its activities.

The creation of the UN Commission on Human Rights served as a springboard for a more specific approach to women's rights. Under pressure from women delegates and NGOs, a subcommission on the status of women was established in 1946 and gained full commission status a few months later. It promptly asserted that its function was to promote women's rights in political, economic, civil, social, and educational fields—an assertion that covered the waterfront.

The Commission on the Status of Women became the focus of women's activities in the UN. Through its network of related NGOs, UN decisions have been broadcast to NGO members throughout the world. It has monitored actions by the official intergovernmental bodies and has inspired studies, conferences, and conventions, including the UN Decade for Women and four women's conferences. Symptomatic of the new global outreach are the locations of these conferences—Mexico City (1975), Nairobi (1985), Beijing (1995) as well as in Europe, Copenhagen (1980).

Through the pressure of women, both inside and outside the UN, women have become an integral part of the organization's agenda. Conventions relating to them have dealt with political, educational, employment, and marital rights. Women have also been partners and activists in general fields, such as environment, population, human rights, food, and, more recently, economic and social development, the World Conference on Human Rights (1993), the Conference on Population and Development in Cairo (1994), and the World Summit on Social Development in Copenhagen (1995).

The Commission on the Status of Women also turned its attention to the UN Secretariat where, despite Charter provisions on equality, most women served in clerical jobs and where there was a glass ceiling between professional women and the top jobs. Despite the dual requirement of equitable geographical representation, on the one hand, and of efficiency, competence, and integrity, on the other, the balance always seemed to tip in favor of the former. There was only a limited supply of trained women from developing countries with unfilled quotas and those from the West were barred because of full quotas. Pension regulations were also highly discriminatory. Women were explicitly treated as "not being men" and, therefore, not eligible for the same benefits as men.

In 1949, in response to U.S. pressure, the first study of the position of women in the Secretariat was undertaken. Out of a total of 1,678 women, only 393 held professional jobs (23.4 percent). Under unrelenting pressure from the Commission on the Status of Women, the percentage of professional women had risen to 31.3 by 1993 and some of the inequities in the personnel regulations had been removed. Women were, and still are, found mostly at entry levels, with few in senior management. The 1995 target set by the General Assembly was for an increase to 35 percent.

One of the most notable achievements of the Commission on the Status of Women was the Convention on the Elimination of All Forms of Discrimination Against Women adopted at the 1980 World Conference in Copenhagen. Women exercised authority—signing the treaty—traditionally reserved for men.

By their patience and skill in steering the draft through the political shoals, women demonstrated their ability as consummate politicians and as feminists. To gain their equality, women had achieved an international legal instrument challenging thousands of years of tradition and custom that had subordinated them to men.

The women's conferences brought thousands of women face to face with each other. Women became acutely aware of the diversity of interests and conditions of people brought up under different political systems, religions, cultures, and economies. In the process, women became sensitized to needs and objectives other than their own. In order to achieve their targets, they had to learn to accommodate and compromise. Without a vote, the delegations in Mexico City managed to adopt the first comprehensive global policy on the status of women.

The Nairobi Conference, ten years later, continued the process, honing still further the diplomatic skills and perseverance of women. At that time, they had set their sights on the future and had adopted a program for the years ahead— Nairobi Forward-looking Strategies for the Advancement of Women. It integrated issues on the basis of gender: the participation of women in development and the recognition that current development strategies were being carried out at the expense of the poor—and, thus, of women; a notable recognition that women's rights were a matter of global concern. The Forward-looking Strategies also asserted the right of women to control the fate of their own bodies and mitigated some feminist objections to an aggressive population policy that was seen as an effort of Westerners to limit the population growth in developing countries. The compromise was to link population policy and women—a linkage reiterated at the 1994 Cairo International Conference on Population and Development.

The 1980 conference at Copenhagen had tested the strength and unity of the international women's movement and its ability to accommodate differences. It landed women squarely in the middle of political dissension—by Israel and the United States on the one hand, and on the other, the Arab states and the developing countries' demands for the reduction of international economic inequalities. Many felt that involving women in such political issues weakened their cause. Others considered that politicization served the cause. Views on both sides were changed by debates over the need for economic equity versus feminist perspectives on why women were oppressed and what should be done about it. Western women came to understand better the economic restraints that severely limited opportunities and options for women in the developing countries, and they in turn became more aware of the relevance of the feminist point of view.

The independence of fifty formerly dependent countries in the 1950s and 1960s and their membership in the UN brought attention to the forefront to the effect of economic issues on women. It provided the impetus for women to debate the nature of their participation in their new nations. This became the conceptual basis for the women and development movement. The All Africa Women's Conference was created in 1962, followed by a series of national and East African women's seminars. At the same time, Betty Friedan's book, *The Feminine Mystique* revitalized the Western women's movement.

The UN became the principal advocate and guardian of the women and development movement. Early in the 1970s, the UN Economic Commission for Africa created a Woman's Programme, after seeking the advice of women. The first global meeting on women and development took place in 1972 at UN headquarters: an Expert Group on the Integration of Women in Development under the chairmanship of Sir Arthur Lewis with a working document prepared by Ester Boserup.

An increasingly important factor in the drive for justice for women are the NGOs, many of whose members are women. As the budget strings tighten, there is growing reliance on the contribution of NGOs in carrying out UN programs. Their importance for achieving economic development and an equitable world order was highlighted in the 1994 Programme of Action of the UN International Conference on Population and Development. NGOs, are, in the words of the Programme, "already rightly recognized for their comparative advantage in relation to government agencies, because of innovative, flexible and responsive

Conclusion 181

program design and implementation, including grassroots participation, and because quite often they are rooted in and interact with constituencies that are poorly served and hard to reach through government channels.''

While the NGOs have strengthened the UN, they have also been strengthened by it. The UN gave the NGOs new contacts and outreach and stimulated the creation of additional projects, often in new fields such as credit for women. It also led to an increasing realization of the need for collective action and a collective voice, if women were to achieve full citizenship. In each of the women's conferences, the NGOs organized a "forum" or "tribune" to discuss, coordinate, and express their views on the conference agendas. Following the Mexico Conference, a permanent Tribune was established to respond to requests for information and to develop communications methods and educational materials for women and men throughout the world.

The struggle for women's equality has also been waged in that cluster of bodies affiliated with the UN which deal with such areas as food, health, and labor. Women's equality as a subject of concern has been slow to percolate their consciousness. The last to entertain the idea was the World Bank (affiliated with the UN but not a Specialized Agency), which was happily oblivious of it for a quarter of a century. Since each of these institutions deals with a limited area and there are fewer women following the deliberations it is not subject to the same broad pressures as the UN. The relative success attained by women has been partly determined by whether or not the institution's headquarters is located in a city with a large cluster of NGOs. Another critical feature is the attitude of the Director-General. Because the institutions are relatively isolated from public view, the Director-General's power is almost absolute.

Despite the torrent of words, official and unofficial, uttered on behalf of women, the customs of centuries are not washed out. Even when the will exists—and it often doesn't—the structure of society still creates a straitjacket for women. Bureaucracies have been created by men and are still run by men. Working women still carry a quadruple burden—as workers, mothers, homemakers, and wives. One of the few senior women officials in the UN had felt it necessary in 1979 to advise women who wanted a successful career to delay marriage until they had established themselves.

Other key problems for women are to meld more effectively the rival concerns of developed and developing countries and to integrate politics and women's rights. Their achievement depends upon a new commitment from senior managers to hire and promote more women and from member states that must be willing to propose qualified women to fill their national quotas. States will also have to allow affirmative action to override strict adherence to geographic representation. Women will have to maintain constant pressure to achieve the critical mass adequate to induce change. This, in turn, requires a strong, well-financed power center at the UN where women can and will make demands commensurate with their needs.

Although a beginning has been made, resources are minuscule. It has been suggested, as a start, that the two UN agencies dedicated to women—the International Research and Training Institute for the Advancement of Women (INSTRAW) and the UN Development Fund for Women (UNIFEM)—need, as a start, $400 million a year to be commensurate for the tasks to be performed. Such support should become a priority.

As women's groups become more strategic in using the UN as a forum to air their demands, the organization must respond by recognizing their influence and their power as a constituency to be reckoned with. Women's political agenda has already left its mark on the UN and promises to do even more in the future. Recent UN conferences have devoted much attention to the specific requirements for women's empowerment.

The spectacular success of women's organizations over the last twenty years is threatened by global uncertainties. At the same time, women's movements have acquired more complex and more political agendas—more complex and more demanding than in the past. As it tries to shape the future, it will need all the resources it can command—both material and diplomatic.

APPENDIXES

APPENDIX I
WOMEN'S RIGHT TO VOTE BY COUNTRY AND DATE

Country	Date	Country	Date
Afghanistan	1965	Dominican Republic	1942
Albania	1945		
Algeria	1962	Equador	1946
Andorra	**	Egypt	1956
Angola	1975	El Salvador	1961
Antigua and Barbuda	1951	Equatorial Guinea	1963
Argentina	1947	Eritrea	**
Armenia	1921	Estonia	1920
Australia	1901	Ethiopia	1994
Austria	1918		
Azerbaidjan	1921	Fiji	1970
		Finland	1906
Bahamas	1962	France	1944
Bangladesh	1947		
Barbados	1951	Gabon	1956
Belarus	1919	Gambia	1960
Belgium	1918	Georgia	1918
Belize	1945	Germany	1919
Benin	1956	Ghana	1941/1957
Bhutan	1953	Greece	1952
Bolivia	1938	Grenada	1951
Bosnia/Herzegovinia	1949	Guatemala	1945
Botswana	1965	Guinea-Bissau	1977
Brazil	1934	Guyana	1953
Bulgaria	1944		
Burkina Faso	1960	Haiti	1950
Burundi	1961	Honduras	1957
		Hungary	1945
Cambodia	**		
Cameroon	1964	Iceland	1915
Canada	1917	India	1950
Cape Verde	1975	Indonesia	1945
Central African Rep.	1986	Iran	1963
Chad	**	Iraq	1980
Chile	1931	Ireland	1918
China	1949	Israel	1948
Colombia	1957	Italy	1945
Comoros	1956		
Congo	1963	Jamaica	1944
Costa Rica	1949	Japan	1945
Cote D'Ivoire	1952	Jordan	1974
Croatia	1949		
Cuba	1934	Kazakhstan	1924
Cyprus	1960	Kenya	1963
Czech Republic	1920	Kiribati	1971
		Kuwait	*
Dem.Rep. Korea	1946	Kyrghyzstan	**
Denmark	1915		
Djibouti	1946	Laos	1958
Dominica	1951	Latvia	1918

Source: Inter-Parliamentary Union (IPU), *Distribution of Seats Between Men and Women in National Parliaments, 1945–1991* (Geneva: IPU, 1991), 1–17. *Distribution of Seats . . . as of June 30, 1994* (Geneva: IPU, 1994), 1–13. UN, *The World's Women Trends and Statistics 1970–1990* (New York: UN, 1991). Telephone communications with IPU and with embassies and UN missions, 27 September 1994.

* Women do not have the right to vote.
**Date not communicated to IPU, but voting rights exist and women serve in Parliament.

Lebanon	1926	Saint Kitts and Nevis	1951
Lesotho	1965	Saint Lucia	1951
Liberia	1949	Saint Vincent and Grenadines	**
Libya	1964	San Marino	1960
Liechtenstein	1984	Sao Tome and Principe	1975
Lithuania	1921	Senegal	1945
Luxembourg	1919	Serbia & Montenegro	1949
		Seychelles	1948
Madagascar	1959	Sierra Leone	1951
Malawi	1964	Singapore	1948
Malaysia	1957	Slovak Republic	1920
Maldives	1932	Slovenia	1945
Mali	1956	Solomon Islands	1945
Malta	1947	South Africa	1930/1984/1994
Marshall Islands	1944/1986	Spain	1931
Mauritania	1961	Sri Lanka	1931
Mauritius	1956	Sudan	1953
Mexico	1947	Surinam	1953
Micronesia,Fed.	1979	Swaziland	1968
Moldova	1978/1993	Sweden	1918/1921
Monaco	1962	Switzerland	1971
Mongolia	1923	Syria	1949
Morocco	1963		
Mozambique	1975	Tajikistan	**
		Thailand	1932
Namibia	1989	Togo	1956
Nauru	1968	Tonga	1960
Nepal	1951	Trinidad and Tobago	1945
Netherlands	1919	Tunisia	1959
New Zealand	1893	Turkey	1930/1934
Nicaragua	1955	Turkmenistan	**
Niger	1948	Tuvalu	**
Norway	1907/1913		
		Uganda	1962
Pakistan	1937	Ukraine	1919
Panama	1941	United Arab Emir.	not yet
Papua New Guinea	1975	United Kingdom	1918/1928
Paraguay	1961	United Rep.Tanzania	1959
Peru	1950	USA	1920
Philippines	1937	Uruguay	1932
Poland	1918	Uzbekistan	**
Portugal	1931/1976		
		Vanuatu	1980
Rep. of Korea	1948	Venezuela	1980
Rep. of Macedonia	1946	Viet Nam	1946
Romania	1946	Western Samoa	1990
Russian Fed.	1918	Yemen	1967/1970
Rwanda	1961	Zaire	1967
		Zambia	1962
		Zimbabwe	1957

APPENDIX II
PRIORITY THEMES FOR THE PERIOD 1992–1996*

A. EQUALITY

1992:	Elimination of de jure and de facto discrimination against women
1993:	Increased awareness by women of their rights, including legal literacy
1994:	Equal pay for work of equal value, including methodologies for measurement of pay inequities and work in the informal sector
1995:	Equality in economic decision making
1996:	Elimination of stereotyping of women in the mass media

B. DEVELOPMENT

1992:	Women and the environment
1993:	Women in extreme poverty: integration of women's concerns in national development planning
1994:	Women in urban areas: population, nutrition, and health factors for women in development, including migration, drug consumption, and AIDS
1995:	Promotion of literacy, education, and training, including technological skill
1996:	Child and dependent care, including sharing of work and family responsibilities

C. PEACE

1992:	Equal participation of women in all efforts to promote international cooperation, peace, and disarmament
1993:	Women and the peace process
1994:	Measures to eradicate violence against women in the family and society
1995:	Women in international decision making
1996:	Education for peace

*Source: CSW, *1990 Report*, 32; CSW, *1992 Report*, 92.

Selected Bibliography

I. BOOKS AND PERIODICALS

Aburdene, Patricia and John Naisbitt. *Megatrends for Women.* New York: Villard Books, 1992.

Abzug, Bella, with Mim Kelber. *Gender Gap: Bella Abzug's Guide to Political Power for American Women.* Boston: Houghton Mifflin, 1984.

Applewhite, Harriet B., and Darlene G. Levy, eds. *Women and Politics in the Age of Democratic Revolutions.* Ann Arbor: University of Michigan Press, 1990.

Asher, Robert E., et al. *The United Nations and the Promotion of the General Welfare.* Washington, D.C.: Brookings Institution, 1957.

Ashworth, Georgina. "The United Nations Women's Conference and International Linkages in the Women's Movement." In *Pressure Groups in the Global System*, edited by Peter Willetts, 125–35. New York: St. Martin's Press, 1952.

Barrow, Nita. "The NGO Decade Forum." *Africa Report* 30, no. 2 (The African-American Institute) (March–April 1985): 9–12.

Barry, Kathleen. *Female Sexual Slavery.* New York: New York University Press, 1979.

Batho, Edith. *A Lamp of Friendship.* Washington, D.C.: American Association of University Women, n.d.

Beckman, Peter, and Francine D'Amico, eds. *Women, Gender, and World Politics.* Westport, Conn.: Bergin & Garvey, 1994.

Bennett, A. LeRoy. *International Organizations: Principles and Issues.* Englewood Cliffs, N.J.: Prentice-Hall, 1988.

Bernard, Jessie. *The Female World from a Global Perspective*. Bloomington: Indiana University Press, 1987.
Blocker, Jack S., Jr. "Separate Paths: Suffragist and Women's Temperance Crusade." *Signs* 11, no. 1 (Spring 1985): 460–76.
Boals, Kay. "Feminism and Political Science." *Signs* 1, no. 1 (1975): 161–74.
Boserup, Ester. *Women and Economic Development*. New York: St. Martin's Press, 1970.
Boulding, Elise. *The Underside of History*. Boulder, Colo.: Westview Press, 1976.
Boulding, Elise. *Women in the Twentieth Century World*. New York: John Wiley, 1977.
Boyd, Nancy. *Emissaries: The Overseas Work of the American YWCA, 1895–1970*. New York: Woman's Press, 1986.
Bridenthal, Renate, Claudia Koontz, and Susan Stuard, eds. *Becoming Visible*. Boston: Houghton Mifflin, 1987.
Bruce, Margaret K. "An Account of United Nations Action to Advance the Status of Women." *Annals of the American Academy of Political and Social Science* 375 (January 1968): 163–75.
Buchanan, Mary E. T., ed. *World Directory of Women's Organizations*. London: Vail & Co., 1953.
Byrnes, Andrew. "The Other Human Rights Body: The Work of the Committee on the Elimination of Discrimination Against Women." *Yale Journal of International Law* 14 (Winter 1989): 1–67.
Cagatay, Nilufer, Caren Grown, and Aida Santiago. "The Nairobi Women's Conference: Toward a Global Feminism?" *Feminist Studies* 12, no. 2 (Summer 1986): 402–12.
Chafe, William H. *Paradox of Change: American Women in the Twentieth Century*. New York: Oxford University Press, 1991.
Chambers, Robert. *Rural Development: Putting the Last First*. London: Longmans, 1983.
Charlesworth, Hilary, Christine Chenken, and Shelly Wright. "Feminist Approaches to International Law." *American Journal of International Law* 85, no. 4 (October 1991): 613–45.
Charlton, Ellen M., Jana Everett, and Kathleen Staudt. *Women, the State and Development*. Albany: State University of New York Press, 1989.
Cook, Rebecca. "International Human Rights Concerning Women: Case Notes and Comments." *Vanderbilt Journal of Transnational Law* 23 (1990): 779–818.
Cook, Rebecca. "Reservations to the Convention on the Elimination of All Forms of Discrimination Against Women." *Virginia Journal of International Law* 30 (1990): 643–709.
Cornia, Giovanni A., et al., eds. *Adjustment with a Human Face: Protecting the Vulnerable and Promoting Growth*. Oxford: Clarendon Press, 1987.
"Dakar Declaration on Another Development with Women." *Development Dialogue* 1, no. 2 (1982).
De Chungara, Domitila Barrios. *Let Me Speak! Testimony of Domitila, a Woman of the Bolivian Mines*. New York: Monthly Review Press, 1978.
De Hedervary, Claire. "Good Grief, There Are Women Here!" In *The Sisterhood is Global*, edited by Robin Morgan, 692–95. Garden City, N.Y.: Anchor Books, 1984.
Divine, Robert. *Second Chance*. New York: Atheneum, 1967.
Dixon-Mueller, Ruth. *Population Policy and Women's Rights*. Westport, Conn.: Praeger, 1993.
Donnelly, Jack. "Human Rights at the United Nations, 1955–1988: The Question of Bias." *International Studies Quarterly* 32 (1988): 275–303.

Duverger, Maurice. *The Political Role of Women*. Paris: UNESCO, 1955.
Earhart, Mary. *Frances Willard*. Chicago: University of Chicago Press, 1944.
Eisler, Riane. *The Chalice and the Blade*. New York: Harper, 1987.
Elshtain, Jane. *Public Man, Private Woman*. Princeton: Princeton University Press, 1981.
Enloe, Cynthia. *Bananas, Beaches & Bases*. Berkeley: University of California Press, 1990.
Equal Times, newsletter of UN Group on Equal Rights.
Etienne, Mona, and Eleanor Leacock, ed. *Women and Colonialism: Anthropological Perspectives*. New York: Praeger, 1980.
Evans, Richard. *The Feminist*. New York: Barnes & Noble, 1977.
Fenwick, Charles. *The Organization of American States: The Inter-American Regional System*. Washington, D.C.: Kaufman, 1963.
Ferguson, Kathy. *The Feminist Case Against Bureaucracy*. Philadelphia: Temple University Press, 1984.
Foster, Catherine. *Women for All Seasons: The Story of the Women's International League for Peace and Freedom*. Athens: University of Georgia Press, 1989.
Franck, Thomas M. *Nation Against Nation*. New York: Oxford University Press, 1985.
Fraser, Arvonne. *The UN Decade for Women*. Boulder, Colo.: Westview Press, 1987.
Friedan, Betty. *The Feminine Mystique*. New York: Norton, 1963.
Friedan, Betty. "Scary Doings in Mexico City." In *It Changed My Life*, 344–65. New York: Random House, 1976.
Galey, M. E. "Promoting Nondiscrimination Against Women: The Commission on the Status of Women." *International Studies Quarterly* 23, no. 2 (June 1979): 273–302.
Gildersleeve, Virginia. *Many a Good Crusade*. New York: Macmillan, 1954.
Goodrich, Leland, and Edvard Hambro. *Charter of the United Nations: Commentary and Documents*. 3d ed., rev. New York: Columbia University Press, 1969.
Grant, Rebecca, and Kathleen Newland, eds. *Gender and International Relations*. Bloomington: Indiana University Press, 1991.
Green, James F. *The United Nations and Human Rights*. Washington, D.C.: Brookings Institution, 1956.
Haas, Peter M. "Epistemic Communities and International Policy Coordination." *International Organization* 46, no. 1 (Winter 1992): 1–35.
Hall, Dorothy V. *Making Things Happen*. London: Headley Bros., 1963.
Harris, Rosalind, and Mildred Persinger. "Report: International Women's Year Tribune." New York: NGO Planning Committee, 1975. Mimeographed.
Heyzer, Noeleen. *Women Farmers and Rural Change in Asia: Towards Equal Access and Participation*. Kuala Lumpur, Malaysia: Asia Pacific Development Center, 1987.
Himmelstrand, Karin. "Can an Aid Bureaucracy Empower Women?" In *Women, International Development and Politics: The Bureaucratic Mire*, edited by Kathleen Staudt, 101–13. Philadelphia: Temple University Press, 1990.
Hoff, Joan. *Law, Gender and Injustice: A Legal History of U.S. Women*. New York: New York University Press, 1991.
Hottel, Althea, ed. "Women in the World." *Annals of the American Academy of Political and Social Science* (January 1968).
International Council of Women. *Women in a Changing World*. London: Routledge & Kegan Paul, 1966.
International Women's Rights Action Watch. "FLS Convention Index. Minneapolis, Minn.: Humphrey Institute, 1991. Mimeographed.

International Women's Tribune Centre. *Newsletter* 1 (1980–current).
International Women's Tribune Centre. *Developing Strategies for the Future: Feminist Perspectives.* New York: 1980.
Jacobson, H. K. *Networks of Interdependence.* New York: Knopf, 1979.
Jancar, Barbara. "Women in Communist Countries." In *Women and World Change,* edited by Naomi Black and Ann Cottrell, 140–41. Beverley Hills, Calif.: Sage, 1981.
Jaquette, Jane S., ed. *Women and Politics.* New York: Wiley, 1974.
Jaquette, Jane S., ed. *The Woman's Movement in Latin America.* Boston: Unwin, 1991.
Jawayardena, Kumari. *Feminism and Nationalism in the Third World.* London: Zed Books, 1989.
Josephson, Harold. *James T. Shotwell and the Rise of Internationalism in America.* Cranbury, N.J.: Associated University Presses, 1975.
Kaufmann, Johan. *Conference Diplomacy.* Leyden, Netherlands: A. W. Sithoff, 1968.
Kennedy, David M. *Birth Control in America: The Career of Margaret Sanger.* New Haven: Yale University Press, 1970.
Kirkpatrick, Jeane J. *Political Woman.* New York: Basic Books, 1974.
Kirshenbaum, Gayle. "Inside the World's Largest Men's Club." *Ms. Magazine* 3, no. 2 (1992): 16–19.
Landes, Joan B. *Women in the Public Sphere in the Age of the French Revolution.* Ithaca, N.Y.: Cornell University Press, 1988.
Lerner, Gerda. *The Creation of Feminist Consciousness.* New York: Oxford University Press, 1993.
Lovenduski, Joni. *Women and European Politics: Contemporary Feminism and Public Policy.* Sussex, England: Harvester Press, 1986.
Lubin, Carol Riegelman, and Anne Winslow. *Social Justice for Women: The International Labor Organization and Women.* Durham, N.C.: Duke University Press, 1990.
Maathai, Wangari, interviewed by Daphne Topouris in "Empowering the Grassroots." *Africa Report* 35, no. 5 (The African-American Institute) (November–December 1990): 31–32.
Marin-Bosch, Miguel. "How Nations Vote in the General Assembly of the United Nations." *International Organization* 41, no. 4 (1987): 195–204.
Maynes, Charles William. "The UN in Today's World." In *The US, the UN and the Management of Global Change,* edited by Toby Trister Gati, 329–42. New York: New York University Press, 1983.
McCully, Patrick. "FAO and Fisheries Development." *Ecologist* 21, no. 2 (March–April 1991).
Meron, Theodor. *The United Nations Secretariat, the Rules and the Practice.* Boston: Lexington Books, 1977.
Miller, Carol. "The Interaction of National and Transnational Women's Networks with the League of Nation's Secretariat." British International Studies Association (BISA), December 1991. Mimeographed.
Miller, David Hunter. *Drafting of the Covenant.* Vols. 1 and 2. New York: G. P. Putnam's Sons, 1928.
Miller, Francesca. "Latin American Feminism and the Transnational Arena." In *Women, Culture and Politics in Latin America,* edited by Emilie Bergmann et al., 10–26. Berkeley: University of California Press, 1990.
Moynihan, Daniel Patrick. *A Dangerous Place.* Boston: Little, Brown, 1975.

Nelson, Barbara J., and Najma Chowdhury. *Women and Politics Worldwide*. New Haven: Yale University Press, 1994.
Newland, Kathleen. "From Transnational Relations to International Relations: Women in Development and the International Decade of Women." *Millenium: Women and International Relations* (special issue), 17, no. 3 (Winter 1988): 507, 513.
NGO Planning Committee. *Forum '80: Final Report*. New York: 1981. Mimeographed.
NGO Planning Committee. *Forum '85: Final Report*. New York: 1986. Mimeographed.
Nicol, Davidson. "Reflections." *UNITAR News* 7, no. 1 (1975): 3–4.
Nijeholt, G. Lycklama. "The Fallacy of Integration: The UN Strategy of Integrating Women into Development Revisited." *Netherlands Review of Development Studies* 1 (1987): 23–37.
Nordic UN Project. *United Nations and the Advancement of Women*. Report No. 16.1990. Stockholm, 1990.
Northledge, F. S. *The League of Nations*. Leicester, England: Leicester University Press, 1986.
Pala, Achola. "Definitions of Women and Development: An African Perspective." *Signs* 3, no. 1 (Autumn 1977): 9–13.
Pfeffer, Paula F. "A Whisper in the Assembly of Nations." *Women's Studies International Forum* (1985): 459–71.
Pietila, Hilkka, and Jeanne Vickers. *Making Women Matter: The Role of the United Nations*. London: Zed Books, 1990.
"Profile of Kofi Annan, UN Personnel Chief." *Secretariat News* 43 no. 5 (30 June 1987).
Puchala, Donald J. "American Interests in the United Nations." In *The Politics of International Organizations*, edited by Paul F. Diehl, 226–41. Chicago, Ill.: Dorsey Press, 1989.
Randall, Vicky. *Women and Politics: An International Perspective*. Chicago, Ill.: University of Chicago Press, 1987.
Ranshoffen-Wertheimer, Egon F. *The International Secretariat: A Great Experiment in International Administration*. Washington, D.C.: Carnegie Endowment for International Peace, 1945.
Rathberger, Eva. "Operationalizing Gender and Development." Paper presented at Association for Women in Development, Washington, D.C., 21 November 1991. Mimeographed.
Rice, Anna V. *A History of the World's Young Women's Christian Association*. New York: Woman's Press, 1947.
Robins, Dorothy B. *Experiment in Democracy*. New York: Parkside Press, 1971.
Russell, Ruth. *History of the United Nations Charter*. Washington, D.C.: Brookings Institution, 1958.
Schuck, Victoria. "Forum '85 and the UN Decade for Women Conference." *Political Science and Politics* 18, no. 4 (Fall 1985): 907–11.
Sen, Gita, and Karen Grown. *Development, Crises and Alternative Visions: Third World Women's Perspectives*. New York: Monthly Review Press, 1987.
Seymour, Jennifer Whitaker. "Women of the World: Report from Mexico City." *Foreign Affairs* 54, no. 1 (October 1975): 173–81.
Sharp, Walter R. *The UN Economic and Social Council*. New York: Columbia University Press, 1969.
Shelton, Dinah. "The Right to Education." *Revue des Droits de l'Homme* 51 (1975).
Shotwell, James T. *Autobiography*. New York: Bobbs-Merrill, 1961.

Snyder, Margaret. "Gender and the Food Regime: Some Transnational and Human Issues." *Transnational Law and Contemporary Problems* 1 (1991): 469–505.
Snyder, Margaret. "Farmers and Merchants: Some Observations on Gender and the State in Africa." *Africa Contemporary Record.* New York: Holmes & Meier Publishers, 1994.
Snyder, Margaret. *Women, Poverty and Politics: A UN Fund for Women.* London: Zed Books, 1995.
Snyder, Margaret, and Mary Tadesse. *African Women and Development: A History.* London: Zed Books, 1995.
Sohn, Louis B., and Thomas Buergenthal. *International Protection of Human Rights.* Indianapolis, Ind.: Bobbs-Merrill, 1973.
Sowerwein, Charles. "The Socialist Movement from 1850–1940." In *Becoming Visible,* edited by Renate Bridenthal, Claudia Koontz, and Susan Stuard, 403–22. Boston: Houghton Mifflin, 1987.
Stanton, Elizabeth Cady, Susan B. Anthony, and M. Jocelyn Gage. *History of Woman Suffrage.* 6 vols. New York: Arno Press, 1969.
Staudt, Kathleen A. *Women, Foreign Assistance and Advocacy Administration.* New York: Praeger, 1985.
Staudt, Kathleen A., ed. *Women, International Development and Politics.* Philadelphia: Temple University Press, 1990.
Staunton, Dorothy. *Our Goodly Heritage.* London: Walthamstow Press, 1956.
Stephenson, C. M. "Feminism, Pacifism, Nationalism and the UN Decade for Women." *Women's Studies International Forum* 5, no. 3 (1982).
Szalai, Alexander. "The Situation of the Women in the United Nations." *UNITAR Report* 18 (1973): 15–16.
Taylor, Paul, and A.J.R. Groom. *Global Issues in the United Nation's Framework.* New York: St. Martin's Press, 1989.
Tinker, Irene. "A Feminist View of Copenhagen." *Signs* 6, no. 3 (1981): 531–35.
Tinker, Irene. *Persistent Inequalities.* New York: Oxford University Press, 1990.
Tinker, Irene, and Jane Jaquette. "The UN Decade for Women." *World Development* 2 (March 1987): 419–27.
UNA-USA, Al-Ber Costa Chapter. "World Plan of Action." *Women in Action.* 1976. Mimeographed.
Vajrathon, Mallica. "The Success of the Copenhagen World Conference: A Feminist Perspective." New York: Tribune Centre, 1980. Mimeographed.
Walters, F. C. *History of the League of Nations.* Vols. 1 and 2. New York: Oxford University Press, 1952.
Whittick, Arnold. *Woman into Citizen.* Beverley Hills, Calif.: ABC-CLIO Press, 1976.
Wollstonecraft, Mary. *Vindication of the Rights of Women.* 1792. Reprint, London: Penguin, 1988.
Women's Environment and Development Organization. *Official Report: World Women's Congress for a Healthy Planet.* Miami, Fla.: Women's Environment and Development Organization, 1991.

II. UNITED NATIONS AND RELATED DOCUMENTS

Conference on International Organization. *Delegations and Officials.* Rev. Doc. 693G/3(2). San Francisco, California. 29 May 1945.

Selected Bibliography 195

Economic and Social Council
- Ad Hoc Group of Experts on Restructuring the Economic and Social Sectors. *Report.* New York: UN, 1975.
- Board of Trustees of the International Research and Training Institute for the Advancement of Women. *Report.* 1981–present.
- Commission on Human Rights (CHR). *Reports to ECOSOC.* 1946–1994.
- ———. Working Group on Slavery. *Report on Traditional Practices Affecting the Health of Women and Children.* E/CN.4/1986. 4 February 1986.
- Commission on Social Development. *Reports to ECOSOC.* 1969–present.
- Commission on the Status of Women (CSW). *Reports to ECOSOC.* 1946–present.
- ———. *Summary Records.* 1947–1978.
- ———. *Study of the Interrelationship of the Status of Women and Family Planning: Report of the Special Rapporteur.* E/CN.6/575 and Add. 1 December 1973.
- ———. *Draft Declaration on the Elimination of All Forms of Discrimination Against Women.* E/CN.6/426. 30 October 1974.
- ———. *International Standards Relating to the Status of Women.* Working Paper. E/CN.6/573. 6 November 1973.
- ———. *International Women's Year: Report of the Working Group to the CSW.* E/CN.6/588. 30 January 1974.
- Council Committee on Non-governmental Organizations. Report. E/4485. 6 May 1968.
- Plenary meetings. 1946–present.
- Population Commission. *Reports to ECOSOC.* 1947–present.
- *Resolutions and Decisions of the Economic and Social Council.* 1946–present.
- Social Commission, *Reports to ECOSOC.* 1947–1968.

Food and Agriculture Organization. *Women in Agricultural Development: FAO's Plan of Action.* Rome, 1990.

General Assembly Official Records
- Committee on the Elimination of Discrimination Against Women (CEDAW). 1st to 14th sessions. *Report.* GAOR Supplement 38. 1981–present.
- Conference on Human Rights. *Final Act of the 1968 Conference on Human Rights.* A/CONF.32/41. New York: UN, 1968.
- Consultative Committee for the World Conference of the IWY. *Draft International Plan of Action.* E/CONF.66/CC/2. 8 February 1975.
- Plenary meetings. 1946–present.
- *Report of the Economic and Social Council.* GAOR Supplement 3. 1946–present.
- *Reports of the Third Committee.* 1946–present.
- *Resolutions and Decisions of the General Assembly.* 1946–present.
- UN Development Fund for Women. *Reports of the Secretary-General.* 1986–present.
- Voluntary Fund for the UN Decade for Women. *Reports of the Secretary-General.* 1978–1985.

World Conference of the Mid-Decade for Women: Equality, Development and Peace. *Report of the Conference, including the World Program of Action and Resolutions.* A/CONF.94/35. New York, 1980.

World Conference on Human Rights. (Vienna). *Report of the World Conference.* A/CONF.157/24. 1993.

World Conference on IWY. *Report of Conference, including the World Plan of Action, Resolutions and Regional Plans of Action.* E/CONF.66/34. New York, 1976.

———. *The UN System and the Elimination of Discrimination Against Women.* E/CONF.66/BP/1 and Add. 1. 1975.

World Conference to Review and Appraise Achievements of the UN Decade for Women: Equality, Development and Peace. *Report of the Conference, including the Forward-Looking Strategies for the Advancement of Women to the Year 2000 and Resolutions.* A/CONF.116/28/Rev.1. 1986.

World Population Conference (Bucharest). *World Population Plan of Action.* A/CONF. 60/19. New York, 1974.

Government of the Netherlands. Ministry of Foreign Affairs. *A World of Difference: A New Framework for Development Cooperation in the 1990s.* The Hague, 1991.

International Bank for Reconstruction and Development. *The Integration of Women into the Development Process.* Washington, D.C., May 1975.

———. *Agricultural Extension for Women Farmers in Africa.* Discussion Paper No. 103. Prepared by Katrine A. Saito and C. Jean Weidemann. Washington, D.C., October 1990.

———. Advisory Group on Higher-Level Women's Issues. *Excellence Through Equality: An Increased Role for Women in the World Bank.* Washington, D.C., April, 1992.

———. *Kenya: The Role of Women in Economic Development.* Washington, D.C., 1989.

———. *Women in Development: A Progress Report on the World Bank Initiative.* Washington, D.C., 1990.

International Civil Service Commission (ICSC). *Recruitment Policy: Report on Progress Made since the Twenty-second Session in Undertaking Special Measures for the Recruitment of Women.* ICSC/24/R.13. 19 June 1986.

———. *Recruitment Policy: Special Measures for the Recruitment of Women.* ICSC/22/R.14. 14 June 1985.

International Labor Organization. *Conventions and Recommendations, 1919–1966.* Geneva: International Labor Office, 1966.

Inter-Parliamentary Union. *Distribution of Seats between Men and Women in National Parliaments, 1945–1991.* No. 18. Geneva, 1991.

———. *Distribution of Seats between Men and Women in the 178 National Parliaments Existing as of 30 June 1994.* Geneva, 20 September 1994.

Organization for Economic Cooperation and Development. *Integration of Women in Development Practice.* Prepared by Winifred Weeks-Vagliani. Paris, 1985.

United Nations Development Fund for Women (UNIFEM). *Development Cooperation with Women: The Experience and Direction of the Fund.* New York, 1985.

United Nations Development Program (UNDP). *Women's Participation in Development* Evaluation Study No. 3. New York, June 1980.

———. *Women's Participation in Development: An Interorganizational Assessment.* Evaluation Study No. 13. New York, 1985.

———. *Women in Development: Project Achievement Reports.* 1989.

United Nations Educational, Scientific and Cultural Organization (UNESCO). Executive Board. *Evaluation of Study and Research Progress on the Status of Women.* Prepared by Denis Kandiyoti. 127 EX/INF.8. 11 September 1987.

United Nations International Children's Emergency Fund. (UNICEF). *NGO/UNICEF Cooperation: A Historical Perspective.* Monograph 5. UNICEF History Series. March 1987.

United Nations Institute for Training and Research (UNITAR). *The United Nations and Decision-Making: The Role of Women.* Edited by Davidson Nicol and Margaret Croke. Vols. 1 and 2. New York, 1978.

———. *Women and Development: The Role of the United Nations System.* Prepared by Fadia Nasr and Marcel Nquema-Mba. June 1975.

United Nations Secretariat

    Center for Economic and Social Information/Office of Public Information. *Women and Men Speak Out: International Women's Day 1975.* New York, October 1975.

    Center for Human Rights. *United Nations Action in the Field of Human Rights.* Geneva, 1988.

    Center for Social Development and Humanitarian Affairs (CSDHA). *Compendium of International Conventions concerning the Status of Women.* New York, 1988.

    ———. *Compendium of Statistics and Indicators on the Situation of Women.* New York, 1990.

    ———. *Improvement of the Status of Women in the Secretariat: Report of the Secretary-General.* A/C.5/42/24. 1987.

    ———. *Improvement of the Status of Women in the Secretariat: Report of the Secretary-General.* A/C.5/44/17. 1989.

    ———. *Integration of Women in Development: Report of the Secretary-General.* E/CN.6/481. 14 November 1972.

    ———. *Measures and Activities Undertaken in Conjunction with International Women's Year.* A/10263. 2 October 1975.

    ———. *National Machinery for Monitoring and Improving the Status of Women.* Background Paper No. 5. March 1988.

    ———. *Report of the Ad Hoc Task Force on the Status of Women in Professional and Higher Categories.* New York, October 1990.

    ———. *Report on Implementation of the Action Program for the Improvement of the Status of Women in the Secretariat.* A/C.5/41/18. 1986.

    ———. *Report on Improvement of the Status of Women in the Secretariat.* A/C.5/40/30. 1985.

    ———. *Status of Women in the Professional Category and Above: Second Progress Report.* A/37/469. 1987.

    ———. *World Survey of the Role of Women in Development.* ST/CSDHA/6. New York, 1985.

    CSDHA, UNICEF, UNFPA et al. *The World's Women: Trends and Statistics, 1970–1990.* New York, 1991.

Department of Social and Economic Affairs. Status of Women Section (DSEA/SW). *Equal Pay for Equal Work.* New York, 1960.
———. *Legal Status of Married Women.* New York, 1958.
———. *Nationality of Married Women.* New York, 1963.
———. *Parental Rights and Duties.* New York, 1968.
———. *Preliminary Report on the Political Rights of Women.* E/CN.6/27. 16 December 1947.
———. *Report on Participation of Women in the Work of the UN.* E/CN.6/132. 1950.
———. *UN Assistance for the Advancement of Women: Report by the Secretary-General.* E/CN.6/435 and Add. 1, 2, 3, 4 (January–February 1965), E/CN.6/450 and Add. 1, 2, 3 (January 1966).
Division for Administration and Management. Administrative Instruction. *Procedures for Dealing with Sexual Harassment.* ST/SGB/253. 29 October 1992.
———. Information Circular. *Guidelines for Promoting Equal Treatment of Men and Women in the Secretariat.* ST/IC/1992/67. 29 October 1992.
Joint Inspection Unit (JIU). *Advancement of the Status of Women in the UN Secretariat in an Era of Human Resources Management and Accountability: A New Beginning?* Prepared by Erica-Irene Daes. JIU/REP/94/3. May 1994.
———. *Report on Personnel Problems.* Vols. 1 and 2. JIU/REP/71/7-A/8454. 1971.
———. *Status of Women in the Professional Category and Above: Second Progress Report.* Prepared by Earl D. Sohm. JIU/REP/82/4. March 1982.
———. *Women in the Professional Category and Above in the UN System.* JIU/77/7-A/33/105. 1977.
Legal Office. *Status of Multilateral Treaties.* 1991.
Office of Public Information. Press Section. *Press Releases IWY/1–69.* New York, 18 June–3 July, 1975.
———. *Yearbook of the United Nations.* New York, 1946–present.
World Bank Group Staff Association. *Technical Report: Status of Higher-Level Women in the World Bank Group.* Washington, D.C., 1989.
World Health Organization (WHO). Executive Board. *Verbatim Records.* Geneva, 1990.
———. *Report to the Director-General.* Prepared by Maureen Law. Geneva, 1985.

Index

Abzug, Bella, 40
Addams, Jane, 3
Afghanistan, 79–80, 88
African Association of Women for Research and Development (AAWORD), 105, 108
African National Congress (ANC), 51
Algeria, 54, 62–63
All-Africa Council of Churches (AACC), 148
All Africa Women's Conference (AAWC), 98, 180
All Pakistan Women's Association (APWA), 17
Altrusa International (AI), 3
American Association for the Advancement of Science (AAAS), 100, 141
American Bar Association (ABA), 6
Anderson, Mary, 6
Angola, 53

Annan, Kofi, 127
Anstee, Margaret J., 123, 128
Anthony, Susan B., 3, 178
Antonio, Don, 40
Apartheid, 35–37, 64, 68, 72, 85, 88; International Convention on the Suppression and Punishment of the Crime of Apartheid, 72; United Nations Special Committee, 51
Argentina, 33, 54, 79
Australia, 21, 34–36, 45, 51, 55–57, 68, 70, 119, 124

Bahamas, 39
Ballantyne, Edith, 144–46
Balogun, 99
Bandanaraike, Sirimavo, 33–34
Bangladesh, 36
Barbados, 55, 65, 68
Baroody, Jamil, 81–82
Barrios de Chungara, Domitila, 40, 145–46

Barrow, Nita, 65, 147
Begtrup, Bodil, 13, 16
Beguin, Antoinette Waelbroeck, 168
Belgium, 12, 38, 51–52, 70, 118–19
Belize, 118
Benitez, Helen, 80–81
Bernardino, Minerva, 7, 11–13, 17, 19
Bertini, Catherine, 128
Beyer, Clara, 98
Bhatt, Ela, 110
Bhutan, 56
Boernstein, Diana, 121
Bokor-Szedo, Hanna, 81
Bolivia, 54
Bondfield, Margaret, 4, 161
Boserup, Ester, 97, 99–101
Botswana, 91
Boulding, Elise, 138
Boulton de Bottome, Mrs., 81
Boutros-Ghali, Boutros, 128
Bravo, Marcia, 40, 141
Brazil, 7, 54, 88, 91
Bretton Woods Conference, 159
British Continental and General Federation for the Abolition of State Vice, 2
British Federation of Business and Professional Women, 12; Roundtable of Women's Organizations, calling for convention on discrimination, 12
British National Council of Women, 157
British Trades Union Congress, 4, 161
Brooks, Angie, 17
Bruce, Margaret, 21, 81, 121
Brunauer, Esther, 7
Brundtland, Gro Harland, 128
Burkina Faso (previously Upper Volta), 55, 88
Butler, Josephine, 2

Cadogan, Lord, 7
Canada, 2, 7, 23, 34, 45, 55–57, 63–64, 66, 107, 119, 162
Carnegie Endowment for International Peace, 6
Carrothers, Violet, 162
Casselman, Cora T., 7
Catt, Carrie Chapman, 3

Chapultepec, 7
Charter of Economic Rights and Duties of States (CERD), 32, 35, 39
Chaton, Jeanne, 80, 82
Chile, 13, 30, 35, 54–56, 119
China, 7, 13, 15, 17, 35, 51, 80, 110, 166
Chinery-Hesse, Mary, 168–69
Chipchase, Ethel, 160
Church Women United, 148
Cisse, Jeanne Martin, 36
Colombia, 30–31, 55, 66, 91, 110
Commission on Arab Women, 15
Commission to Study the Organization of Peace, 6
Commonwealth Secretariat Office of Women in Development, 90
Comoros, 118
Conference of Non-Aligned and Developing Countries, 55
Conference of Nongovernmental Organizations in Consultative Status with ECOSOC (CONGO), 40, 136–37, 139, 144–47, 150
Costa Rica, 30, 55
Council of Europe, 21
Crowdy, Dame Rachel, 5
Cuba, 20, 33, 49, 53–54, 143
Czechoslovakia, 12, 36, 52

Daes, Erica-Irene, 129
Dakar Declaration on Another Development with Women, 104
Danish Council of Women, 146
Davis, Angela, 40
Declaration of Mexico, 33, 37, 39, 41, 51, 55, 64, 68–69, 85, 142
de Hedervary, Claire, 118
Dembinska, Zofia, 81
Democratic Yemen, 106
Denmark, 5, 12–13, 39, 51, 99, 119, 140
de Perez Dias, Lucila L., 7
de Urdaneta, Isabel Sanchez, 7, 119
Development Alternatives with Women for a New Era (DAWN), 104–5, 108, 112–13, 149
de Vidal, Isabel P., 7
de Vries, M. G., 107
Dominican Republic, 7, 12–13, 30, 55

Doss, Leila, 125
Dowdeswell, Elizabeth, 128
Drummond, Sir Eric, 5
Dumbarton Oaks, 7

Echeverria Alvarez, Luis, 32
Echeverria Alvarez, Senora, 141
Ecuador, 55, 87
Egypt, 21, 23, 33, 35, 53, 66, 69, 80, 97
Eichelberger, Clark, 6
El Salvador, 54
Emara, Leila, 63, 69
Ethiopia, 68
European Economic Community (EEC), 21, 51

Feminist International for Peace and Food, 149
Fiji, 56, 118
Finland, 21, 80, 162
Fonda, Jane, 40
Food and Agriculture Organization (FAO), 14, 80, 86, 98, 156–58, 162–63, 167, 169; Plan of Action, 169; staff, 168–69; Women in Development, 169; Women in Food Production and Food Security, 163; World Food Conference, 98, 158
Fosdick, Dorothy, 7
France, 12–13, 20, 22–23, 35, 51, 64, 80, 162
Fraser, Peter, 12
French Women's Suffrage Union, 4
Friedan, Betty, 40, 97, 142, 180

Gabon, 35, 55
Gachukia, Eddah, 65, 147
Gany, Diaroumeye, 67
Gardener, Robert, 98
General Federation of Women's Clubs, 2
German Social Democratic Party (SPD), 2
Germany, 22, 37, 51–53, 62, 64, 70, 85
Ghana, 15, 38, 55, 80–81, 97–98, 100, 168
Gildersleeve, Virginia, 7
Gindy, Aida, 97
Giogis, Konjit Sine, 68

Goegg, Marie, 2
Gompers, Samuel, 4
Grass Roots Organizations Operating Together in Sisterhood (GROOTS), 110
Greece, 12, 30, 35, 56
Green Belt Movement, 110, 113
Greer, Germaine, 141
Grenada, 53
Group of 77, 23, 32, 37–39, 47, 49, 62–64, 69, 72, 85, 100
Grown, Karen, 104
Groza, Madam, 53
Guatemala, 54–56
Gueye, Lena, 49
Guinea, 36
Guinea-Bissau, 162

Habachy, Suzan, 127
Hague Conference on Nationality, 5
Haiti, 20, 106
Hammerskjold, Dag, 13, 119–20, 177
Hansen, Annelise, 146
Harris, Rosalind, 40, 100, 137
Harvard University, 6
Hazzard, Virginia, 65, 147
Henderson, Julia, 13, 122
Herz, Barbara, 107, 165
Herzog, Chaim, 41
Heyzer, Noeleen, 100
Holy See, 35, 38, 52, 55–56, 72
Honduras, 54
Horsbrugh, Florence, 7
Housewives in Dialogue, 68
Hoveyda, Fereddun, 81
Hudson, Manley O., 6
Huggard, Marianne, 145
Hull, Cordell, 6–7
Human rights, 6–7, 14; UN Commission, 7, 13–14; UN Covenants on Civil and Political Rights and on Economic, Social and Cultural Rights, 14; UN Division of Human Rights, 14, 17, 81, 119, 121; UN Universal Declaration, 14, 18–20, 78, 82, 84; UN World Conference on Human Rights, 179
Hungary, 38, 68, 81

Hussein, Aziza, 80, 97
Hutar, Pat, 30

Ider, Ms., 81, 89
India, 7, 12–13, 34–35, 52–54, 104, 119
Indian Women's Charter of Rights and Duties, 13
Indonesia, 51, 106
Inter-Allied Suffrage Conference (IASC), 4
Inter-American Commission on Women (IACW), 3–4
International Alliance of Women (IAW), 3, 5, 81, 178
International Association of Women, 2
International Bank for Reconstruction and Development (World Bank), 107, 109, 111–12, 124, 156–57, 159–60, 163, 168, 172, 181; Group Staff Association, 171, 172; relations with nongovernmental organizations, 167; staff, 168, 171–72; Women in Agriculture, 166; Women in Development, 165–66
International Civil Service Commission (ICSC), 170
International Communist Conference of Working Women (ICCWW), 2
International Confederation of Free Trade Unions (ICFTU), 17
International Conference of Socialist Women (ICSW), 2
International Conference on Population and Development, 150, 180
International Conference on the Question of Palestine, 123
International Congress of Women (ICW), 3
International Congress of Working Women (ICWW), 6
International Council of Nurses (ICN), 3
International Council of Women (ICW), 3, 177–78
International Federation of Business and Professional Women (IFBPW), 18
International Federation of Catholic Alumnae (IFCA), 2

International Federation of University Women (IFUW), 2, 18
International Federation of Women Lawyers (IFWL), 18
International Federation of Working Women (IFWW), 6
International Food and Population Conference, 30, 50, 137, 139
International Labor Organization (ILO), 3, 5–6, 14, 17–18, 50, 78, 155, 157–58, 160–62, 167–69; Action Group for Equality, 168; Declaration and Resolution Concerning a Plan of Action for Women Workers, 160; Governing Body, 162, 168; instruments regarding equality, labor inspection, maternity, night work and underground work, 6; relations with nongovernmental organizations, 167; resolutions on political rights, opportunities and equal treatment, 17–18, 160; staff, 168–69; Staff Union, 168
International Monetary Fund (IMF), 107, 111, 112
International Planned Parenthood Federation (IPPF), 21, 80
International Political Science Association (IPSA), 16
International Research and Training Institute for the Advancement of Women (INSTRAW), 39, 50, 57, 99–100, 108, 113, 182
International Socialist Congress (ISC), 2
International Social Service (ISS), 40
International Women's Day, 123, 126
International Women's Rights Action Watch (IWRAW), 90
International Women's Rights Conference, 2, 177
International Women's Suffrage Alliance (IWSA), 3
International Women's Tribune Centre (IWTC), 40–41, 100, 144, 149
International Women's Year (IWY), 1, 15, 21, 30–31, 33–34, 41, 50, 84, 112, 135, 150
Interparliamentary Union, 112

Index

Iran, 32, 38, 47, 49, 70, 81, 99
Iraq, 35, 51
Israel, 33, 35–36, 38–39, 41, 45–48, 52–57, 62, 68, 70, 180
Italy, 51
Ivory Coast, 55

Jahan, Rounaq, 143
Jain, Devaki, 104
Jamaica, 33, 38, 55, 85, 99, 123
Japan, 55–56, 64, 72, 128, 140
Jiaggie, Judge Annie, 81, 97
Johnston, Suzanna, 125
Jordan, 36, 55
Jurdek, Angela, 13

Kane, Maimouna, 49, 51–53
KANU/Maendeleo ya Wanawake, 148
Karibu, Women's Centre for Women of All Faiths, 148
Kaul, Sheila, 52
Kenya, 30, 51, 61, 64–65, 70–71, 103, 166; African National Union, 167; External Trade Authority, 148; Family Planning Association, 167; International Women's Study Institute, 148; National Council of Women, 109; Water for Health Organization, 109, 167; Women's Bureau, 148
Kenyatta, Margaret, 65–66, 69–70, 98
Kenyon, Dorothy, 13, 16, 19, 119
Keyes, Alan, 70
King, Angela, 127
Kissinger, Henry, 41
Kollontai, Alexandre, 2

Labarca, Amanda, 119
Law, Maureen, 170
League of Arab States, 51, 158
League of Nations (LN), 3–5, 11, 136, 177–78; Advisory Committee on Traffic in Women and Children, 5; Articles 7(3), 23(1), 23(c) of the Covenant, 4; Assembly, 4; Commission on International Labor Legislation, 4; Committee of Experts on the Legal Status of Women, 5–6, 13; Committee on Social and General Questions, 5; Conference on the Codification of International Law, 5; Convention on the Traffic of Women and Children, 5; Liaison Committee of Women's International Organizations, 5; Permanent Mandates Commission, 5; Political Committee, 177; Secretariat, 5
Lebanon, 13, 20, 54
Ledon, Amelia, 16
LeFaucheux, Marie-Helene, 12–13
Lehman, William, 103
Leijon, Anna-Greta, 162
Lesotho, 53, 55
Lewis, Sir Arthur, 97, 180
Liberia, 17, 30
Libya, 22, 36
Lie, Trygve, 117–18
Lopez, Cecilia, 66–67
Lutz, Berta, 7
Lycklama à Nijeholt, Goertje, 104–5

Maathai, Wangari, 110, 113
McDiarmid, Alice, 7
McKenzie, Jeane, 12
Madagascar, 22
Maendeleo ya Wanawake, 148
Mair, Lucille, 49–50, 57, 85, 99, 123, 146
Mali, 88
Manalo, Rosario, 63–64, 66, 68–69
Marcy, Mildred, 98
Margrethe, Queen of Denmark, 51
Marriage: family law, 19–20; minimum age, 20; nationality, 4, 18–19
Martinez, Aida Gonzales, 162
Mauritius, 35
Medical Women's International Association (MWIA), 3
Mehta, Mrs. Hans, 13
Menon, Lakshmi, 119
Mexico, 7, 16, 23, 31–32, 37, 40, 51, 55, 71, 80, 82, 87–88, 119
Miller, Billie, 68
Miller, Frieda, 162
Minority Rights Group, 19
Moi, Daniel arap, 65
Molotov, Vyacheslav, 7
Mongolia, 81, 89

Morocco, 19, 35–36, 64, 72, 79, 88
Mother Teresa, 40
Mozambique, 54
Mudalier, Sir Ramaswami, 12
Mullan, Sylvia, 120
Mwangola, Margaret, 109
Myrdal, Alva, 13

Namibia, 36, 144
Nason, Rachel, 81
National Women's Trade Union League, 6
Nepal, 80, 165
Netherlands, 12, 20, 51, 67, 70, 88, 107, 111, 119
New, Mrs. W. S., 13
New International Economic Order (NIEO), 21, 32, 35, 46–48, 50, 54, 70, 85, 100
New Zealand, 12, 55, 71
Nicaragua, 47, 54, 70
Nicholson, Sir Harold, 117
Nicol, Davidson, 125
Niger, 22, 67
Nigeria, 30, 34, 99, 160
Nikolaeva, T. N., 63
Non-Aligned Movement, 47, 49, 54–55
Nongovernmental Organizations (NGOs), 1–3, 15, 21, 31, 48, 61, 68, 112–13, 119, 135–51, 180–81; Article 71 of United Nations Charter, 136; categories, 137; Committee on Arrangements for Consultation, 136–37; Conference of Nongovernmental Organizations in consultative status (CONGO), 136–37, 139, 144–47, 150; Fourth World Conference on Women, 137, 150; League of Nations, 5; World Conference of the Mid-Decade for Women, 144–47; World Conference on International Women's Year, 140–44; World Conference to Review and Appraise the Achievements of the United Nations Decade for Women, 147–50
NORAD (Norwegian Directorate for Development Cooperation), 111
Nordic Women for Peace, 146

Norway, 12, 34, 107, 111, 119, 124, 128, 170

Ocloo, Esther, 100
Ogata, Sadako, 128
Ojeda, Paullada Pedro, 32, 39
Olin, Doctor Ulla, 106
O'Neil, Maureen, 63
Organization for Economic Cooperation and Development (OECD), 98, 107–8, 112; Development Advisory Committee, 98; Women and Development Committee, 107
Organization of Petroleum Exporting Countries (OPEC), 47
Ostergaard, Lisa, 51
Overseas Education Fund, 148

Pahlavi, Princess Ashraf, 31–32, 34, 81, 99
Pakistan, 17, 33, 53–54, 67, 69
Pala, Achola, 103–5
Palestine Liberation Organization (PLO), 21, 35–36, 41, 45, 47, 51, 53–54, 103
Palme, Olaf, 35
Palmer, Elizabeth, 144–45
Palmer, Ingrid, 50
Pan Africanist Congress of Azania (PACA), 51
Panama, 35
Pan American Union (PAU), 3–4, 178; Conference of American States, 3; Declaration of Lima in Favor of Women's Rights, Inter-American Commission on Women (IACW), 3–4, 13, 110; treaty on Nationality of Married Women, 4, 18; Women's International Committee, 3
Papua New Guinea, 56
Paqui, Hilda Rwabazaire, 145
Paraguay, 54–56
Paris Peace Conference, 3–4; Commission on International Labor Legislation, 4
Pasticci-Ferencic, Dunja, 99
Perez de Cuellar, Javier, 65, 111–12, 127–28
Perkins, Frances, 162

Persinger, Mildred, 40, 100
Peru, 54–56
Philippines, 22, 30, 33, 38–39, 62–63, 81, 84–85, 97, 99
Poland, 13, 16, 20, 80–81, 84
Population: International Conference on Food and Population, 30, 50, 137, 139; International Conference on Population and Development, 150, 179–80; Tribune, 137; UN Population Commission, 12; UN Population Fund, 14, 21, 98, 113, 128; World Plan of Action, 21, 139; World Population Conference, 21, 30, 40, 50
Portugal, 56
Prostitution and sexual exploitation, 18; Conventions on Traffic in Women and Children, 18, 20; Protecting Women's Human Rights from Sexual Exploitation, Violence and Prostitution, 163–64
Pulido de Briceno, Mercedes, 125, 126, 127

Racism and Zionism, 38–39, 41, 51–52, 62–64, 68–70, 72
Radziwell, Gabriella, 5
Reagan, Maureen, 63, 64, 71
Riby-Williams, James, 98
Ripert, Jean-Paul, 63
Rollet, Christine Stettner, 124
Romania, 30, 52, 53, 67
Roosevelt, Eleanor, 11, 12, 13
Roosevelt, Franklin D., 6
Rwanda, 106

Sadik, Nafis, 128
Saifullah, Kulsun, 67
Salas, Rafael, 98
Saudi Arabia, 81
Sauerwein, Virginia, 100
Schlueter-Hermkes, M., 169
Schneiderman, Rose, 6
Schwalb, Susan, 146
Scott, Gloria, 107, 124
Self-Employed Women's Association, 110
Sellami-Meslem, Chafika, 62, 63, 89

Semler, Vicki, 100
Sen, Gita, 104
Senegal, 49, 55, 85
Sevigny, Therese, 128
Shahani, Leticia, 38, 62, 97, 99, 123, 142
Shotwell, James T., 6
Sipila, Helvi, 21, 31–33, 39, 80, 122, 142, 143
Slavery, 18; Advisory Committee on Traffic in Women and Children, 5; Convention on the Traffic of Women and Children, 5; Supplementary Convention on the Abolition of Slavery, the Slave Trade, Institutions and Practices, 20
Smeaton, Dame Mary, 122
Society for International Development, 143
Sohn, Louis, 6
Solomonescu, Olimpia, 67
Somalia, 36
South Africa, 22, 35–37, 46, 54, 68, 70, 72, 144
South West Africa People's Organization (SWAPO), 51
Soviet Women's Association, 33
Spaak, Paul Henri, 12
Spain, 35, 56
Spens, Terese, 99
Sri Lanka, 33–34, 35
Stanton, Elizabeth Cady, 3, 178
Steinem, Gloria, 40, 141
Stemberg, Gertrude, 162
Stettinius, E. L., 7
Street, Jessie, 119
Sudan, 36
Suffrage for women, 16; Convention on Political Rights, calling on governments to grant women the right to vote and exercise all political functions, 16; questionnaire and resolution calling for immediate granting of political rights for women, 16
Summerskill, Shirley, 99
Suriname, 53, 55
Swaziland, 55

Sweden, 35, 64, 70, 87–88, 97, 98, 107, 119, 139, 162
Syria, 52, 53
Szilagyi, Eva, 68

Tallawy, Mervat, 66
Tanzania, 111
Tereshkova, Valentina, 33
Thailand, 30, 55, 56
Thant, U. *See* U Thant
Thatcher, Margaret, 128
Thorsson, Inga, 97, 98, 122
Tomsik, Vida, 97
Trickle Up Program, 149
Trinidad and Tobago, 22, 55
Tsien, Patricia, 120, 121
Tukan, 55
Tunisia, 54
Turkey, 64

Union of Soviet Socialist Republics, 7, 12–13, 16–17, 19, 33, 35, 38, 46, 49, 51–52, 63, 71–73, 84–86
United Arab Emirates, 72
United Arab Republic, 80
United Kingdom, 2, 5, 7, 12, 16, 21, 22, 37, 39, 52, 53, 55, 62, 64, 70, 99, 117, 119, 128
United Nations Ad Hoc Inter-Agency Committee, 31
United Nations Centre for Social Development and Humanitarian Affairs (CSDHA), 101, 123
United Nations Commission on Human Rights (CHR), 7, 12–13, 19–20, 29, 178
United Nations Commission on Social Development (CSD), 96
United Nations Commission on the Status of Women (CSW), 7, 12–15, 29–31, 49, 62, 73, 77–81, 92, 96, 119, 123–24, 127, 150, 178–79; collaboration with UN bodies, 14–16; comparative legal studies, 13–14, 16; discrimination, 20, 77–89, 92; long-term program, 20, 30; nationality and marriage, 18–20; preparing women's conferences, 21–24, 49, 62; program of concerted international action for the advancement of women, 97; Secretariat, 14, 17, 119–20; working group on slavery, 19–20
United Nations Conference on International Organization (UNCIO), San Francisco, 7–8, 136
United Nations Conference on the Human Environment, 138–39
United Nations Conference on Trade and Development (UNCTAD), 50
United Nations Convention for the Suppression of Traffic in Persons, 18
United Nations Convention on the Elimination of All Forms of Discrimination Against Women (CEDAW), 18, 51, 77–92, 179; Committee on the Elimination of Discrimination Against Women, 78, 81, 89–90; Convention ratified, 78; drafting convention begun, 84–87; 1979 GA adopted convention, 88; 1963 draft resolution introduced in the GA by developing and Eastern European countries on eliminating discrimination against women, 78–80; 1963 draft resolution introduced in the GA by developing and Eastern European countries on women, 78, 81, 89–90; 1965 CSW begins drafting declaration, 80–82; 1967 GA adopted Declaration, 84; 1980 Convention signed, 51, 56
United Nations Council for Namibia, 50–51, 66
United Nations Decade for Women, 1, 15, 21–23, 29, 47–48, 61–62, 68, 71, 73–74, 81, 86, 99–101, 105, 108–10, 125, 135, 138–40, 146, 149–50, 159–60, 163, 178
United Nations Department of Economic and Social Affairs (DESA), 13, 63
United Nations Department of Public Information (DPI), 137
United Nations Development Fund for Women (UNIFEM), 32, 39, 57, 99–101, 103, 108–13, 182; Forward-looking Assessment, 108, 113
United Nations Development Program

Index

(UNDP), 99–101, 103, 106–9, 111–12, 141, 156, 160, 162
United Nations Division for the Advancement of Women, 31, 62, 73, 89, 91
United Nations Division of Human Rights, 14, 17, 81, 119, 121
United Nations Economic and Social Commission for Asia and the Pacific (ESCAP), 17
United Nations Economic and Social Commission for Western Asia (ECWA), 50, 53, 158
United Nations Economic and Social Council (ECOSOC), 7–8, 11–18, 20, 22, 31–32, 41, 49, 64, 77–78, 81–82, 84, 100, 112, 120, 126, 136–40, 142
United Nations Economic Commission for Africa (ECA), 37, 97–98; African Training and Research Centre for Women (ATRCW), 37, 98–99; Women and Development Program, 98
United Nations Educational, Scientific and Cultural Organization (Unesco), 14, 22, 78, 80, 146, 155–56; ad hoc working group on equal opportunities for women, 170; Consultative Committee on Women, 164; Convention on Eliminating Discrimination in Education, 18; relations with nongovernmental organizations, 167
United Nations Environment Program (UNEP), 128, 149; Liaison Center, 149
United Nations Fund for Population Activities, 14, 21, 98, 113, 128
United Nations General Assembly (GA), 8, 11, 13, 20, 22, 24, 30–32, 41, 46–49, 57, 62–63, 70–71, 77, 79, 84, 86, 88, 91, 96, 99, 103, 108, 110, 120, 126–27, 136–37, 150; Fifth Committee, 118; Sixth Committee, 19; Third Committee, 15, 49, 63, 79, 81, 84, 87–88, 92, 122
United Nations High Commissioner for Refugees (UNHCR), 50, 53, 128
United Nations Institute for Training and Research (UNITAR), 125, 141;

colloquium at Schloss Hernstein, 121–22
United Nations International Children's Fund (UNICEF), 14, 65, 96–98, 101, 110, 113, 158
United Nations International Court of Justice (World Court), 6, 11
United Nations International Law Commission (ILC), 19
United Nations Population Commission (PC), 12–13
United Nations Secretariat, 17, 117–30, 179; Administrative Tribunal, 120; Articles 8 and 101, of UN Charter, 117–18, 120; discrimination de facto, 121, 124; discrimination statutory, 118–20; general service category, 119, 123; geographical representation, 117–18; Group on Equal rights, 121, 126–27; Joint Advisory Committee, 124; Joint Inspection Unit, 122–23, 129; Office of Personnel, 126–27; professional category, 119, 121–22, 126–29; Schloss Hernstein colloquium, 121–22; Staff Council, 125; Staff Union, 120–21
United Nations University, 50
United Nations Water Conference, 139
United Nations World Conference of the International Women's Year (Mexico), 21, 29–42, 51, 56, 77, 85–86, 89, 92, 99–101, 108, 110, 112, 140–44, 146, 160; Committee I, 36–38; Committee II, 38–39; Consultative Committee, 32; Feminist Caucus, 141; goal of equality, development and peace, 30, 34, 81, 101, 159–60; Plenary, 34, 39; Secretariat draft plan, 32; Tribune, 33–34, 39–40, 140–44; Western Declaration, 37–38; World Plan of Action, 21, 29, 33, 38–41, 49, 63, 100, 141–42
United Nations World Conference of the Mid-Decade for Women (Copenhagen), 22, 45–58, 62–63, 77–78, 87–89, 100, 103, 123, 125, 140, 146, 149, 180; Committee of the Whole, 51, 55–56; First Committee, 51, 52–53, 55;

Forum, 56–57, 144–47; Group of 77, 47, 49; Preparatory Committee, 22, 45, 49–50; Programme of Action, 45, 49–50, 54–57, 63, 87, 103, 146; racism/Zionism, 51–52; Second Committee, 51–55; United States' role, 45
United Nations World Conference on Human Rights, 21, 179
United Nations World Conference on Women (Beijing), 24, 137, 150, 178
United Nations World Conference to Review and Appraise the Achievements of the United Nations Decade for Women (Nairobi), 23, 57, 62–74, 100, 103, 108–10, 140, 147–50, 179–80; Committee One, 66–68; Committee Two, 68–69; Forum, 61, 65, 90, 147–49; Forward-looking Strategies, 23, 61, 64, 66, 68–74, 109–10, 150, 180; General Committee, 64; Plenary, 66, 69–71; Preparatory Committee, 62–64, 67
United Republic of Cameroon, 56
United States Agency for International Development (AID), 33, 103
United States of America, 2, 7, 11–13, 16–17, 19, 21, 23, 30, 32, 35–39, 45–47, 49, 51–57, 62–64, 66, 70–73, 79, 81, 85–86, 88, 103–4, 113, 119, 124, 126, 140, 162, 164, 180
Uralova, Evdokia I., 12
Urbina, Maria Lavalle, 80, 82
Uruguay, 7, 36, 54–55
U Thant, 96

Vajrathon, Mallica, 48
van den Assum, Laetitia, 67, 88
Venezuela, 51, 62, 81, 119, 125–26
Vietnam, 35

Waldheim, Kurt, 31–32, 49, 51, 103, 122, 146
Walker, Anne, 100
Walsh, Michaela, 100
Ware, Helen, 68
Warzazzi, Halina Embarek, 19
Weil, Alice, 125
Whiteman, Marjorie, 7

Wilkinson, Ellen, 7, 12
Willard, Frances, 2
Wollstonecraft, Mary, 177
Women and Development, 95–113; Commission on Sustainable Development for Women, 137; Dakar Declaration on Another Development with Women, 104; Development Alternatives with Women for a New Era (DAWN), 104–5; Development Fund for Women (UNIFEM), 39, 57, 99; First Development Decade, 96; International Conference on Population and Development, 150, 179–80; International Development Strategy, 57; International Research and Training Institute for the Advancement of Women (INSTRAW), 39, 50, 57, 99–100, 108; Second Development Decade, 31, 96–97, 159; Third Development Decade, 57; United Nations World Survey of the Role of Women in Development, 109
Women for Peace, 147
Women Living Under Muslim Laws, 91
Women's Anthropology Conference, 148
Women's Caucus, 150
Women's Christian Temperance Union (WCTU), 2, 177
Women's Consultative Committee on Nationality, 5
Women's International Democratic Federation (WIDF), 30, 41, 137, 143, 147
Women's International League for Peace and Freedom (WILPF), 3, 5, 143–45, 147, 149
Women's Network, 110
Women's World Banking, 100, 142
Woodbury, Mildred Fairchild, 17
World Conference on Agricultural Education, 158
World Conference on Human Rights, 179
World Congress in East Berlin, 30, 41; Statement and Appeal to Women of the World, 41
World Council of Churches, 148

World Federation of Trade Unions (WFTU), 17
World Food Conference, 98, 158
World Food Program, 128, 158
World Health Organization (WHO), 14, 19, 50, 80, 155–56, 159, 164–65, 167, 170–72; Ad Hoc Working Group on the Employment of Women, 170; ombudsman, 170; program manager for staff development, 170; staff, 170–72; World Health Assemblies, 165
World Peace Council, 147
World Population Conference, 21, 40, 137; Plan of Action, 21; Tribune, 137
World Summit on Social Development, 179
World Union of Women for International Concord (WUWIC), 3
World Women's Christian Temperance Union (WWCTU), 2–3
World Young Women's Christian Association (WYWCA), 2, 40, 65, 80, 144, 177
Wu, Yi Fang, 7

Yalta Conference, 7
Yugoslavia, 71, 97, 99

Zaire, 56
Zambia, 91
Zetkin, Clara, 2
Zimbabwe, 64, 163
Zonta International, 3

About the Editor and Contributors

VIRGINIA R. ALLAN served on the U.S. delegation to three of the UN Women's Conferences—1975, 1980, and 1985. She chaired President Nixon's Taskforce on Women's Rights and Responsibilities and served as a member of the Citizen's Advisory Council on the Status of Women. She is past president of the National Federation of Business and Professional Women, former deputy assistant secretary for public affairs in the U.S. Department of State, and the first president of the U.S. Committee for the UN Development Fund for Women.

ARVONNE S. FRASER served as the U.S. ambassador to the UN Commission on the Status of Women in 1994, the second woman to hold that post. Previously she was a senior fellow at the Hubert Humphrey Institute for Public Affairs, University of Minnesota, and the director of the International Women's Rights Action Watch.

MARGARET E. GALEY served as congressional staff advisor to the U.S. delegation to the Mid-Decade Conference (1980), the Nairobi Conference (1985), and the UN General Assembly. She attended the Conference on the IWY for the Commission to Study the Organization of Peace. Besides preparing reports for the commission and the House Committee on Foreign Affairs, she has published many articles, including the "Regime for Financing the UN" (*Howard*

Law Journal), "The International Seabed Authority as a Creator of Grants" (*Ocean Development and International Law*), and "Congress, Foreign Policy and Human Rights" (*Human Rights Quarterly*). She is currently an independent scholar and consultant.

JANE S. JAQUETTE is professor of politics and chair of the Diplomacy and World Affairs Department at Occidental College. She has written extensively on issues of comparative women's political participation, women in development, and international feminism. *The Women's Movement in Latin America: Participation and Democracy* was published in 1994. She is past president of the Association for Women in Development and president-elect of the Latin American Studies Association.

CHARLOTTE G. PATTON is an adjunct assistant professor in the Political Science Department, York College, City University of New York. She participated in the 1994 UN Conference on Population and Development as a staff member of the NGO Forum. She is the NGO representative at the UN for the International Studies Association.

MILDRED E. PERSINGER has represented the World YWCA at the UN for many years and chaired the NGO Organizing Committee for the tribune, the unofficial sessions held in 1975 during the Mexico City UN Women's Conference. Subsequently she founded the International Women's Tribune Centre and was its first president.

MARGARET SNYDER is the founding director of UNIFEM and a cofounder of the African Training and Research Centre for Women. Currently a Fulbright Scholar, she was a visiting fellow at Princeton University while completing *Women, Poverty and Politics: A UN Fund for Women* and coauthoring with Mary Tadesse *African Women and Development: A History* (1994).

CAROLYN M. STEPHENSON is associate professor of political science at the University of Hawaii at Manoa. She received her B.A. from Mount Holyoke and her M.A. and Ph.D. from Ohio State University. She was an NGO observer to all three of the UN Decade for Women conferences. Skaggs Foundation supported her research in Nairobi.

KRISTEN TIMOTHY is deputy director of the United Nations Division for the Advancement of Women and coordinator for the Fourth World Conference on Women. Ms. Timothy has served at the UN since 1970. She has a B.A. in political science (Tufts University), an M.A. (Makerere University), and an M.P.A. (Kennedy School, Harvard University).

ANNE WINSLOW was former editor in chief and director of International Organization's Program, Carnegie Endowment for International Peace. She served subsequently as training officer, United Nations Institute for Research and Training (UNITAR). Her publications include three chapters in a 1991 UNITAR volume, *The United Nations System at Geneva* and as coauthor with Carol Riegelman Lubin of *Social Justice for Women: The International Labor Organization and Women* (1990).